"I found *The Waiting* to be one of the most eloquent, moving, irresistible true stories I have ever read. It begins with a sudden and terrible crime against a completely innocent schoolgirl that could have sentenced her to a life of tragedy. But Minka was no ordinary girl. After giving up the child the crime caused her to have, she began to search and wait for decades for the moment she knew somehow had to come—the moment when she would at last be reunited with her daughter. Authors Cathy LaGrow and Cindy Coloma, with the help of the families involved, have eloquently captured this magnificent story of tragedy overcome by love, hope, and perseverance. Most readers will discover, as I did, that as the pages turn, they will shed more than a few tears but they will also find their faith in humanity restored and their hearts more than a little bit lighter."

HOMER HICKAM
#1 *New York Times* bestselling author of *Rocket Boys/October Sky*

"*The Waiting* will engross you. It is a powerful story of love and fulfillment, told with amazing detail and sparkling prose. Rarely has a book moved me so completely."

BILLY COFFEY
Author of *When Mockingbirds Sing* and *The Devil Walks in Mattingly*

"A poignant story, masterfully told with heart. Minka's journey comes to light in this beautiful work. And it is a story to be treasured."

LIS WIEHL
Bestselling author and FOX News legal analyst

"*The Waiting* is a story of a life conceived from one horrible act and a mother's love. Minka chose the best for her daughter, only to discover a family that was greater than she ever imagined. The beauty of this story is that it's about an ordinary life, yet an extraordinary love. As someone who met my own birth father at age twenty-eight—and who has adopted three children—I couldn't stop the tears from flowing. Families are created in different ways, but *The Waiting* reminds us that love conquers heartache and that the smallest flame of hope can lead to answered prayers. I highly recommend this book!"

TRICIA GOYER
USA Today bestselling author of over forty books, including *Plain Faith: A True Story of Tragedy, Loss and Leaving the Amish*

"Every woman's nightmare. Every mother's wonder. . . . Author Cathy LaGrow's captivating family memoir is rooted in silence and shame, where grief is denied and hope is an unspoken prayer. *The Waiting* is a stirring testimony of God's goodness and grace to a troubled young girl and an inquisitive aging woman."

KAREN SPEARS ZACHARIAS
Author of *Mother of Rain*

"An amazing story that proves God hears our prayers and does sometimes give us the desires of our hearts. Written with heartfelt, poetic prose, *The Waiting* will move you as you read about this unlikeliest of reunions."

TRAVIS THRASHER
Bestselling author of *Home Run* and *Never Let Go*

the waiting

The true story of a lost child,

a lifetime of longing,

and a miracle for a mother

who never gave up

∽≈≈⋙≈≪≈∽

CATHY LaGROW

with Cindy Coloma

TYNDALE
MOMENTUM

An Imprint of
Tyndale House Publishers, Inc.

Visit Tyndale online at www.tyndale.com.

Visit Tyndale Momentum online at www.tyndalemomentum.com.

TYNDALE is a registered trademark of Tyndale House Publishers, Inc. *Tyndale Momentum* and the Tyndale Momentum logo are trademarks of Tyndale House Publishers, Inc. Tyndale Momentum is an imprint of Tyndale House Publishers, Inc.

The Waiting: The True Story of a Lost Child, a Lifetime of Longing, and a Miracle for a Mother Who Never Gave Up

Designed by Nicole Grimes

Published in association with the literary agency of Books & Such Literary Management, 52 Mission Circle, Suite 122, PMB 170, Santa Rosa, CA 95409.

Scripture quotations are taken from the *Holy Bible*, King James Version.

Library of Congress Cataloging-in-Publication Data

LaGrow, Cathy.
  The waiting : the true story of a lost child, a lifetime of longing, and a miracle for a mother who never gave up / Cathy LaGrow, with Cindy Coloma.
    pages cm
ISBN 978-1-4143-9190-8 (hc)
1. Disbrow, Minka, 1911- 2. Lee, Ruth, 1929- 3. Christian biography. 4. Adoption—Religious aspects—Lutheran Church. I. Title.
  BR1700.3.L34 2014
  277.3'0820922—dc23
  [B]   2014005504

Printed in the United States of America

20	19	18	17	16	15	14
7	6	5	4	3	2	1

For Minka, who waited

Preface

SHE'D HAD ONLY THE PHOTOGRAPH, all these years.

The old woman had viewed the cherished black-and-white image thousands of times in secret. She knew every detail by heart. There was the wisp of a baby with a sweet, sleeping face, always the first place her eyes went. And off to the side, gazing at the baby, a young mother, her damaged hands lying across the skirt of a good dress. Those same hands, now thickened and spotted by age, held the precious photograph carefully.

Had she really been so young once?

Her tidy apartment was quiet, as usual, with a warm ocean breeze filtering through the open windows. But the silence no longer echoed emptiness. In recent days the space had been filled to overflowing, like her heart.

She was ninety-four now, undeniably old. And after all this time, along with everything else that had been restored, her letters had come back to her. So many pages, hundreds of them, written over years and years.

The trauma of that long-ago time covered her memory like a fog, but she remembered the pain revealed in the words—the pain and the love. She remembered those well. They had been her constant companions for nearly eighty years.

Her bent fingers reached for the pages, and time unspooled.

Her hands stopped at a letter bearing a signature other than her own, a letter she'd never seen before. This one was written by the dear Reverend, long dead now, like nearly everyone else mentioned in these letters.

She read, and the words opened the door to another time, another century. Another August day, like this one and yet nothing like it at all . . .

Board of Foreign Missions
Ev. Luth. Synod of Iowa
And Other States

OFFICE OF SECRETARY
REV. W. F. KRAUSHAAR, M.A.

Aberdeen, South Dakota
April 3, 1929

My dear madam,

     I have an unfortunate girl in my congregation that expects to give birth to a child about the end of this month. I have investigated her case and am convinced that she was the victim of a dastardly crime of assault. She comes from a good family and has been staying with relatives in Sioux City. Could you take her in and help her when her time comes? Her family is not wealthy, but they will pay whatever your regular fees are.

     I must mention too, that her people want her to give her baby away since the father is a fugitive criminal, but the girl seems rather inclined to keep it, possibly you can give them the best advice. Do you find good homes for such children? Of course, they would prefer a Lutheran home.

     I would greatly appreciate an early reply.

Faithfully yours,
Reverend Kraushaar

PART ONE

Loss

Chapter One

AUGUST 1928

FOUR AND A HALF HOURS before her life would change forever, Minka stood in a dusty parking lot, twisting her handkerchief as she willed her family to hurry up. If they took much longer, she might just pick up her ankle-length skirts and run all the way home.

Her stepfather, Honus, leaned against the black side of the family's milk truck, blocking out the white *D* in Sunnyside Dairy, his hands jammed into the pockets of his summer suit. It was not yet noon, but the air was already thick and hot. Around them, engines loosely clattered as men cranked up Model Ts. Women called out good-byes to one another and gathered children before climbing inside their cars.

Minka's sister, Jane, and their mother were still on the circular brick steps of Zion Lutheran Church, visiting with friends. On any other Sunday Minka might have lingered too, joining in conversations if she felt bold enough, speaking whichever language was being used—English, German, or Dutch. The church

3

community, largely made up of immigrants, had finally voted ten months earlier to conduct all services and business meetings in English, but once they were outside, people's native tongues were loosed.

Today, Minka had fidgeted through the entire service. She couldn't wait to get back home.

Minka DeYoung was sixteen years old, taller than average and as thin and straight as a stalk of wheat. Her fine brown hair was cut in a loose bob and pinned back on one side with a frilly ribbon. Her gaze was lively and intelligent, though she often ducked her head bashfully and, like other people who fought shyness, had a habit of holding herself very still in public. Minka knew her nose and ears were too large for her face; she didn't realize her delicate cheekbones were beautiful. She was always careful not to draw attention to her hands, which had been damaged long ago.

Honus removed his fedora, but rather than fan his face with it, he held it in both hands and squinted at the pale sky, watching a thrush flap its way to the top of the church's steeple.

Minka glanced toward the church. Her mother had moved to the bottom of the steps, but Jane was still deep in conversation, leaning close to her friend Jette and smiling about something. Minka wished they'd hurry.

This afternoon was the event she'd been waiting for and thinking about for weeks: her sewing class picnic at Scatterwood Lake. Back home, a new dress waited on a hanger, freshly pressed. She would put on just the right jewelry and redo her hair, and then, for a few hours at least, she'd be like a normal teenaged girl, not a full-time worker who split her time between the family dairy and a meatpacking plant.

But Minka couldn't do a thing until her mother and Jane *hurried up.*

One row over, a car rolled by, carrying a banker from First National. Its paint was an exquisite dark blue, shiny enough to reflect trees. Minka's eyes followed it. She loved beautiful things, even if they weren't hers.

Honus nodded to the banker behind the wheel. The man returned the gesture.

"Dat is one of de new Fords, called Model A," Honus said to Minka.

"Are they better? Than the tin lizzies?" Minka asked. She usually managed to contain all the questions that popped into her head when adults were talking—she'd been raised with perfect manners, after all—but excitement about the picnic loosened her propriety with her stepfather.

"Dey are supposed to haf a ride . . . not so bumpy. Dey are fast. But also *duur* . . . expensive, I think." *Think* came out sounding like *sink*. Like Minka's mother, Jennie, who'd sailed to America just months before Minka was born, Honus had emigrated from Holland. He would speak with a thick Dutch accent all his life.

They watched the car turn onto Jay Street and disappear. So many things had changed in the decade since the Great War ended. There was still a hitching post on the other side of the church building, and some farmers came to church by horse and buggy. Minka remembered when that was the only transportation *anyone* had.

A few years back, she and her siblings had gone to a picture show for the first time. As they'd watched people and scenery move silently across the white cloth screen, her mouth had dropped open and stayed that way until her tongue dried out and she'd had to swallow painfully. Jane and John, always quick to tease their sister, hadn't so much as nudged her. They too had been staring, goggle-eyed.

Every month seemed to bring a new innovation. Most homes in Aberdeen, South Dakota, now boasted electric lights indoors, and a few had a newfangled mechanical box for cold food storage, an improvement over root cellars, so long as the toxic chemicals used for cooling didn't spill onto human skin. There were radios in living rooms, and skirt hems that ended more than twelve daring inches above the ground.

Honus's house had an indoor bathroom, a luxury to which Minka and her family had quickly—and gratefully—grown accustomed. Before moving in with him, they'd lived for twelve years at Uncle's farm on the prairie, where Jennie worked as housekeeper and conditions were more primitive. Three years ago when Uncle retired, Honus Vander Zee came calling, and shortly thereafter, with no announcement or fanfare, Jennie had gotten married.

The marriage gave Jennie's children a permanent home, but it upended the only life they'd known. Honus was starting up a new dairy and needed strong workers, and he believed that high school was "for city kids who haf nothing else to do." When each DeYoung child reached the age of fourteen, he or she was put to work milking cows full-time. Minka's older brother, John, soon escaped to the navy.

In the parking lot, Honus cleared his throat.

"It will be a hot day." He looked at his hat, eased it through his hands. "Hotter den yesterday, maybe."

"Yes, sir." Minka lifted her arms away from her body. She didn't want to start sweating in her church dress. During the sermon the sanctuary had rippled with a sea of paper fans, and Minka had kept shifting on the hard wooden bench, thinking of her new dress, the waiting lake, the hours of freedom in front of her. She couldn't resist bringing it up. "Maybe it'll be cooler by the lake this afternoon. At the picnic."

"Ja, maybe."

Minka didn't know that her mother had convinced him to let her go. Honus hadn't married until he was nearly thirty-five years old, and young women were a mystery to him. Raised in Europe, he had absorbed the austere attitudes of a different century regarding children, work, and rewards. From his perspective, duty trumped pleasure—and there was plenty to be done at the farm every single day. Any time away created more work that needed making up.

Sometimes on warm Saturday evenings after milking chores, Honus would lean through the kitchen doorway and say in his quiet way, "Come go for a drive." Since bedtime came early at the dairy, there wasn't time to freshen up or change out of work overalls. Minka and Jane climbed into the stuffy back of the milk truck, and Honus drove them and Jennie to the ice cream shop in town. After buying one malted shake in a tin canister and requesting four paper straws, Honus brought it to the truck and passed the shake around. When they'd each had an equal number of sips and the last bit of ice cream was gone, Honus returned the canister and drove home. To him, such an impractical treat—likely more than he'd gotten as a boy—was enough.

As clusters of the congregation moved toward vehicles, Minka spotted girls from her sewing group. She watched the friends wave to one another before climbing into their cars.

Across the parking lot, Minka overheard a girl named Dorothy call out to a friend, Clara. "We will get you in an hour!" Dorothy slammed the door to the already-rumbling Model T.

Minka clenched her fists and blew air into her cheeks. Her eyes jumped to Mom and Jane, who had yet to move, and then up to Honus, still leaning contentedly against the side of the milk truck. He usually didn't allow dawdling; despite Reverend Kraushaar's sermons about the Sabbath, there was work to do every day of the week. But Honus merely glanced at Minka, deflating the hope that he'd wave her mother and sister away from the church steps.

Though every day of her life was consumed with heavy labor, work had never bothered Minka. Her bony frame masked a surprising stamina. Often, the longer she worked, the more invigorated she felt. She knew that her natural gifts were physical, and she was proud of them. Maybe she couldn't light up a room just by walking into it, like Jane, but she could work as long and accomplish as much as anyone she knew, including adults.

It was the loss of her education that scraped at Minka's spirit. She'd been raised poor but with self-respect. Even as a child, running barefoot in the summer dirt at a farm that wasn't her family's own, she'd carried herself with a sense of dignity, had felt as worthy and capable as any other girl. Now, at sixteen, Minka felt ashamed. What if milking cows was all she was good for—what if an uneducated milkmaid was all people would ever see when they looked at her?

This afternoon's picnic would allow her to once again feel "as good as." Her heart pounded, partly from nerves, partly from excitement. Perhaps if her mother and Honus saw that today's outing didn't affect her work, she'd occasionally be allowed to go on future adventures.

Finally, here came Jane across the field. Her arm was linked through her mother's, and she leaned against her, giggling about something. Jennie was smiling. In this pressing heat, they moved slowly. Minka wanted to drag them forward. She turned and opened the truck's back door. Its metal handle was hot to the touch, and the hinges squealed. As she climbed up, she banged her knee on the wooden crates that served as seats, and her handkerchief fluttered onto the metal floor. She'd been twisting the cloth so anxiously that it looked like a wrung-out chicken's neck.

* * *

Minka stood at the mirror in her mother's bedroom, trying on strands of necklaces. Despite growing up on a hardscrabble farm, she'd always loved pretty jewelry. Jennie had brought some simple accessories from Holland many years ago, and Minka had often capered around Uncle's house wearing every strand she could find, all draped together around her neck. Jane and John had nicknamed her "Gypsy."

Jane wasn't calling her sister names today. Minka's younger sibling had been trying not to sulk ever since they'd arrived home from church. With excitement such a rare commodity in their lives, the sisters nearly always shared it; the night before, Jane had volunteered to help Minka bake cookies for the big event.

But Jane was the charming "baby" of the family, unaccustomed to standing in the shadows, and now the sharing of joy stretched taut. Minka's new dress was the best item in their shared closet. Only Minka would be going on the picnic. Jane's steps had been heavy and a pout had crimped her pretty lips as she changed into work clothes for her usual afternoon of chores.

The summer sewing class was made up of girls from Zion Lutheran. Although store windows now overflowed with finished goods, from ready-made clothes to canned food to toiletry items, sewing was still an expected skill for a future housewife. Like most farmers, the Vander Zees took care of their own animals, grew and preserved their own food, performed their own mechanical repairs, made their own soap and clothes.

Jennie sewed skillfully and would have made a fine teacher if she'd had time, but she was too busy with chores. So Minka went off to sewing class, where she demonstrated an innate creativity and quick skill that surprised and pleased her. She produced the most immaculate stitches in the group—she'd heard her teacher praising her work to Jennie. Minka loved the feel of new fabric in her hands. Sometimes, while doing chores or riding in the car, she daydreamed of expensive silk in bright colors, falling like water over her shoulders and resting perfectly against her thin hips.

For this first dress Minka had chosen a modern shift pattern with a dropped waist in a fetching green-and-white cotton. She couldn't resist adding a decoration: an apple-and-leaf appliqué, cut from a contrasting fabric and stitched below her left shoulder. Compared to this fresh style, even her best church dress seemed dowdy.

As Minka fastened a strand of beads behind her neck, Jennie came through the doorway. She covered her mouth when she saw her daughter, her quietest and most diligent child. The mirror reflected the woman Minka would soon become.

"Je ziet er mooi uit," she murmured. *You look so pretty.* Then, louder: "You are a fine seamstress, Minnie."

Minka savored the compliments. Since babyhood, her pretty sister had always been the center of attention. Minka was happiest out of the spotlight, but sometimes when she watched Jane fling herself into their mother's lap, she longed to do the same. In a household marked by Dutch reserve, compliments were few and physical touch came only to those who demanded it. Minka was too shy—and too stubborn, really—to demand anything.

"Dey are picking you up here?" Jennie asked, crossing the room to lift Minka's overalls from the bedstead.

"Yes, Mom." Minka pushed at the bottom of her hair. She'd dampened it in the bathroom and attempted to make some finger waves, but it had dried too quickly in this heat and now looked straggly. She supposed the other girls would have the same problem today.

"And you be back in time for de milking, ja?" That chore commenced at five o'clock at *both* ends of the day, and the cows' full udders wouldn't wait, picnic or no.

"Yes, Mom, that's what they said."

Jennie bent and wiped the tops of Minka's shoes, then set them where Minka could slip into them. The clunky leather shoes would make her feet sweat, but they would have to do. Mary Janes did not come in a large-enough size for Minka. Jennie's children had inherited a scattering of oversized genes from some unknown branch of the family tree—John would eventually stand well over six feet, much taller than his father had been. And at a time when most girls' feet were a dainty size 4 or 4.5, Minka's were twice that big.

Minka's hands were large too, although that was not the reason she made a concerted effort to hide them. She was most bothered by their disfigurement. Daily hours of milking had taken a toll, but the real damage had been done when she was a small girl. At Uncle's, out of necessity, children had been put to work as soon as they could walk in a straight line. John helped with the horses and out in the fields, while Jane loved to hang close to her mother's skirt, doing chores underfoot. As the oldest and strongest girl, Minka took on the most arduous household work. She toted buckets of water, hauled pails of animal feed, and lifted bulky sheaves of wheat at threshing time. Minka volunteered for these tasks, relishing the nod or smile from Jennie as she did so. It made her happy to help her busy mother. But by the time she was thirteen, Minka's fingers were permanently deformed, the bones bent inward at the ends where her tiny joints had grasped and lifted a thousand heavy handles.

Through the open window a noisy engine signaled the arrival of Minka's ride. She glanced in the mirror once more, automatically pushing her hands into her sides so the folds of fabric obscured them. She was giddy enough to let a vain thought cross her mind: She had never looked better. She spun and hurried toward the kitchen, where her dinner basket waited.

"Don't forget these," Jane called after her. She held out the cookie tin. After the whole batch had cooled last night, Jane had chosen the twenty most perfect cookies, enough to share with all the girls and chaperones. Minka had stacked and restacked them onto two big cloth napkins, which she neatly tied up and placed in the tin.

"Danke." Minka had nearly rushed out without the treats.

"Tell them I helped," Jane said, looking wistfully at the package. And Minka—even though this was *her* special day, and even though she'd spent her whole life on the sidelines watching Jane accept easier chores and more praise—felt sorry that her little sister couldn't come along.

✳ ✳ ✳

On the road to Scatterwood Lake, large plumes of airborne dirt billowed behind the caravan of vehicles. The cars trailed one another at quarter-mile distances to avoid being completely engulfed in dust.

Three girls in the backseat made lively chatter as Minka stared out the front side window toward the hazy countryside. Agatha's mother was driving her husband's big Chrysler Imperial, gripping the steering wheel so hard that her knuckles turned white. She'd made a couple of polite inquiries at first, asking after Minka's mother and the dairy, but now she seemed focused on maneuvering the car past the occasional oncoming vehicle. Minka studied a flock of sheep bunched together in the shade of some cottonwoods, then tugged at the hem of her dress and silently practiced sentences. She was determined to join in the girl talk once they arrived at the park.

The heat was stifling, almost made worse with the windows down. Dust-filled air swept against the girls' skin and collected in their lungs. With a clean, embroidered handkerchief, Minka tapped at the sweat that flattened her hair along the edge of her face and against her neck. The other girls beat at the air with wood-and-lace fans. Minka didn't own a fan, only handkerchiefs made from former dresses that had moved down the ladder from Sunday best to work dresses to scraps.

The park at Scatterwood Lake drew locals from all around Aberdeen. In addition to dance pavilions, the grounds offered roller-skating, swimming, picnic areas, fishing, and baseball fields, although the main draw today would be the water. Several years earlier, a young North Dakotan musician named Lawrence had played to a surprisingly large crowd there after rain canceled the county baseball championship and sent spectators running to the pavilions for cover. Years later, that singer would inspire Midwestern pride as he reached worldwide fame with *The Lawrence Welk Show.*

The large size of the park and surrounding lake also appealed to travelers passing through the area. Drifters were as common as grasshoppers in a cornfield. Jobs that had been plentiful after the Great War were vanishing, although the coming Depression was still a mostly hidden threat.

The caravan of vehicles pulled into a field to park, and girls spilled out of cars, smoothing hair and brushing at crisscrossed lines wrinkled into their dresses. Many continued to fan themselves as they came together, calling out names of girls from other cars. After a few moments of uncertain pointing toward various picnic spots, the group headed to an unclaimed grove of trees that provided patches of shade. It felt like they were walking through a hot oven.

Minka spread out her blanket next to Clara, a quiet girl to whom Minka often gravitated. She uncovered her dinner: baking-powder biscuits Jennie had made that morning, a milk bottle filled with now-warm water, and fried chicken from a bird that had been scratching around the yard just the day before. Minka had plucked the feathers herself, first softening the quills by dunking the chicken in a pot of boiling water. She'd been dressing fowl for so many years, she could practically do it in her sleep.

Underneath a sky bleached milky-white by the glaring sun, diamond patterns glimmered and danced on the lake's surface. The roller rink, some distance away, appeared mostly empty that afternoon. Minka certainly wouldn't skate even if the day cooled off. While several girls owned skates, wheeled contraptions that strapped over their shoes, Minka had never tried the sport. Her sewing teacher had said that skates were available at the rink, but Minka knew there wouldn't be shoes to fit her, not in ladies' sizes.

Minka studied the other girls, and when it looked as though most of them had finished their chicken or sausages or roast beef sandwiches, she lifted the tin of cookies from her basket. The nervous pang that twisted her stomach made her feel silly. Rather than make an announcement, she decided to approach each girl casually.

"Would you like a cookie? I made them. Jane and I made them."

Eager hands reached for the cookies. Not a single girl declined, and as they swallowed the first bites, they handed out compliments. "These are really good, Minka! Did you use butter in them?" They rearranged blankets and nudged each other over, and soon all the girls were in one big, lopsided circle. Minka sat down, her wide mouth curved into an irrepressible smile.

The conversation bubbled all around Minka, mainly about people in town whom Minka didn't know. Over the last two months, she'd heard enough scandals, rumors, and transgressions to make her head spin. She'd heard where the basement saloons or speakeasies were rumored to exist. It was hard to believe that regular people, not just criminals, gathered and broke Prohibition laws together—and in her own town. Perhaps some of them were the very people her family delivered milk to, although surely not anyone who sat in the church pews on Sunday morning.

There were other whispered rumors on the blankets. One of the girls who came infrequently was said to skip sewing class to meet a boy from town.

"You know what that means," talkative Agatha had said one day, and the other girls' faces creased with identical knowing expressions. To Minka, it made them look grown-up and wise, while her face burned. She had no clue what Agatha was talking about, but whatever it was, it was surely terrible. Growing up with a mother who never shared gossip or idle talk, Minka found the chatter both unsettling and titillating.

In this way, sewing class had educated Minka on more than patterns and needlework. Her only other glimpses of the outside world came in occasional letters from her brother, John, which the whole family passed around and eagerly read, or from weekly visits from Honus's friend Charlie. Each Saturday evening, the two men settled into the living room and spoke in Dutch about world events, the economy, and local businesses.

Minka and Jane listened to these conversations. In recent months, the men had discussed the debate over whether tourists would truly be attracted to barren South Dakota for the sight of four presidential faces chiseled from some granite cliffs in the Black Hills. Many believed it was an enormous waste of federal money.

Minka didn't understand much about economics or tourist attractions or why people risked jail for a drink or why a girl would leave sewing class to meet a boy, but she was curious about everything beyond a world of cows and overalls.

Today the girls' talk turned more benign, probably due to the nearness of the chaperones. But Minka's naivete was about to be shattered, and more thoroughly than anyone could have imagined.

❈ ❈ ❈

With the picnic packed up, the group spread around the park so the girls could put their feet into the murky water, or mill around the skating rink, or remain in the shade, weaving more conversation. Minka heard the inner ticking of the day descending toward evening milking time. Soon her escape would end. She drew near Clara again.

"Do you want to walk around the lake?" Minka was far more comfortable with a single person than with a group, and undemanding Clara was a good companion.

They followed a small fishing trail that wove in and out of the trees and brush. Minka threw stones across the mirror surface of the water and wondered what it would be like to swim. She'd never learned.

The lake made her think of her real father. She had no memories of him, just a single studio portrait taken when he was seventeen years old and a handful of stories that Jennie told time and again. Those scraps of information were precious to Minka, and she held them in her heart, paging through them like a journal when she felt lonely for the father she'd never known. She knew that his last day on earth had been hot like this one, although he'd died at a different South Dakota lake.

Minka didn't realize how far they'd walked on secluded trails until she and Clara saw three men, and realized with a start that they were out of sight of anyone else. The strangers were adults, perhaps thirty years old. They closed in on the girls with friendly smiles. Minka immediately felt the familiar shyness well up inside her. She dropped her eyes and stepped to one side.

"Hi! What're you girls doing on this hot day?" one of the men said. Another one wore a cowboy hat and stood without speaking, his hands shoved deep in his pockets.

Minka said nothing. Clara murmured a greeting and then turned to Minka with a hesitant expression. Minka felt herself inwardly shrinking from them, as though that would somehow send them away.

"Come on, let me at least take your picture," the talkative one called.

Their camera brought the girls in close; what would it hurt to let them take a picture? Yet one of the men circled behind the girls and stood looking back the direction they'd come. The talkative one took hold of Clara and tugged her away, toward a thicket of trees. Minka stared after them, glancing into Clara's panicked eyes. As Minka began to move toward her friend, the one with the cowboy hat approached her.

He might have said his name was Mack, but now everything seemed to have slowed down, like a phonograph on the wrong speed; at the same time, Minka had the sense that events were moving away from her faster than she could run. She couldn't understand whatever words Mack was saying. Her vision had telescoped. He looked tiny now, as though he were standing on the other side of a wide street.

She couldn't fathom what was happening, even as his hands pushed her down and lifted her dress. Shyness and shock kept her from saying a word in protest. She simply focused on his hat.

Afterward, Minka knew that something dreadful had occurred. The pain, the intimacy of the act, the look on Mack's face as he stood over her for a moment before turning and leaving without another word—all of these impressions were infused with shame. Somewhere to the right Clara was crying, but Minka was too paralyzed to go to her friend.

Minka had drawn her legs up beneath her dress and wrapped her arms around her knees. Dry thistles poked through the fabric of her outfit and matted her hair. Her wrists and knees stung, as did other parts of her, places filled with a new, throbbing humiliation.

She got to her feet. One of her shoes was under a bramble of weeds, and her dress was crumpled. Her fingers shook as she struggled to pull thistles from the skirt.

Clara's cries quieted after a few minutes, and then she came into view, walking hunched into herself, as though something was wrong with her back. She looked more horrified than Minka felt. Minka had the sense that Clara could shed some light on *It*, this thing that had just happened, but she couldn't bring herself to ask.

What time is it? Minka wondered. Clara didn't look her way, just mumbled something about having to get back. Minka hurried now, wincing with every move. She felt a stinging sensation, although she wasn't sure where it came from. She brushed dry grass from her hair and swiped at her cheeks. They were damp. Her teeth seemed on the verge of chattering, even in the oven-like air.

Minka felt the blood before she saw it. She touched the back of her dress, afraid a stain had soaked through, but found only thistles. She had nothing but dried leaves to try cleaning between her thighs. Finally, she followed Clara, who moved unevenly along the path. They pushed out of the shade of the trees and back into sunlight. To the right, swimmers splashed and called to one another. The sewing group girls were standing near the cars, holding grass-flecked blankets and empty baskets. One of them shaded her eyes with a hand, peering toward the trees.

"There they are!" the girl called and waved.

Neither Minka nor Clara waved back.

Clara climbed into the backseat of one of the cars and pressed against the side, wiping her face. She ignored a concerned query.

"What is wrong with her?" Agatha muttered to another girl.

Minka waited until the engines came alive and their sewing teacher was counting heads before she sought a different vehicle, any vehicle but the one Clara was in.

On the drive home to Aberdeen, Minka squeezed her eyes shut against the golden hues slanting over the wheat fields. She was sticky with sweat, not just her own, and nearly overwhelmed by the desire to leap from the car and scrub herself clean in some deep, cool well.

Minka made a promise to herself as the car bounced down the dirt road. She was a thoroughly honest person, but Minka knew that she must keep this day folded up and buried inside. She would not tell a soul what had just happened. As long as Clara didn't tell either, it would disappear and be forgotten.

But Minka would be unable to keep her vow of silence. She could not imagine it now, but an agonizing journey lay ahead. And every day in the years to come would be inexorably linked to this solitary afternoon at Scatterwood Lake.

Time would scrub from her memory whatever words her assailant spoke, the clothes he wore, the contours of his face. But that cowboy hat, moving back and forth against a bleached-out August sky, was the image that endured.

Minka would never forget that single detail for as long as she lived. And that was going to be a very, very long time.

Chapter Two

"GIRLS."

Honus's soft voice came from the bottom of the stairwell. After three years at the dairy, that one word was all the alarm clock Minka and Jane needed to wake every morning.

It was pitch-dark, and the air on the other side of their goose-down blanket was cold, although not yet freezing as it would be by the end of the year. The bedroom's paltry heat emanated from the stovepipe, which came up through the floor in one corner and exited into the ceiling on its way to the roof.

Jane's cat had returned from prowling during the night and now lay curled between the girls, adding welcome warmth. Jane insisted that they leave the window open a few inches for him when they went to bed, even when it was snowing outside. Often, the damp paw prints he left scattered across the bedcovers would turn to ice by morning.

Today, November 10, was Minka's seventeenth birthday, although she didn't remember the date when she woke. Her family didn't celebrate birthdays, so this morning felt no different from any other—unlike that morning three months ago, when she'd woken up with sore places under her nightgown and the previous day's event huge in her mind.

The day when *It* had occurred.

She'd tried to put *It* out of her mind. The memory had stubbornly crept back at the oddest moments: when she was sitting on a milking stool or hanging out the wash; or especially when she sat in the bathtub on Saturday nights, the places *he* had seen and hurt all exposed beneath the water. Sometimes panic had bubbled up and she'd fought a longing to escape her life, to just pack a bag and board a train and go anyplace else, to *be* someone else. Other times she'd wanted to run all the way back to Uncle's and hide in his dark, quiet root cellar, where no one would think to look for her.

The week after *It* happened, she'd dropped her dinner tin at the meatpacking house where she worked in the afternoons, twisting sausages alongside grown men. One of the Germans had knelt beside her. As he handed up the tin, he said, "Ach, Minnie, Sie mussen achtgeben." *Minnie, you must be careful.* Though his words were innocuous and his tone gentle, he'd been so close that she could smell his sweat and something he'd cooked, maybe cabbage. Minka's skin had gone clammy, and it had taken half an hour for her hands to stop trembling.

She was better now. She'd stopped drifting to a soundless place where she didn't hear people right next to her, a habit that caused Jane to ask crossly, "What's wrong with you?" Time passed, and her body healed. She hadn't told a soul. Most people had secrets, didn't they? Jennie had kept it secret when she married Honus. To this day, none of the children knew when or where their own mother's wedding had occurred—they'd just been packed off to Honus's to live one day, and that was that.

"Hurry," Jane said on this unnoticed birthday morning.

Minka swung her legs to the edge of the bed. She usually had to prod Jane along, but this was the third time this week that her sister had gotten up first. Everything seemed harder to do lately, starting with getting her legs out from under the covers.

There was no lantern in their room, but Minka and Jane knew every inch of the plain bedroom by heart. They grabbed their overalls and bulky work shirts from the iron bedstead. Jane murmured good-bye to the cat, then followed Minka down the stairs. The cold floorboards leached warmth from their bare feet.

During the winter they dressed in the dining room, where a coal heater kept the air toasty. A faint, red glow showed through narrow openings in the grate, providing them with enough dim light to see armholes and buttons. As she reached the last step, Minka's head began to swim. She put a hand on the wall to steady herself.

She'd been getting these light-headed flashes lately. Probably she wasn't eating enough. Her appetite had been poor, and several times she'd asked her mother for the bright-blue bottle of Bromo-Seltzer, hoping the salty medicine would ease her indigestion.

After stepping into their overalls and adjusting the straps, the girls passed through the kitchen and said good morning to Jennie, who sat peeling potatoes at the table. She'd already lit the fire in the cookstove, and its heat was beginning to swallow the chill in the room. The girls pulled on their leather boots and stepped outside.

The predawn air slapped away any remaining sleepiness. Frost coated the ground, glittering in the moonlight and crunching beneath the girls' boots. The quiet was broken by clanks and rumbles at the Milwaukee train yard across the road. The girls passed the coop where Jennie's chickens still slept and headed for a wedge of light spilling from the door of the main barn. Honus had already lit lanterns along the barn posts inside. It was warmer there, where cows shifted in the stalls, udders bulging between their legs. Round, black eyes turned toward the sisters, and low moans rolled like murmurs from the more impatient heifers.

Jane took one side of the barn; Minka, the other. After filling the corn bins in front of each cow, Minka wound a chain around the leg of the first animal on her row. This one was a kicker, and Minka wore the large, dark bruises to prove it. Last week, the cow had deliberately fallen over on her. Minka's leg had been pinned, and she'd spilled a full pail of milk—a wasteful accident on a farm where frugality was prized.

Minka was leaning against the warm side of a cow when the day's first light spilled through the half-open barn door. As she shifted on the hard stool, straw dust floated upward, irritating her nose. Her strong fingers gripped a teat, pulling and squeezing downward. Warm milk hissed into the pail in a smooth rhythm.

The cow shifted its back foot, almost coming down on her toes. She pushed her shoulder into its leg, and the cow swung its head, giving her a disinterested glance before dipping back into its corn bin. When the stream of milk turned to drops, Minka lifted the bucket and poured the milk into a large metal canister. She moved on to the next cow.

At least today was Saturday, which meant she didn't have to think about classes going on without her over at the high school. She'd hoped to stop feeling the loss of her education, given enough time, but it continued to niggle at her mind like a pesky little sibling with a pointed stick. She would've learned on her own if she could have. But there were no books at Honus's, and she didn't have time to go to the public library in Aberdeen, as inviting as she found its large, columned front porch and rooms full of books.

It didn't help that Honus occasionally brought her along on deliveries, saying she "needed to learn the route." They'd pass Central High School, the pretty, redbrick building with its triple rows of gleaming windows, and it was as if Minka could see big letters splashed across the front in white paint, spelling out a message: *This Is Not for You.*

Ironically, when they'd lived at Uncle's, Minka had often

dreaded going to school. The din in the one-room prairie school-house had been so loud that she couldn't think straight. She didn't know that her vision was poor, that eyestrain caused her frequent headaches—she assumed that everyone was born with a headache. When she squinted at the blackboard or held a book up to her face so she could see the letters, the spinster teacher barked impatiently at her.

Her favorite part of each school day had been the long trek there and back, walking through neighbors' fields and climbing over splintery fences. As she'd passed under a dome of endless sky and felt prairie winds sweep across the open acres, she'd had a delicious sense of freedom, of solitude, even with John and Jane chattering beside her. Sitting in the schoolroom, by contrast, had made her feel like she was in captivity.

Minka didn't realize how much she needed the nourishing pride of learning until after her education ended, at the conclusion of eighth grade. School had tried her quiet personality, but it had also fed her hungry mind, giving her a sense of moving forward through life. She'd had something precious, and now it was gone.

And she would have given most anything to have it back.

✳ ✳ ✳

Milking the dairy's dozen cows was only part of Minka and Jane's twice-daily routine. Once the gray, ten-gallon canisters were full, the girls lugged them to the cooling room, set up in a separate building away from earthy barn odors that could spoil milk. After running the milk through a cooler to prevent bacterial growth, they carried the cans to the house, where a large room held the bottling machine. This was the easiest and most satisfying part of the job, pulling levers and watching glass bottles fill with the milk they'd worked so hard to collect. During the last step, the machine stamped paper caps on the bottles and set them down in uniform rows. Both girls loved the clean, soothing pattern of it.

Minka could remember when a fondness for order, combined with her iron will, had gotten her in trouble. As a little girl, she'd wanted everything in its proper place, including the food on her plate. She didn't want the meat touching the carrots, or the potatoes slopping onto the biscuits. Sometimes, if Jennie was in a hurry dishing out food, the separate components of Minka's meal all slid together.

A well-raised Dutch girl wouldn't dream of sassing an adult or voicing a complaint. Instead, Minka would sit back in her chair and cross her small arms. As everyone else dug into their food, Minka stared at her plate.

Jennie usually chose to ignore her daughter's silent protest, but on a bad day it might strike Uncle wrong. He'd set down his fork, raise a thick finger, and bellow.

"Schmeiss sie in den Keller!" *Throw her in the cellar!*

Minka would push back her chair and march to the cellar door with the grave air of someone unjustly convicted of a crime. She'd take the rickety stairs down and sidle along the dirt floor in front of the canning shelves. Plopping next to the potato mound, she'd wait in the dark for the basement salamanders to creep over. Then she'd play with them until everyone had finished supper and Jennie called her back upstairs.

Minka no longer staged childish protests over slopped food, although she still often felt that old stubbornness rise up. It seemed as much a part of her as her brown hair and big feet. These days, more and more, she wielded that determination, used it to force herself from bed to perform her work as required, to not be pressed down by despair, to hold out hope for some kind of future that involved anything but cleaning and cows.

She used that obstinacy to keep *It* pushed to the furthest corner of her mind, a place she could *will* herself not to access. Of course, the never-ending daily physical work kept those thoughts at bay too.

When all the milk bottles were filled that November morning, the girls carried the heavy crates out to Honus's truck. Jane brought a container of skimmed cream to the house. Near the kitchen doorway they passed Honus leaving for his morning deliveries.

Jennie had breakfast waiting: thick oatmeal bubbling in a pot, salty strips of bacon, and potatoes fried into crispy wedges. Coffee simmered on the stove, bitter and ready for the sweet cream to smooth it out. The scents mixed in the air, filling the room with a warm and satisfying homeyness.

But Minka's stomach rolled with a wave of nausea.

"I'll just have oatmeal this morning, Mom." Minka spooned some from the pot. The thick porridge settled into lumps in her bowl, looking as if someone had been sick in it. She sat down, pushing away the thought. Jane stood by the stove, picking strips of bacon out of the frying pan.

Jennie twisted toward Minka, peering at her with a concerned expression. A drop of bacon grease fell from the wooden spoon in her hand and splattered onto the rag rug beneath her feet. A new thought leapt into Minka's mind: *Is something wrong with Mom?*

Minka felt too tired to think of a way to ask. She picked at her oatmeal.

"Would you girls like to go to the house of Janssens dis afternoon?" Jennie asked from where she knelt scrubbing at the grease spot with a towel. "I talk vit Mrs. Janssen, and she said dat we come for a visit. After dinner, maybe?"

Jane looked up quickly, eyes flashing with delight.

"Yes! Can we? Oh, maybe Nellie will play piano for us. I'm going to wear my blue dress—is it clean?"

Jennie chuckled. "Ja, Jane, is clean. In de closet." She looked at Minka. She seemed to be waiting for something. Looking for something.

"That sounds fun, Mom." The bland response didn't seem

sufficient, even to Minka. "I'll wear my plaid dress." She smiled at Jennie, trying not to look as tired as she felt.

Minka was always happy to get away from the dairy, and a girls-only visit was a rare treat. She just wished she weren't so tired. And she hoped this indigestion would be gone by then.

✳ ✳ ✳

Minka sat in the Janssens' living room, poking her fork at a slice of still-warm spice cake Mom had baked. The Janssens were fellow Dutch, and Minka saw them at church every Sunday. Like most of the other teenaged girls in town, the sisters, Jette and Nellie, attended high school, went to school football games and dances, and regularly saw movies at the theater. They had little in common with Minka or Jane, could not relate to their callused hands or their ignorance of higher mathematics. But Jette and Nellie had been properly brought up and were polite to the DeYoung girls. They sat on the couch, chatting with Jane.

Jane, as always, was perfectly at ease.

Spice cake was Minka's favorite, and treats were rare in their household, where Honus and Jennie sat and pored over each monthly grocery bill. But today the cake tasted sickeningly sweet; she had to force every forkful into her mouth.

Maybe I caught something riding along the milk route on Thursday, she thought. She'd been the one hopping out of the truck to retrieve empty bottles off porches, replacing them with quarts of fresh milk, helping Honus carry crates into the grocery stores, speaking politely to the clerks. Ever since the horrible, worldwide Spanish flu pandemic a decade earlier, everyone worried about diseases and infections that spread from one person to another. Two months earlier, a Scottish scientist had discovered something he called "mould juice," but no one had yet realized the significance of the find; it would be a dozen more years before penicillin was put into production.

"Nellie." Mrs. Janssen stepped in from the kitchen, where she'd been visiting with Minka's mother.

The girls stopped talking and turned in her direction. When adults spoke, children hushed—it was a law of the universe, as surely as the way a stone cupped in your palm and then released would drop straight to the ground.

"Why don't you play something on the piano for our guests?" Mrs. Janssen gestured toward a tall, brown instrument pushed against the wall.

Nellie hesitated, glanced at Jane and then Minka. "Would you like to hear something?"

There were no instruments at Honus's. Minka and Jane nodded at once.

As Nellie raised the sleek lid, revealing the white and black keys, longing and envy vied for Minka's emotions. She watched Nellie flip through a songbook, the thick pages rasping against each other, a prelude to the music. Nellie couldn't play as well as Mrs. Johnston, the organist at church—but she produced a real song. She was making *music*.

Minka looked down at her ruined fingers, now clasped together. It was possible that even if she had a piano, and even if she were offered lessons, she'd never manage the keys smoothly, not with her crooked bones. But if she were Nellie, Minka was sure that she would play every day. She'd play until her hands were too tired to move.

Self-pity was an unknown trait in Minka's world. Jennie didn't complain about her misfortunes, about the backbreaking work that had fallen to her every day since her first husband had died. Minka's earliest memory was of her mother polishing the cookstove at Uncle's with a soft cotton rag, one of a hundred daily tasks she performed from sunup until sundown. This work ethic had been imprinted on Minka's and Jane's souls, and they emulated it faithfully, unconsciously.

But lately Minka felt plagued by a discontent that filled her like a sickness. Nellie's song stirred a wave of sadness and guilt that threatened to bring tears to her eyes. Minka swallowed hard and gritted her teeth to keep from crying, to keep from embarrassing all of them, to keep from drawing another strange look from Jennie. She shifted in Nellie's direction and then caught her mother's eyes already upon her. Minka wished she could go home.

Cleaning and milking were better than this turmoil, these emotions, whatever *this* was.

✳ ✳ ✳

The following day after church, Jennie asked Minka to help hang the washing.

Minka carried the heavy basket outside and set it on the cold, crusted ground. Rays of weak sunshine poked through the clouds, but a steady breeze from across the prairie pushed against her face, chilling her skin. Wet laundry was hung outside no matter how cold it was, even if the clothes froze stiff and had to be thawed inside before folding.

Minka pulled one of Honus's damp shirts from the pile, draped it over the line, clipped it in place. She reached for another. Her mother worked next to her, hanging a pair of Honus's pants. After a moment, Jennie spoke.

"Minnie, where are your rags?"

Minka was distracted, thinking about the cute little boy with soft, black curls and a missing front tooth who'd sat in the pew in front of her that morning. He'd kept turning around and making faces at Minka until his mother whispered fiercely in his ear.

"Hmmm?" she said.

Jennie repeated her question, adding, "Your monthlies."

"Oh." *That*. Those had been blessedly absent for a while. "I haven't been getting them." She hauled a long sheet over the line.

"Not getting? Since when?"

"I don't know. A couple of months now."

Jennie had stopped moving.

"Since de *summer*?"

Minka thought for a moment. "Well . . . I think so. Yes."

Jennie stared at Minka, her soft face anxious. There was a long pause.

"Minnie," her mother said. "Haf you . . . haf you ever . . . been wit a boy?"

A jolt of adrenaline raced through Minka. Even though her mother's words didn't make sense, at the word *boy*, her mind flashed back to *It*—to hot, dry grass crushed under her back, to a trickle of blood, to a cowboy hat against a blazing sky.

"What do you mean?" Her voice came out high-pitched.

"I mean . . . haf you been alone wit a boy? Wanneer hij . . . jou aangeraakt?" *When he touched you?*

How does Mom know about that? Minka thought. *How could she possibly know?* Did someone see and tell her? Had Clara said something, or had Mack come around?

Minka stammered. She couldn't seem to form words.

"Minnie." This time Jennie's voice was firmer. She dropped the sheet she was holding, right on the dirt. She took Minka by the hands and pulled her close. "Tell what happen."

So Minka told. She told about the skating rink, about the walk with Clara, about the camera and the men. Red faced and halt-ingly and staring at the ground, she told it all.

"Oh, Minnie." Minka looked up at the sound of her mother's torn voice. Jennie's gentle eyes spilled over with tears. The white sheet lay around her feet like a wet cloud.

"Minnie . . . I think you are going to haf a baby."

Chapter Three

REVEREND WILLIAM F. KRAUSHAAR's office at Zion Lutheran Church was a fitting backdrop for the dignified minister Minka had known all her life. Important-looking documents hung in fancy frames on the walls, and glass-fronted cabinets were stuffed with thick books. The large desk was wooden, scratched but shiny. The office looked capable of imparting wisdom and serenity to anyone who merely sat in it for a while, which would have been a welcome miracle for Minka. Her entire body seemed to radiate a deep and horrid shame, one that was surely visible to everyone.

She'd never entered the office before today, had never walked down the private hallway that led here. It was another place meant for adults, with closed doors and austere furnishings and silence. She'd tried to step lightly, but the sound of her shoes knocking on the wooden floor echoed much too loudly.

Minka had dressed well for this meeting. In the back of the family's one shared closet at home, she'd caught a glimpse of the white-and-green dress she'd sewn with such expectation, as if the garment might open a door to a new life. Now it hung in a dark corner, worn only that day at Scatterwood Lake and then passed over, time and again, ever since.

As Minka took in the room, her fingers touched the soft pearls that lay against the bodice of her nicest church dress. She was wearing a favorite of her mother's necklaces. Jennie had taken it from a drawer that morning and fastened it around her daughter's neck. The feel of Jennie's arm brushing her shoulder and the familiar smell of the homemade soap she'd used on the dinner dishes had filled Minka's eyes with tears.

Now Minka sat beside Jennie, wishing with all her might that she were somewhere else. A week earlier, when Jennie had made her baffling pronouncement—"You're going to have a baby"—Minka didn't understand at first.

"You mean the stork is coming?" she'd asked.

In an anguished mixture of Dutch and English, her mother had explained that, no, there'd never *been* a stork; well, there were storks, but they were only birds, not mythical messengers skimming heaven and returning with newborns.

The adults in Minka's life, like their parents before them, had taken great pains to play out the cherished fable from their Old World tradition. Some years earlier the family had visited Jennie's brother, who'd also immigrated to America and then married a housemaid. Jennie and Aunt Teresa were talking in the kitchen while Minka and Jane played with their toddler cousin. Abruptly, the sharp wail of a baby sounded from another room.

"Oh my goodness." Teresa covered her mouth in surprise. "Where is dat coming from?"

Minka and Jane looked at each other, eyebrows raised.

"Go on." Teresa prodded the girls. "Go see what it is."

The girls crept into Teresa's bedroom and found a newborn baby lying on the bed, squalling. The window was wide open, the curtains blowing against the wall.

"De stork brought another baby!" Minka's aunt and mother exclaimed.

Minka had raced to the window, trying to catch a glimpse of flapping wings, of this magical bird she'd never seen.

She'd never questioned the story. Although they'd been raised on a farm, there had been a tangled code of propriety governing what she and Jane were exposed to. When Jennie cut off the heads of chickens or geese, the girls stood by to boil the bodies and pluck the feathers, but they weren't allowed near the barn when the big animals—the cows or pigs—were being slaughtered. They knew Uncle drowned the occasional sackful of unwanted barn kittens, but the girls never knew exactly where those kittens had come from, since they were kept from seeing any births.

Until her painful awakening, Minka had pictured storks as heavenly creatures that drew up close to God and returned with soft, wrinkly gifts. She'd looked forward to some distant day, after she was married, when the graceful bird would fly to her home and deliver the babies who were meant for her.

But not a word of it was true. Jennie had explained that a child grew *here*, touching her own stomach. It filled Minka with dread and the sense that she was falling through an unfamiliar space. What more did she believe that was untrue? What other facets of life lacked the wonder and beauty she hoped existed beyond dust, barns, and crates of milk bottles?

With a week to ponder these revelations, the story Minka had trusted all her life sounded silly. She couldn't believe she'd never questioned why Aunt Teresa and some of the church ladies occasionally gained weight—concealed under billowing aprons, yes, but still *there*—then mysteriously lost it. She couldn't believe that in seventeen years, Mom had not found the right moment to turn the page on childhood, to tell her daughters the truth. Minka felt duped.

And now they'd come to Reverend Kraushaar's office.

The Reverend entered the room with a warm hello and sat down behind his desk. When his chair scraped the floor, Minka flinched. She couldn't tell where he was looking, because she kept her eyes locked on the worn edge of a hymnal resting near his arm. She had an urge to pick it up and flip through the pages, to lose herself in the words of familiar songs. To focus on something else for the next half hour.

He already knew, of course. Jennie had visited him earlier this week. At least Minka would not have to sit through hearing the story again—or worse, tell it herself. When Minka was a toddler, her family had attended the small Lutheran church in Warner, near Uncle's farm. Every Sunday, after conducting services here in Aberdeen, Reverend had driven his buggy ten miles to minister to that country congregation too. He was a kind man with daughters of his own, but Minka couldn't imagine telling the Reverend about *It*.

"Minka," he said in a gentle tone, then hesitated. Minka heard him sigh. Her eyes stayed locked on the hymnal. "Your mother told me what happened."

Minka had believed herself incapable of more embarrassment, but hearing him allude to *It*, her face flushed hot all over again. Her head spun until she gripped the arms of the chair to steady herself. Manners dictated a reply.

"Yes, sir," she said, trying and failing to look at his face. Her eyes moved to a seam along the edge of his dark wool suit.

"We've been talking about the best course of action. What would be the best for you and the . . . ah, the child."

Jennie placed a hand on Minka's left arm. Minka was grateful for the pressure. Perhaps it would keep her from sliding away through the floorboards.

The Reverend continued. "While this is certainly a troublesome situation, a terrible wrong bestowed upon you, we have a solution in mind. A way for you to . . . retain your good character. Which I am in no doubt of." To emphasize, he placed one broad hand on his chest, right where Minka was staring. "I know this was not your fault. You are innocent of any wrongdoing. But now we must . . . we must think of your future. And that of the . . . the child to come."

Jennie was evidently not going to interject. Her hand stayed on Minka's arm.

"You see, there is a place I know of. A place down in Sioux Falls where they help girls . . . like you. Girls who have found themselves in, ah, delicate situations. When your time approaches, I will write them and ask for their help.

"In the meantime, your mother and stepfather have decided you will stay with Mr. Vander Zee's aunt in Iowa."

Minka looked at her mother and saw the drawn eyebrows and pressed lips she wore when worried. So this was true. They were sending her away? This felt like a punishment. She'd never been to Sioux Falls or to another state, but she knew these places were far away from home. Minka had dreamed of escaping her dairy life, but not like this.

"It is best if you tell no one of this," the Reverend continued. "Not even your sister. You will deliver the baby, and then . . . there are people who will want to adopt the child. To give it a good home. And you can then return back here. No one will know what happened. You can go on with life as before. . . ."

His voice was drowned out by Minka's own frightened thoughts. Never before had she so wished that children's questions were not *verboten*. Who was going with her? How would she sleep without her sister on the other side of the bed? Would she ever see her family again?

And how could she possibly prepare for this event that was coming?

＊ ＊ ＊

Back at home, Jennie patted Minka's back and suggested she "go lie down," something unheard of in the middle of the day if a person was not deathly sick. Minka did feel unnaturally exhausted, as if she'd been out in the garden hoeing rows all day. But pulsing through her was a strong need to be *doing* something, to lose herself in the familiar rigors of work. After grabbing a dusting rag from a kitchen drawer and stopping in the family's closet to change into overalls, she fled to the second story. She sought escape from her mother's anguished eyes, her sister's puzzled glances, the chattering in her own mind.

But the chattering came right along with her.

So this is it. Everything decided, before she'd walked into Reverend's office. She would have a baby, and then she wouldn't have a baby.

She placed one hand on her stomach. Minka now understood how *It* had become this. Minka's "troubles," as the Reverend referred to her situation, were something that was supposed to happen after marriage, with her husband, not forced upon her by a stranger. Jennie had explained it last week. Minka still struggled to accept it all.

She could hear Jane walking around downstairs, closing doors and drawers as she dusted the first floor. Jane wouldn't pepper their mother with questions. Minka knew those would be saved up for *her*, once they were alone in their room tonight. And she was going to have to be dishonest, again.

"What is wrong with you? Are you sick?" Jane had asked her one morning this week while shaking Minka awake. Honus's simple "Girls" hadn't roused her. And although Jane wasn't as observant as Minka, she'd noticed that their mother treated Minka differently now, almost as she'd always treated Jane. As if she were more fragile, needed some tending to.

Minka had never lied or kept anything from her sister; she'd never had anything to hide until Scatterwood Lake. A baby seemed an impossible thing to conceal, but in the Reverend's office this afternoon, Minka had been assured that she needed to do just that. For her own sake.

Minka took the cloth rag and scrubbed at the banister surrounding the staircase, as though the repetitive movement could wipe away her distress. During warmer months, when windows were left open for circulation, this dusting had to be done every afternoon, even when the air upstairs was hotter than a kettle of boiling peaches at canning time. Between smoke and soot billowing from the trains, and dust being churned up by cows in the nearby stockyard, everything in the house was coated with grime every day.

Now the windows were closed tight against the winter weather and dusting was needed only twice weekly. This had always been Minka's favorite chore—she savored the time alone. She usually practiced singing in front of the mirror, pretending she was the great opera diva from the radio, Madame Schumann-Heink. She envisioned Douglas Fairbanks, or one of the other dark-haired silent film stars who made her pulse flutter, appearing in a doorway, tossing her dust rags and whisking her away from the farm.

Those hours of daydreaming had been a harmless way to pass dull afternoons, but today her thoughts raced. Jane still believed in storks bringing babies. Minka wanted to warn her. Not a stork, but *It*. What if the same thing happened to Jane?

A longing for her sister's friendship rolled over her, a desire for a stronger connection. Their differences often created a wedge between them, with Jane mercilessly teasing her shy sister and Minka envying Jane's ease with strangers, with their own mother. But they'd been each other's only companion all these years, and in rare moments such as this, Minka realized how tightly they were bound together.

After finishing the banisters and baseboards in the hallway, Minka moved into the first of four upstairs bedrooms, the one she and Jane shared. The room was plainly furnished with a double bed and a wooden dresser. The bedspread was creaseless; the rag rug below lined up perfectly with the dresser. Weak daylight spilled in from the side window, and when Minka saw her reflection in the mirror, half of her was illuminated in the soft light and the other half appeared smudged, as though she weren't entirely there. She placed a hand on her stomach again. It was as flat and firm as ever. Yet somewhere in there was a baby, underneath the skin and blood and bones. How could a real baby be that tiny, smaller than a mouse?

Minka had never had many toys, but she had owned a doll once. At Uncle's, the money Jennie earned by selling butter or chickens in town usually went to buy fabric, school shoes, and kitchen supplies. One Christmas Minka had opened a paper-and-twine package and was amazed to find a fancy doll with a leather body and china feet and hands. The doll's eyes closed when it was laid flat. Minka had treated the plaything like a live baby, holding it close and staring at it for long stretches of time. A short time later, toddling Jane had gotten ahold of it and promptly poked its eyes out. But Minka could remember clearly how much she'd treasured that doll, even after it was damaged.

She'd spent countless moments the last week imagining the baby inside of her. She'd pictured herself holding it, patting its back. She'd held Aunt Teresa's baby a few times—she knew how soft a baby's skin was. How helpless they were. Maybe her baby would be a boy, like that boy she'd seen in church last week.

And yet she and this child were destined to be strangers. Would this baby grow up to look like her? Would she know her own son or daughter, if she saw the child on the street?

Minka couldn't guess how long she'd been standing in one spot, looking at the mirror but seeing one scene after another flash by, possibilities and ultimatums and uncertainties. Memories tangled together with thoughts of the future. Maybe if she didn't move, none of these things would happen. She would just be suspended in time, right here, with no decisions to be made or actions to be taken.

Terrible reality slapped Minka awake, leaving no room in her mind for pretending. She, and *It*, had made an actual baby. An unmarried teenager was going to become a mother. And, as Reverend and Mom had made perfectly clear, that girl was going to come home without that baby. This, too, was another piece to process.

What woman received a baby only to give it away?

＊　＊　＊

Her mother was the best person to chart a path for Minka, but even at thirty-nine years old, Jennie didn't know how to break down the stiff boundaries between parents and children. During her childhood in Holland, though Jennie never doubted the love of her mother and father, they did not speak the words. They didn't share their thoughts or affectionately touch their children. It had never occurred to Jennie to tell her own children "I love you," although she did love them, with everything in her.

A week ago, in the middle of the night, Jennie's eyes had flashed open with the possibility of what was wrong with Minka. It couldn't be—and yet, as she'd discovered, it *was*. As her daughter revealed what she had endured and kept locked inside, Jennie's heart felt sliced in half. Since then Jennie had performed all her daily tasks—preparing food and scrubbing floors and feeding chickens and washing clothes—with a deep, sharp ache inside.

She already knew the crushing weight of sudden tragedy. She knew it all too well.

Jennie could not help wondering if this would have happened in the world she'd grown up in. She'd come to this foreign country as a young wife, the first in her family to emigrate, full of hope for adventure. Old memories rushed to the surface, mingling with this new trouble until the weight of it threatened to sink Jennie. Might she be to blame, somehow? Had her youthful choices paved the way for this outcome?

She'd come to America, and America had stolen her daughter's innocence.

Just as, fifteen years ago, it had claimed her husband's life.

* * *

July 1911.

One day after Americans celebrated their country's 135th birthday with fireworks and parades, the SS *Potsdam* entered New York Harbor and sailed past an enormous statue of a robed lady holding a torch. Her brown copper facade, starting to tinge into the soft green that would eventually cover her, reflected a blistering, bright sun. The region was in the middle of a deadly streak of hot weather, and faint harbor breezes brought little relief.

It had been a trying voyage for Tjiske de Jong. When she'd sent her husband, Bouche, ahead of her in April, she hadn't known that their second baby was already nestled deep within her. Now she was nearly five months pregnant, and the heat pasted her long skirts to her legs and swollen stomach. During the journey she'd eaten soda crackers; tended to her toddler son, John; and repeatedly patted her pockets, feeling for the twenty-five American dollars that Bouche had sent her, which she couldn't afford to lose. She'd practiced the new names they'd be using in this new country: Ben and Jennie. The names sounded flatter than she was accustomed to, and her tongue struggled with the muted tones. *Ben and Jennie. Ben and Jennie DeYoung.*

She and her son were spared the large crowds and long waits inside the Ellis Island terminal, an arduous experience reserved for steerage passengers. As a second-class ticket holder, Jennie was allowed to undergo medical examinations aboard the ship. Once released, she and John walked carefully down a gangway and into the chaos of the world's second-largest city.

Using a combination of Dutch, German, and English words with clerks who were used to dealing with immigrants, Jennie collected her luggage and purchased train tickets. Then she and little John boarded the first in a series of rattling railcars that wound along the upper United States and around the Great Lakes. Her new country's vastness kept her staring out the windows. After three days on stuffy trains, past towns and cities dotting an endless expanse of hills, woods, and rolling prairie, Jennie had traveled only halfway across America.

When they'd decided to move, she and her husband had likely never even seen pictures of their destination—the local Dutch newspapers featured only written descriptions and the occasional hand-drawn illustration. But America's fame had grown as large as the country itself, and to millions of Europeans, the stories were irresistible. Free land. Extravagant opportunities. Enough independence to make a man feel like a king.

Before making the ocean crossing three months earlier, Bouche and two friends had been offered jobs by a Dutch acquaintance who'd already settled in a place called South Dakota. They would be working at a dairy—a modest start, but there was plenty of time for future grand plans. Bouche was only twenty-four years old, and although small of stature, he was hardy and a good worker.

When Jennie finally stepped onto the dusty planks of the train station in Aberdeen, South Dakota, her eyes took in glimpses of her new home, but she sought one face. And then she saw Bouche . . . no, *Ben* now . . . with his dear, solemn face and his carefully combed blond hair. His gaze landed on their little boy, her rounded belly, her eyes. He smiled.

Their new town seemed wild and bare and so *young*. Most of the streets were still unpaved, and passing buggies churned up clouds of dirt, leaving deep ruts in the street. There were no wind-mills, no tree-lined canals, no centuries-old cathedrals.

But the family was happy to be together again, and Jennie busied herself with organizing their one-room cabin and sewing clothes for the coming baby. That November she gave birth to a girl they named Minka Bernard DeYoung. The family spent the first days of the baby's life huddled near their cookstove, as the temperature outside hovered near zero and snow piled to alarming heights. Christmas Eve ushered in an even colder snap of weather, and then in January 1912, Aberdeen measured the coldest tem-perature ever recorded there, before or since—a bone-shattering forty-six degrees below zero.

The DeYoung family survived that first harsh winter in their small cabin. The following year, John learned to put together words and sentences, Minka learned to crawl and babble, and Jennie discovered she was pregnant again. The couple felt their lives were blessed. They were saving money, one dollar at a time. Someday they would buy a place of their own. And who knew how many children they would have? They were used to big families—Jennie's own father had produced nine children.

Wrapped up in all these youthful dreams, how could they have guessed what was coming?

※ ※ ※

Sunday, June 29, 1913. Jennie was on bed rest, nursing a nine-day-old newborn, Jane. Minka, now nineteen months old, toddled around after her brother, John. With household supplies running low, Ben decided to go to Aberdeen for groceries. Maybe little John asked to go too—he was nearly four years old—but in the end, all three children stayed home with Jennie. Hours passed. Then more. The cabin grew dim, so Jennie lit a lantern. The chil-dren fell asleep. Ben did not return.

Fear clenched at Jennie's stomach, cold and hard, but there was no one to send to town to find Ben. She kept pacing and peering outside until she could stand it no longer.

Leaving the children in bed, Jennie crept out the door into the warm, dark air. She walked slowly down the road, trying not to jar her still-tender body. Finally, she heard a familiar sound: the clop of horses' hooves, the rattle of buggy wheels. She held the lantern up, its feeble light spilling in front of her, and called out for her husband.

"Is dat jou, Bouche?"

It wasn't Ben. It would never be Ben again.

His friends mournfully explained what had happened. It had been so very hot that day. By the time Ben completed his errands in town, it was late afternoon, and the sun was high and fierce. When he ran into some Dutch friends in Aberdeen, a swim sounded like the best idea in the world. They drove their buggies to Lake Minne-Eho, a popular swimming hole that townspeople had recently carved out of a former slough. It was only a mile or so from home. Ben wanted a quick, cooling dip before starting another hot week at the dairy.

He was not a great swimmer. But there was a small island in the middle of the lake, solid and enticing, and all his friends headed toward it. As Ben followed them, he lost his rhythm. Then his sides began to cramp.

Surely he fought hard, willing his mind to override the sharp pain stabbing through his muscles. As his head bobbed beneath the water, he must have thought of his young wife, his three little ones. His friends moved toward him, calling his name, then shouting to strangers for help.

By the time they reached him, Ben had sunk into a hole formed where an old roadbed crossed the slough. His friends dove again and again. Someone rowed over with a boat. But thirty minutes passed before they could grab hold of Ben's leg. It was far too long.

His friends picked up his heavy, sodden body and placed it

into a buggy. They made the agonizing drive back home. Before they got there, they were met on the dusty road by a twenty-three-year-old woman who, for a few more moments there in the lantern light, did not yet know she was a widow.

For years afterward, Jennie recounted the story to friends, while the children listened silently. She told about the drive to the cemetery, when the cart driver had hurried across the dirt roads, jostling the wooden casket behind him. This bit of indignity would hurt Jennie for the rest of her life. Her beloved lay inside that bouncing box, the man with the full lips and the boyish nose whom she'd married when she was just a teenager. The father of her babies deserved more respect.

Jennie stood at the grave site, holding her newborn in one arm, gripping the hand of her toddler daughter in the other.

"John," she said to her son, "houd mijn rok vast . . . en nooit loslaten." *Hold on to my skirt . . . and never let go.*

After just two years in America, most of that time spent in a cabin with her children or with other immigrants, Jennie still struggled to speak English. She had no professional skills. But she knew how to keep house, how to stretch a dollar, how to work harder than anyone else. Now solely responsible for the survival of a family of four, she would have to make do.

She certainly wasn't going anywhere without her children—that point was nonnegotiable. When farmers came to interview Jennie for housekeeper positions, she'd point firmly to the corner, where her children played and the baby slept, and say one English word, over and over. "Mine. Mine."

Where I go, she meant, *they go.*

Jennie gratefully accepted her first job offer from a young farmer, who seemed to fancy the Dutch widow. But he was less enamored with the children. He took John to the hayloft and left him there alone. He put Minka into a trunk and closed the lid over her. He pushed baby Jane near to the stove, close enough to singe her feet.

After a few weeks, Jennie gathered up her children and left. She wasn't going to sacrifice their safety, not even for their survival. And finally salvation came in the form of an older German farmer named Pansegrau. The children couldn't pronounce his name.

They simply called him "Uncle."

※　※　※

In the end, for all her efforts to survive with her children and to shelter them from the tragedies of life, Jennie was not able to protect her quiet daughter. Minka had always been such an obedient girl, so uncomplaining. She could be stubborn, to be sure, but she'd never caused Jennie to wonder how she'd "turn out." Independent John and carefree Jane were the ones who needed close watching.

There was one thing left in Jennie's power: she would do everything she could to soften the repercussions for Minka. The baby would be placed in another home with a real family. Minka deserved a good life, free from disgrace. She needed to go away before her thin body started to swell with the proof of her *situation*. Jennie knew this. Honus knew this. The Reverend knew this. And no one else needed to know anything.

Minka would be going south as quickly as possible. By next summer, it would all be over. And just maybe, for Jennie's precious daughter, it could somehow be as if nothing bad had ever happened.

Chapter Four

OVER THE WEEKS, Minka caught her sister eyeing her, once when Minka reached for a cow's udder and a sharp pain made her gasp, and several times when she lifted her nightdress over her head.

"You're getting fat," Jane finally said one Sunday morning when Minka struggled with the buttons of her dress.

What overalls could hide all week, Minka's church dresses could not. Her breasts had grown, making her figure resemble that of a curvy movie star. Minka shrugged at Jane's comment. She was afraid to offer an excuse her sister would see right through.

When Jane repeated the observation to their mother over breakfast, Jennie replied without pause. "Minnie seventeen, no little girl now."

For weeks, Minka had fought the compulsion to rub her hands over her growing stomach. She was ever mindful of her sister, who didn't hide her frustration about the underlying changes that had occurred within the house. Their mother treated Jane with a thread of impatience, while being kinder to her older sister. Even Honus tiptoed around them more than usual. And Minka acted oddly, avoiding her sister even at bedtime. There were secrets woven into their lives now, but of course Jane could not suspect the enormity of the deceit.

Shortly after Christmas, Jennie told Minka that she and Honus would be driving her to Tante Hogerhide's house in Iowa the following week. Minka barely knew Honus's aunt, but the girl knew she needed to leave soon.

When the day came, Jane was not happy to be left behind. A couple of Honus's friends were helping with the milking and deliveries, and Mrs. Janssen would check on Jane every day, but Jane would be alone with her routine unchanged—except for Minka's glaring absence. That morning Jane barely said good-bye as she stomped to the barn, looking pretty as usual, even in her worn overalls.

Jane had been told that Minka was headed to Tante's house, but she knew that the dead of winter was not the typical season for visiting distant relatives. Who on earth went traipsing around the countryside when they could get caught in a snowstorm? She worked at the reasons behind her sister's departure, dropping hints, watching for reactions. Maybe Tante Hogerhide needed help or was sick or dying, and her grown sons were of little assistance. But then why couldn't they just tell Jane that?

Or perhaps Honus and Jennie were already seeking a husband for Minka. The sisters knew one or two girls, barely older than Minka, who'd already gotten betrothed.

As Minka, wearing her Sunday best under her wool coat and clutching a borrowed luggage bag, waited for Honus to bring the truck around, she knew she appeared to be a favored child going on an adventure.

In reality, she was so nervous she felt like throwing up.

If Jane only knew.

✳ ✳ ✳

A great unknown waited over the frozen plains, beyond the icy morning horizon. Minka, who'd never been more than fifteen miles from Aberdeen, was filled with both apprehension and curiosity.

The milk truck jostled down slushy roads and the occasional paved highway, moving toward a future that felt like puzzle pieces, scattered and loose in the wind. And no matter how tightly Minka wished to grasp all that remained behind her—her sister, the dairy, and the routine that divided each day and week into a steady, predictable rhythm—hour after hour this unknown approached, and the familiarity of home receded.

With one hand resting on the door for balance and the other holding the blanket around her winter coat, Minka rode on a milk crate in the enclosed back of the rattling truck. The luggage bag sat at her feet. She'd never used such a thing before.

As Honus drove, his eyes stared forward, flashing on occasion to the rearview mirror, then back to the road. Jennie sat stiffly in the passenger seat, rarely speaking except in short conversations with Honus that Minka did not try to hear.

Minka had never been an excitable girl, except during threshing time at Uncle's, when the sight of the big machines thundering up the lane made even grown adults giddy. Minka remembered running to hang off fences when the great threshing caravan arrived on a late-summer morning. But now her emotions threatened to overwhelm her. Her breath came shallow, and her pulse pounded in her throat, prompting her to undo several buttons near her neck. She'd already added to the waistline of this dress when her flat stomach started rounding out, but her belly still constricted against the fabric at every deep breath.

She wiped her hand across the cold glass where her breath kept clouding out the landscape. The prairie's continuity made her think of her mother's descriptions of the endless ocean that had carried Jennie from Holland. The familiar vista of open farmland helped to steady Minka.

A visitor to South Dakota might not see the variations in the landscape. But Minka watched how the land took on different characteristics over the miles: rising up tall like enormous piles of hay, or bunching up like a porch rug rumpled against the front door. Then the rolling hills flattened out for miles, as if pressed down with an iron.

Farms cut up sections of prairie, but at this early time of year they were stripped bare of crops and dusted with snow. Stands of elm, willow, and cottonwood trees reached bare arms skyward or stood like sentries protecting rivers and streams. Towns, some large and others barely outposts, were a welcome distraction. Whenever the truck passed through one, Minka drew close to the glass, holding her breath to keep the view clear as she studied people and buildings.

In one town, as Honus slowed to navigate between pedestrians and autos and wagons, Minka caught the eye of a young girl who stood yanking at her mother's long coat. The mother was engrossed in a heated discussion with a butcher wearing a bloodstained apron. The girl stared at the truck, then waved at Minka, who lifted a hand in return as the milk truck continued by.

Minka had once been that girl watching people travel on, wondering if they were headed to the exciting places she heard about on the radio, places she had seen only in newsreels at the movie theater, where the black-and-white images seemed not particularly connected to the real world. She knew there were exciting and dangerous places like New York—Jennie had told of her first glimpse of America, in a city that seemed big enough to swallow up all of Holland—or shimmering playgrounds like Hollywood, where palm trees stood tall and the weather was so warm that men and women lounged around wearing bathing suits as revealing as

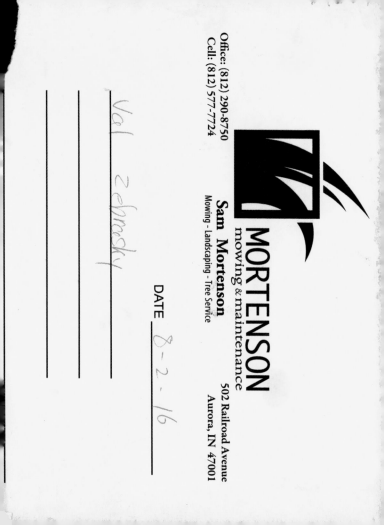

MORTENSON
mowing & maintenance

Sam Mortenson
Mowing - Landscaping - Tree Service

Office: (812) 290-8750
Cell: (812) 577-7724

502 Railroad Avenue
Aurora, IN 47001

Val Zebresky

DATE _8-2-16_

underwear. These worlds half-existed to Minka, like the imaginary lands in fairy tales.

Now she traveled not just to another town but to a different state. Minka would have given anything to go home, but her sentence had been handed out. Not until this baby was born would Minka be allowed to return.

*   *   *

After a short break for lunch and then more cold miles in the truck, Honus pulled to a stop in front of a two-story bungalow with white clapboard siding and a tidy front porch. They were in northern Iowa, not far from her ultimate destination of Sioux Falls. The houses here were lined up with trim lawns and long walkways, and it was *quiet*. This place was nothing like home, where barns and silos were surrounded by acres of crops and a clanking rail yard stood across the street.

Minka stretched her aching limbs as she stepped from the truck. It was warmer here than in Aberdeen, although in this case "warmer" was still well below freezing. Honus carried Minka's bag with a kind of silent compassion that had been subtly on display since her troubles began.

Tante Hogerhide opened the door as they reached the porch steps. She ushered them inside, out of the biting afternoon air.

"Welkom, welkom, kom je maar opwarmen bij het vuur," Tante said. *Come and warm yourself by the fire.* She touched Minka's shoulder, drawing her deeper into the house. Her gentle hand brought a small relief. At least Minka wasn't being abandoned into the hands of a tyrant.

"Danke," Minka murmured. Her face flushed. Kind aunt notwithstanding, this whole thing was deeply embarrassing.

Minka stood at the small coal stove and discreetly glanced around. This house was as neat and clean as her own home, but it didn't smell the same—there was no overlying scent of train smokestacks and barn animals. The three adults excused themselves, speaking quietly as though at a funeral. Lowered voices moved up the stairs and through the rooms as Tante showed Honus where to place Minka's bag and they discussed plans for the girl.

Honus and Jennie remained for less than an hour. They were needed at the dairy and hoped to return before the evening milking. A thick lump rose in Minka's throat, threatening to choke her. She had a childish urge to wrap her arms around her mother's legs, to beg Jennie to take her with them.

In Minka's whole life, she'd only been away from her mother once before. She'd been around eleven years old and had just had her tonsils out. Her mother couldn't leave Uncle's farm, so Minka spent a week in Aberdeen with another Dutch family, to be near the doctor. Although recovering from surgery, Minka had been expected to get up and help tend to a passel of little kids for the week. She'd been terribly homesick and had been weak with relief when she got back to Uncle's, back to Jennie.

Now, she'd be much farther away, for months. And she was facing a much more frightening ordeal.

Minka walked outside with her mother and stepfather. "I write. Will try . . . every day," Jennie said and embraced Minka, clinging a moment longer as if she too fought against this good-bye. Then Jennie dropped her arms. Mother and daughter stood facing each other, eyes locked in an acknowledgment of shared resilience. In that moment, Jennie saw herself all those years ago, facing insurmountable obstacles and being completely alone. She couldn't spare Minka from this burden, no matter how much she wished it.

Minka understood the basics of the days ahead. She would live with Tante Hogerhide and her adult son Bill for the coming weeks. Minka's stomach would get bigger. It still amazed her to think a life was growing there. She would have a baby, then not have a baby. Eventually, the milk truck would return her to the dairy, to Jane, to milking cows and working at the slaughterhouse.

It would be as though nothing had changed. Was that even possible?

Minka watched her mother and Honus climb into the milk truck without a backward glance. The windows were fogged, but she thought she saw her mother swipe at her cheeks.

With her arms wrapped above the small bulge of her stomach, Minka remained stock-still until the truck disappeared down the street. She turned inside without protest or tears. She did not run after the milk truck, as her heart and feet yearned to do. As Minka closed the door behind her, she wondered what she should do next.

At home, nearly every moment was filled with scheduled chores. Now she stood awkwardly until Tante told her to sit. Minka clasped her hands tightly in her lap. She wished Jane were there with her easy chatter. Minka believed that if her sister tried, she could charm a starving man into handing over his last piece of bread. Jane would never have let this room descend into such uneasy silence.

That first night, Tante refused Minka's help getting supper on the table. Her son Bill came home, parking his car in the garage and joining them in the dining room. Minka tried releasing the tension she felt around them both, particularly around Bill. She caught herself straightening her posture, then remembering and trying to cover her stomach. Her face burned when Bill seemed to notice.

"You'll like it here, I think. It's nothing like Minneapolis or Chicago, but it's a sight better than Aberdeen," Bill said with a jovial wink.

"Aberdeen is a nice town too," Tante said with a frown to her son. "South Dakota . . . it is all a nice place. Dey have lakes, and de Black Hills . . ."

"Yes," Bill said. "But do they have a president-elect?"

Tante tilted her head in acknowledgment.

"No, I suppose not. But is still a nice place."

Having trounced his Roman Catholic opponent the previous fall, Republican Herbert Hoover was awaiting his March inauguration. Hoover had been born in eastern Iowa, and although he'd left ages ago, proud Iowans claimed him as their own.

Minka smiled at Tante's attempt to defend Aberdeen, and she realized that for the first time adults were speaking to her as if she were one of them, including her in the conversation.

Minka ate quickly. The meal, like the house and everything else here, was pleasant but different, enough to make her feel unsettled. Afterward, Tante wouldn't allow Minka to help with the cleanup.

"You must be tired, ja? Rest now."

Bill invited her to listen to the radio, but Minka excused herself to the quietness of her upstairs bedroom. A cast-iron apparatus Tante called a radiator took the chill from the room. Minka slowly unpacked her belongings, refolding linens several times, setting them into an empty wooden dresser. This was the first time she'd had a room to herself.

Daylight had vanished outside, and when Minka held up a lantern near the window, she could see snow falling in the dark. The delicious feeling of solitude drained away and was replaced by a sense of lonely abandonment. She changed into a loose nightgown and slid between the cold sheets. Minka felt convinced that she'd never sleep, not with her thoughts crowding one on top of the other, not without Jane's warmth beside her. Change had really come—there was no going back. It was terrifying.

Minka woke to a sensation that something was wrong. Then she remembered where she was. Someone walked past her door and into another room.

The night passed in restless dozing, interrupted by spans of being fully awake, staring into the pitch-black night. The suburban quiet, unbroken by sounds of animals and trains, was disconcerting.

Long before winter dawn touched the horizon, Minka sat up in bed, drawing her knees to her chest. Jane would be awake, putting on her overalls and heading to the barn. How had her sister slept on her first night alone? Minka wondered.

Minka thought of her sister every morning as the first day turned to the first week and to the first month. There wasn't a single night that she didn't miss Jane's presence in the bed, or a morning she didn't mentally walk through the milking chores with her. It was even harder for her sister, Minka guessed. It was always harder to be left behind.

While Minka ached for home, she was surprised by how well she'd adapted to a new life. The queasiness in her stomach passed. Even without the protection of her family, she did not fall to pieces. Physically she seemed to be as strong as ever, and she eagerly performed as many chores around the house as Tante permitted. The older woman exclaimed at how clean everything was with a girl instead of only boys in her house.

Tante moved with the same briskness as Honus, but less rigidly. There were no hugs or understanding talks, no direct mention of Minka's pregnancy—that was danced around with comments: "until you leave" or "when your time draws near." But Tante's welcome was implicit in her kind words and generous nature, and Minka appreciated it. Tante even brought her a pattern and fabric for a new dress, one with an expanded waist.

Tante sometimes insisted that Minka rest. Since empty spaces of time could magnify the loneliness, Minka wrote letters. She addressed them to Jennie, but knowing that Jane would eagerly read whatever she wrote, she omitted any mention of her pregnancy.

By March the icy streets had thawed, and when Tante took her to church on Sunday or out shopping in the bustling city shops, Minka began to notice women pushing babies in frilly carriages. She was thankful that a large wool coat could help mask her now-obvious belly, but sometimes she caught someone giving her a long glance—and her face burned like a confession.

It was not uncommon for girls her age to be married, of course, and none of these people knew she wasn't—that was the whole reason for her having come to this city full of strangers. Still, the thought that passersby might know her condition made her want to hide away in the house.

One sunny day Tante coaxed Minka outside to visit the Sergeant Floyd Monument, a striking, hundred-foot sandstone obelisk towering over the Missouri River, built to honor the one member of the Lewis and Clark expedition who died during the journey. Much later, in 1960, the monument would become America's first National Historic Landmark.

Tante did not treat Minka like a child. She spoke openly of her own concerns, lamenting over her son's drinking. Prohibition was the law of the land, but alcohol was fairly easy to come by, especially in corn-rich Iowa. Some nights when Bill pulled his car into the garage at an especially late hour, Minka could hear Tante helping her son to his room and murmuring, "Oh, Bill, Bill, Bill."

When Minka was alone, she unabashedly held her stomach and winced in troubled wonder at the sharp kicks and movements. How much larger could she possibly grow?

✳ ✳ ✳

Back in Aberdeen, the Reverend Kraushaar had followed through on his promise to contact the facility in Sioux Falls that aided expectant unmarried young ladies. Not long after, he received the reply he'd been waiting for.

April 5, 1929

Dear Rev. Kraushaar,

*We have your letter with reference to a case in your congregation who may need such care as we are able to give.
. . . our rates here are $25.00 per month while the*

*patient is with us. Then there is the charge of $50.00
covering confinement care. All confinements are taken care of
in one of our local hospitals, which insures the patient of the
best of care, and they have made us this special rate covering
each case.*

*Mothers are required to return from the hospital with the
child and remain in the home one month before final plans
are made for the child.*

*We require patients to furnish, before entering, a doctor's
certificate, showing that she is free from venereal disease as
we are not equipped to care for diseased cases and we must
protect the others who may be here. . . .*

*We do have a home finding department which finds good
Christian homes for babies . . . and Lutheran babies are
placed in Lutheran homes. . . .*

*We shall be very glad to cooperate in the care of this case,
and shall be glad to hear from you again.*

Very sincerely,

*Miss Bragstad
Lutheran House of Mercy*

One hundred and fifty miles east of Tante's home, a mother of
sons longed for a girl. Nine years earlier, Olava Nordsletten and
her husband had adopted a baby son only weeks after her own
newborn's death. She'd taken him into her arms so soon that she
was able to nurse him, a comfort to them both. The years following brought her more pregnancies, and these didn't end with
death, but with two healthy boys.

As the three boys grew older and explored the world outside,
Olava imagined frilly dresses, matching aprons, and a little girl
asleep in her lap. She went to her husband. Adoption was once
again on her mind.

"I want a daughter to call my own."

Chapter Five

"The Lord gave, and the Lord hath taken away."

Those meditative words had been with Reverend Kraushaar since he'd woken beside his wife on this Sunday morning in April, even though that Scripture from Job was not part of the liturgy he would follow today. The lectionary calendar of the season called for more joyous verses on this week. Yet the sober words from the Old Testament had followed him to the church.

Perhaps the season brought the verse to mind. Easter Sunday was just behind them, most certainly a reminder of the ebb and flow of Christ being given to mankind and then taken by man's own hand, given again through the Resurrection, and then finally taken away by the Ascension. This Second Sunday of Easter began the anticipation of Pentecost, a new giving from God to His people.

Now the Reverend stood in his pastoral robe before the congregation he knew like family, taking in their faces. He'd preached along with the seasons the people lived and worked by, comforting and instructing immigrant farmers through sorrowful times: the Great War and the Spanish flu, droughts and fires. He'd shared their major life events of weddings, funerals, births, and baptisms. And he'd been with them in more private moments, the broken tears, the anger with God. The Reverend's stalwart flock took adversity in stride, and his weekly instruction and private counsel eased their burdens, even if only in a small way. Often there was no reasonable explanation for heartbreak, for loss.

Thus the passage from Job seemed a theme in this land of hardship, among these people. To remember that "the Lord gave, and the Lord hath taken away" was to remember God's goodness. It helped the Reverend himself to lean on God's divine will, to trust in His sovereign, sometimes mysterious ways.

As he read the day's appointed Scripture verses from the pulpit, Reverend Kraushaar's eyes lingered a moment on Jennie Vander Zee. Her husband sat on one side and her younger daughter, Jane, on the other. Jane appeared not to be listening. Her eyes skimmed the congregation even though her face was turned respectfully toward the front.

In the months since Jennie had first come to him about Minka's troubles, Jennie had visibly aged, though she was not yet forty. But today, Reverend Kraushaar had news he hoped would comfort the couple and provide the best arrangement for their oldest daughter.

The minister brought the sermon toward a conclusion a short time later. He'd been preaching and shepherding these people and this church since August 9, 1908. Now, over twenty years later, his time in South Dakota was about to end.

The Lord gave. The Lord took.

God had opened a new path for him and his family as president of the Lutheran College of Seguin, Texas. He felt honored by the offer, and he relished the new challenge at this time in his life. Yet it meant leaving the congregation he'd served for so long. He'd come to feel what he sensed was God's divine love for this flock.

Around him it seemed a season of taking away, he thought, as his eyes again rested on the Vander Zee family. The call to help the girl and the family was heavy upon him. His work in Aberdeen was not quite done.

He'd known Jennie Vander Zee when she was still Jennie DeYoung, a widowed mother of three young ones who lived and worked as a housekeeper to the elderly Gus Pansegrau. In those days, Reverend Kraushaar had been an almost itinerant preacher, and so young! Then he'd served as a chaplain in the Great War and had earned the kind of knowledge that comes not from seminary books but from sharing mankind's heaviest burdens.

The Scriptures charged the church with the care of widows and orphans. The still-young widow Jennie had done well for herself compared to others in her situation. The Reverend had been comforted by the security her family found during their many years with Uncle.

Jennie's children had been raised with a firm yet loving hand. Her marriage to Honus Vander Zee further improved her situation, and the minister enjoyed watching two dedicated churchgoers— from his two different flocks—come together in such a pleasing union. The joined family appeared to flourish after they bought the dairy. They ran it well, although Jennie's oldest child, John, had resisted the transition and had chosen a military life over milking. John was a tall, strong, fatherless boy. For such as he, the Reverend knew, soldiering was often a good fit.

If only John's sisters had been allowed to continue their education, at least through high school. The Reverend placed a high value on education. But after two decades with his congregation, he understood his community. Times were hard, and immigrant families worked together. Education was considered a luxury by most.

God had been good to Jennie DeYoung and her children. The tragedies of other families, those who had lost sons to war or farms to drought, put that into perspective. They were safe, together, thriving with the new business it seemed. They, and their dairy, were an integral part of Aberdeen. But missing now from his congregation was Jennie's middle child.

The Lord gives and takes away. As Reverend Kraushaar's mind touched on this verse, he thought of the most oft-repeated question he heard as a minister, the one most wrestled with in the human experience: "Why?"

The Reverend knew the answer to that was usually a long time coming.

❋ ❋ ❋

After the Lord's Supper and the closing of the service, the minister stood near the back of the church, bidding his congregation farewell, watching the slow approach of the Vander Zee family as Jennie and Jane spoke to other women and daughters. When Honus reached him, the Reverend leaned close as they shook hands.

"If I may have a word with you and Mrs. Vander Zee in my office."

Honus nodded. He caught Jennie's eye and gave a slight motion of his head. She excused herself from a lively discussion. Jane remained behind but watched them with a slight frown.

"I received word from the facility that I spoke to you about," the minister said after he closed the door to his office. He spoke German fluently but had noticed that parishioners seemed to prefer speaking English with him. Perhaps it seemed more proper.

"In Sioux Falls?"

"Yes, at the Lutheran House of Mercy." Handing Jennie a piece of paper, he continued. "This is the letter I received. I have known the superintendent for many years, and Minnie will be well taken care of here, if it's acceptable to you both."

He noticed how Jennie gripped the letter as she read, concern etched into the wrinkles of her forehead. She winced, and he guessed she'd read the price or about the required test for vene-real disease—an awkward matter, but understandably necessary. Jennie's finger touched a place on the letter as she glanced at Honus, who leaned close to read it. This was most likely the price of Minka's stay and the doctor's fees.

"We pay," Honus said without hesitation. The cost, $50 plus room and board, was a steep one, especially for a frugal Dutch family who diligently managed each penny, and in a time when bread cost eight to ten cents a loaf and a head of cattle could be sold for $59 each.

None of them could have guessed that by the end of that very year, the stock market would crash, ushering in the Great Depression. In five short years, the price of cattle would plummet to $17.50 per head.

"Dit is het beste," Honus said to Jennie. *This is best.* She nod-ded and dropped her hands to her lap as relief came over her features, but also something else—the mask of sorrow, or perhaps shame, that had marked her face over the past half year.

"She come home soon after child," Jennie said. She didn't want Minka to be with the baby after its birth—it would make everything harder. The minister took in the mother's concerns. Jennie knew her daughter better than anyone. Minka reminded the Reverend of his own three daughters, sheltered and completely susceptible to such a vile act. This was an example of the evils of the world preying upon the innocent.

"I will do all I can to get Minnie promptly installed at this place," he promised.

As the couple left his office, Reverend Kraushaar opened his desk and withdrew two pieces of clean stationery. Today was the Sabbath and his family would be waiting with dinner, but Reverend Kraushaar could not delay. The time was coming quickly. First he wrote a quick note to Minka.

Then to Miss Bragstad of the Lutheran House of Mercy.

To Miss Bragstad,

. . . The girl referred to is Minnie DeYoung, at present at 3315 E. Ave. Sioux City, Iowa. Her case is a peculiar one, since her parents insist that the baby must be given away and Minnie return home as soon as possible.

There are other children in the family, esp., another younger sister, from whom they wish to hide Minnie's condition, and then, too, Minnie's rehabilitation here would be practically impossible were she to return with a baby.

Minnie is as innocent a girl as I have ever met. She is the victim of a foul assault. . . . The mother thinks that the child should be taken from Minnie directly after birth and Minnie return home about three weeks thereafter, but can you take care of such a small child until its adoption?

I want to do as much for Minnie as I would for my own daughter. . . . Thanking you for any kindness shown this unfortunate girl.

Sincerely yours,
Rev. Kraushaar

❋ ❋ ❋

"It appears we will have a new arrival in a few weeks," Miss Bertha Bragstad said to her assistant, Miss Julia Questad. As they sat together reviewing the schedule for the week ahead, Miss Bragstad's eyes brushed over the response she'd been writing to Reverend Kraushaar. "Her name is Miss Minnie DeYoung."

"When is her expected time of confinement?" Miss Questad asked as she scribbled down the name.

"Toward the end of May. I must write to explain our policy, however, that she must stay here for a month afterward. Her family wants her to return home immediately, but I have faith they will understand. This young woman comes highly recommended from her minister. She is innocent of the situation she finds herself in."

"That is most difficult," Miss Questad said.

Miss Bragstad caught Miss Questad's raised eyebrow. The matron of the house steadied her gaze at the young woman. "With this one, *I* believe in her innocence as well."

"Oh yes, of course." The doubtful look vanished, and Miss Questad's back straightened.

Miss Bragstad pushed up from the smooth wooden desk with a gentle sigh.

"Receive this not as a reprimand, but a reminder. In your time here, you've heard every story of innocence. Sometimes it is the truth; usually it is not. Regardless of the circumstances, our duty is to treat every young woman without prejudice and with the best possible care. Believe me, they will have a difficult journey ahead, whether innocent or not."

"I apologize." Miss Questad shifted in her seat with eyes lowered to the page open on her lap.

Miss Bragstad walked toward the door, giving the young woman's shoulder a reassuring squeeze. "No apology necessary. Now let us start our rounds."

The younger woman held back as if still embarrassed, but Miss Bragstad knew it would pass. Such reminders were necessary for all of them, herself included. The Lord called them to be compassionate and full of grace at the Lutheran House of Mercy.

Whatever circumstances brought the unwed mothers to their door, Miss Bragstad wished them to leave with a renewed hope that they might become women of character and dignity as they reentered the world outside.

The two women walked the long hallway, reviewing current issues: repairs needed to the stairway railing, a suitable substitute for the cook while she visited family, the review of a recent adoption, adjustments to their tightening budget. They passed the parlor and grand stairway. The sound of breakfast dishes being washed chimed from the kitchen as the cook and her assistant made the transition from one meal to the next.

Several young women occupied the house at the moment, three waiting for their children to be born. One girl was preparing to leave with her baby, under the determined belief that the child's father would accept them once he saw his newborn son.

"When does Miss Sheldon leave?" Miss Bragstad asked before ascending the stairs. She was planning to talk once more to that hopeful new mother.

"Next Sunday. I'll arrange to have her room prepared for the new arrival."

"Very good," Miss Bragstad said. She savored moments like this when the house and office ran well. She had developed a well-oiled system for arrivals and departures, for the housekeeping and kitchen staff, for the arrangements that she coordinated between adoptive parents, the state of South Dakota, and birth parents.

Miss Bragstad had taken the position of matron superintendent at the Lutheran House of Mercy eight years earlier, in 1921. Now, at the age of forty-three, Bertha Bragstad had settled into her role as a spinster. She'd experienced her own disappointments in life, but in her current position—an appointment to be proud of—she'd found a place where she excelled and where others respected her.

Painful childhood losses had prepared her to run this home, where she tried to counter the humiliation carried by arriving girls with the kind of empathy that would guide them into new lives. If an orphaned girl like herself could become the matron of such a respected establishment, these women could also set a fresh path for their own lives.

There were few boundaries between her personal and professional life. Miss Bragstad took on every necessary role without complaint. She lived in the downstairs quarters and was on call day and night. There were plenty of midnight wake ups. In emergencies, Miss Bragstad became a stand-in nurse or temporary doctor. She counseled the young women on their options, listened to their plans for the future, provided arms to soothe heartache, and carefully disciplined the girls when rules were broken.

Over the full twenty-eight years of her career, Bertha Bragstad would easily slip into the shoes of mother and grandmother to hundreds of teenaged mothers and the infants they brought back to the House of Mercy from the hospital. But she would never marry or have children of her own.

"Instead of Miss Sheldon's room, let us put our new arrival in the Rose Room," Miss Bragstad said, pausing in her steps as she considered the Reverend's letter again. Miss Questad appeared surprised but marked the change in her notes.

The Rose Room was Miss Bragstad's favorite upstairs room, the one into which the best light spilled this time of year. Reverend Kraushaar's recommendation meant something to her. If he would treat the girl as his own daughter, then she would as well.

The girl had been through enough already, and Miss Bragstad knew all too well that the worst was yet to come.

Chapter Six

MINKA HESITATED in the back of the milk truck as the engine quieted. She stared through the window at the grand house where she'd be spending the next two months. Her mother opened the truck's back door and motioned toward her.

"Come, Minnie."

Minka held the door frame to steady herself as she stepped down. Honus retrieved her luggage bag. As Minka crossed her hands in front of her rounded stomach, her eyes looked up and along the beautiful white, two-story house that sat perched at the crest of a tree-shaded hill. The home presented a warm greeting with its neat yard, sweeping porch that gazed down across the bright lawn, and vivid flowers that peeked from a gated garden around the corner of the house. The buds on the trees had recently burst open, like thousands of green butterflies emerging from their winter cocoons. Normally, such a lovely sight would thrill her.

But normal had departed Minka's life months ago.

Honus and Jennie had come back to Tante's to deliver Minka

to the Lutheran House of Mercy, and on the drive from Iowa to Sioux Falls, Minka had felt panicked by the draining away of time. The anticipation of the reunion with Jennie had buoyed Minka's spirits for weeks, but now they had just a few hours together.

And the calendar was pushing her ever closer to the great unknown of childbirth.

She'd barely thanked and said good-bye to Tante Hogerhide. Tante had appeared sad to see her go, holding the girl's shoulders tightly as she reminded Minka to return for a visit.

Once in the truck, Minka's thirst for news had loosened her tongue. Much had been left unsaid in the letters she and Jennie had regularly exchanged.

"How is Jane? What has she been doing? Does she ask about me?" Minka had inquired, leaning through the window to the front of the truck. By a few miles into the drive, Minka had already asked about the dairy, the Janssens and other Dutch families, even Honus's dog. She wanted any news from Aberdeen, no matter how trivial.

But Jennie and Honus had not become more talkative in the months Minka was away. The pauses and silence between her questions reminded Minka that to her mother and stepfather, she was still a child, and children spoke only when spoken to. Jennie did mention a couple in church who'd been married earlier that month, and then, most shockingly, that Reverend Kraushaar would be taking a new position as president of a college in faraway Texas. Minka tucked that information away to process later. Too many other emotions and details were vying for her attention.

The meager responses to her questions were disappointing. Jennie seemed anxious about reaching their destination and reminded Minka twice that she should display gratitude for her acceptance to the House of Mercy. With a sigh, Minka settled back for the ride.

It was a perfect spring day. Minka wore the only thing that

fit her now, a cotton shift dress that hung formlessly around her. Their route followed the winding Big Sioux River, which was swollen after a recent rainfall. Following months of cold, the warm sun and fresh-smelling air blowing through the front windows gave Minka moments of giddiness.

Then reality twisted her stomach. Her exile was almost at an end, but first she had to adapt all over again to another new place. And now she was not staying with a relative, but in a house for other disgraced girls. Here she would wait to have the baby . . . and then what? She suspected there were other details she'd yet to be told.

She wondered if she would have to earn her keep, if the people at the House of Mercy would expect her to clean or to go to town on errands. Although she was still plenty strong, her swollen stomach made it difficult to maneuver. And she no longer wore the winter coat that had hidden her new shape. She hated exposing herself and garnering curious glances.

✳ ✳ ✳

Now she stood in the driveway, looking up at this House of Mercy. The air seemed so quiet and still. She detected no movement inside the home or in the yard.

"The superintendent wrote back and said it would be okay if I arrived today," Minka said. She felt suddenly uncertain. "Well, someone did. The note wasn't signed. I wrote that I'd do anything they needed, but they didn't say what to do. . . ." She took one step closer to Jennie.

Just then the double doors to the house swept open and two women in neat, modest dresses descended the stairs to greet them. Minka walked forward, between her mother and Honus. Behind her, the milk truck she'd once detested seemed a haven.

"Welcome. My name is Bertha Bragstad, and I am the superintendent of the Lutheran House of Mercy." The woman who spoke was about Jennie's age. She smiled directly at Minka, as though the girl wasn't a disgraced outcast but a friend. Minka's muscles relaxed.

Miss Bragstad greeted Honus and Jennie and introduced her assistant, Miss Questad. Then she turned back to Minka.

"And you are Minnie," she said. She sounded pleased to be meeting her.

"Yes," Minka said. "Well . . . my name is Minka, but everybody calls me Minnie. How do you do?"

"I am very well, thank you. Which name do you prefer to go by: Minnie or Minka?"

"Oh, I've always been called Minnie."

Miss Bragstad waited as if this wasn't an answer, but when Minka didn't offer any more information, the matron invited them inside for a tour of the house. Honus excused himself to remain on the front porch, where a couple of wooden rockers offered an escape from a houseful of pregnant girls.

The inside of the house was neat and clean, and the decorations bore a light, feminine touch. Freshly cut irises brightened table-tops. The furniture, lamps, and rugs appeared carefully chosen for each room.

Upstairs, Minka was introduced to several other girls. One was knitting in her room with her hands resting on her stomach, and another was reading from a stack of books on a small desk. The door to one room was closed, and Miss Bragstad explained that the baby inside might be napping and shouldn't be disturbed.

Minka felt like that particular door was the entrance to a secret room. She'd soon find herself behind such a door, with a baby asleep beside her.

When they moved back downstairs, Minka held the railing of the stairs to keep her balance. Miss Bragstad paused at the large dining room table. "We take our meals together. Otherwise, the girls are free to rest or to care for their babies."

Jennie's eyes jumped to her daughter, and a wave of anxiety washed over Minka again. Her mother would leave her soon, leave her to face the mystery of childbirth alone. Because of the distance between Aberdeen and Sioux Falls—just over two hundred miles—it wouldn't be practical, or maybe even possible, for Jennie to be summoned when labor came on. Mother and daughter would not see each other again until the day when Minka would say good-bye to her newborn child.

"We can retreat to my office and discuss any questions you may have," Miss Bragstad said.

Miss Questad bid them a good-bye. Minka hung back, wondering what she should do and how long her mother would remain at the house.

"Minnie, you should join us," Miss Bragstad said. The matron of the house and her mother had stopped to wait for her. When Minka reached Jennie's side, they walked together, as if the mother, too, finally realized that her daughter was no longer a child.

Minka gazed around her, remembering Reverend Kraushaar's office, which breathed of wisdom and the mysteries of study and education. Miss Bragstad's office was different, organized yet warm, like the woman herself. Minka enjoyed hearing Miss Bragstad talk. She spoke in perfect English without a Dutch or German accent. Her voice held an air of authority without any hint of cruelty. She carried herself with a confidence that Minka could only dream of having one day.

Looking at Jennie, Miss Bragstad said, "I understand that you had wished for Minka to return to you quickly, but Reverend Kraushaar wrote that he explained our system. Is that acceptable to you?" Her tone was pleasant, and she seemed to be addressing both mother and daughter.

Jennie nodded. Minka wanted to ask how long she'd have to wait before going home, but instead she listened to Miss Bragstad go through the rules of the house. The explanation didn't take long.

"We will talk later today, Minnie. But do you have questions now?"

Half-formed questions thickened her tongue, but Minka shook her head and held herself very still, trying to will away the tears she could feel pressing around her eyes. This unfamiliar weepiness seemed to be ever-present these days.

"May you and I talk alone?" Jennie asked.

"Certainly," Miss Bragstad said. She turned to Minka and nodded. Her smile held so much gentle understanding that Minka realized she was going to lose her fight against the tears. She turned, grabbed for the doorknob, and hurried out of the room.

❋ ❋ ❋

As Minka walked to the front porch, trying to keep her feet straight to hide the waddle in her step, she could not guess the depth of pain her mother felt on this day, or the many days before.

An ache had formed within Jennie since discovering Minka's condition—an ache that grew over the months and now threatened to split her apart. She'd planned to offer her daughter more guidance during this visit, knowing the leap from fairy-tale storks to the reality of childbirth and the devastation of giving away a child would be brutal. She'd planned to tell again the story of the death of Minka's father. How Jennie had held nine-day-old Jane in her arms, waiting for the husband who would never return. She'd wanted to tell Minka about childbirth, just enough to help her feel ready and assure her it would be all right.

But here again, she was failing her daughter. The right words seemed just beyond her grasp.

"She know nothing of . . . her time and . . . after," Jennie said, twisting her skirt in her hands.

"We will prepare her."

"She will want to keep de child. I know dis. Her life would be ruin. And de child too. A child cannot grow up wit such as dis."

Miss Bragstad nodded, understanding too well the ramifications of a child born outside of matrimony. If the story of this child's conception were to follow him or her . . . society would be cruel.

"It is her right to decide. But I understand the special circumstances. I will talk to her."

* * *

After Honus and Jennie said good-bye, Minka did not watch the milk truck disappear down the street. She knew she might fling herself after it, and there was no point in making things worse. The time with her mother had been too short—it had not soothed her as she'd hoped. Loneliness threatened to hollow her out, even as every inch of her torso seemed taken up by the unborn baby.

Now there was nothing standing between her and the frightening coming event.

Miss Bragstad invited her to the garden, the older woman's place of refuge. Minka tried to be polite as they walked, but as the matron of the house named varieties of flowers and pointed out spots where others would soon bloom, the information seemed to skip right by Minka.

Miss Bragstad noticed and decided to change the subject.

"My father died when I was young. My mother was ill, so my older brothers and I had to stop attending school to go to work," Miss Bragstad said. She carried a basket hung over her arm while she clipped stalks of a delicate purple flower that Minka did not recognize. She glanced at Minka but mostly watched her hands and the flowers, giving the girl plenty of time to observe *her*.

Miss Bragstad had already noted plenty about her new charge. Some girls came to this place in resignation, bearing the inner wounds caused by cruel parents or guarding souls hardened by having no parents at all. Others came almost brazenly, full of the kind of careless confidence that prettiness often brings. Miss

Bragstad saw all kinds of unfortunate girls, and she had grown adept at finding the right words for each of them, even those from whom she never received much response.

This one was different. This Minnie was reserved and polite. She had clearly come from a protected environment. Yet she carried herself with a solidness that Miss Bragstad seldom saw in girls this young. It was not quite confidence, but there was a strength there that intrigued the matron.

Miss Bragstad had been a teenager herself when a terrifying hurricane, the worst in US history, swept across a faraway place called Galveston, Texas, in 1900, taking thousands and thousands of souls with it. She'd heard how the Lutheran church building on Galveston Island had withstood the fearsome storm. As everything else turned to rubble, the historic Lyceum had served as a refuge for shattered citizens.

Miss Bragstad had a sense that this slight girl in front of her would likewise survive even the greatest storms in life. She had something rare within her. *Fortitude.* That was the perfect word for it.

Minka studied the older woman too. Did she know that Minka had left school to work? And that her father had died? Why else would Miss Bragstad talk about her own father? Minka realized that Jennie surely had shared some of her background with the matron. Still, she found it nearly impossible to believe that such a sophisticated woman might have a story similar to her own.

With the pleasant distraction of this conversation, the scent of lilacs on the air, and sunshine warming her hair and shoulders, the pain of her mother's departure was draining away.

"What do you enjoy?" Miss Bragstad asked, as she straightened up and scanned the garden.

The question surprised Minka. She could not remember an adult asking such a question since her days at school, when the teacher would ask the students to write on a subject of interest. She had to cast about for an answer.

"I like to sew." She folded her hands behind her back as they walked. "I wish I could play the piano."

Miss Bragstad smiled.

"You will do well here, Minnie."

✳ ✳ ✳

Nights were challenging, though Minka no longer found it strange to sleep alone—her large belly made her grateful for the extra space, and she was glad her tossing and turning wouldn't bother anyone else. But she seemed to wake constantly, needing to relieve her squashed bladder. And at night, there was nothing to distract her from her homesickness. One night, she heard another girl weeping. Other times, a baby cried, and Minka would fearfully rub her own stomach. How would she care for one of those tiny creatures all on her own?

Minka saw the other girls of the house during meals. No one spoke of the circumstances surrounding their pregnancies, but they chatted about shared physical complaints. And the expectant girls listened closely as two new mothers talked about their babies.

Minka worked on her hand-stitching along the edges of cloth diapers until she could sit still no longer; then she wandered the grounds. She daily cleaned her room until she could find nothing else to clean. Then she took a dust rag to the rooms downstairs, until the housekeeper shooed her away as if Minka were trying to steal that position.

"Your family has paid for your stay here. You should rest or do something else," the housekeeper said.

"Minka, dear. You are a guest here," Miss Bragstad told her when they spoke again.

"But I've always worked," Minka said. She didn't know how to explain that work was what she did best, that it grounded her and gave her a sense of rightness.

"Here you will rest and take care of yourself and the baby when that time arrives. Come, you can walk with me to the garden. There are some aphids in the roses, and we need to put soapy water on the leaves." She smiled, then added, "Outdoors is always a good place to think, to refresh your mind."

For the first time in Minka's life, she had someone to talk to about anything. Miss Questad also quickly became a friend like Minka had never had before, sharing stories about the House of Mercy. She told Minka a story about a baby born before they could reach the hospital and another about a boyfriend who showed up with roses and a marriage proposal. No longer was Minka only to be seen—now she had a voice, as well. Day after day, her questions and thoughts opened like the petals on the chrysanthemums.

After each conversation Minka considered what Miss Bragstad had explained to her, putting the pieces together with what she'd known—or thought she'd known, while at home—about love, marriage, children, life. While the older woman was honest with Minka, she spoke with a propriety that made the girl wonder if she'd understood correctly. She'd often return to Miss Bragstad for clarification. *You said the baby will come from my stomach and out of where? And how much pain?*

Minka now understood why the story of the stork had first been told, and she'd never wished more for it to be true.

As the weeks passed, the House of Mercy was in constant change. Some girls departed; new ones came. Another one had her baby at the hospital, then returned to the house, where she spent even more time in her room with the door closed. Minka knew that secret door would open to her soon enough. In the meantime, she wanted to spend hours with Miss Questad and Miss Bragstad.

Minka's back ached every day. Her fingers and ankles were

swollen like plump sausages by noon, and the stairs took her breath away by the time she reached the top.

Then one day, a pain sliced through her abdomen, pushing her forward with its force.

Minka did not have to ask. The hidden door of motherhood was opening to her at last.

Chapter Seven

MINKA AWOKE in a sterile room, groggy and shivering.

"There you are," a woman said, leaning close and coming into focus. Her white nurse's hat reminded Minka of her brother John's sailor cap. The curtains over the window were shut, but bright daylight leaked in around the edges. Minka's thin hospital gown was clean, as were her blankets. The smell of bleach and antiseptic permeated the room.

"It's over?" Minka asked. Her tongue felt like a dried-out piece of leather. The room wasn't cold, but she was. She tried to push higher up on the bed and moaned as a sharp pain cut through her in the same place she'd felt pain the morning after *It* had occurred.

"Careful now. It will take time to heal. You gave us a scare," the nurse explained.

"What scare?" Minka asked, still groggy.

"You were on the table too long."

Minka didn't know what that meant. Disjointed memories flooded her—memories of pain, bright lights, faces, humiliation, and confused panic.

When Minka had arrived at the large clapboard house that

served as Sioux Falls's hospital, she was immediately sedated. The hours after descended into a blur as her doctor followed the most modern procedures of the time, outlined in the obstetric textbook by Dr. Joseph DeLee. The intent was to prevent problems, which unfortunately meant few women escaped damage. At the approach of the pushing stage, Minka was given a dose of ether, knocking her unconscious. The doctor gave her an episiotomy, and then with forceps, he delivered Minka's baby.

The nurse pulled away the blankets and lifted Minka's gown. Minka's reflex was to cover herself, but the nurse pushed away her hand and gave her a quick exam. Minka clenched her muscles until the nurse covered her once again.

She realized her stomach had deflated, though it was not fully back to normal. That thought brought her awake.

"The baby?" she asked.

"Let me finish my rounds."

The nurse left.

Minka tried propping herself up. Every movement sent a sting of pain ripping through her, but she succeeded in moving her feet around to the side of the bed and sitting up. A gush of something wet flooded the sheets. She looked under the covers at bright-red blood. Her monthlies had never been like this, and Minka wondered if that was normal.

"I'm bleeding," she said to another nurse passing her bed. The woman paused.

"Yes, you will for some time," she said and disappeared. Minka closed her eyes, listening to the nurse's feet padding away. Then the first nurse's voice broke in again.

"Are you ready to see her?"

"I . . . there's blood. . . . A lot. . . ." Then Minka took in the words, and her eyes popped open. "Did you say 'her'?"

"You have a girl," the nurse said.

The small bundle was lowered into Minka's arms.

Minka stared at the little face, taking in every detail. The baby's tiny lips were puckered. Her eyelids were closed and touched with a blush of pink. Wisps of light hair fanned across her head, hardly more substantial than the hair on Minka's arms. Her lips moved and her eyes fluttered.

The feel of her reminded Minka of melting butter.

"She is mine, my baby?" Minka glanced up at the nurse in disbelief, then back to the newborn in her arms. She felt a flood of warmth coursing inside her. The sensation seemed to be in her chest. Her head swirled. *This . . .* this was extraordinary.

The nurse lifted the bundle from Minka's arms. "Let me have her. We need to clean you up."

"But . . ." Minka mumbled. *I don't ever want to be away from her. Please let me have her.*

"Can you help a moment?" the nurse said, turning toward a younger woman walking by in a different uniform.

"Certainly," the girl said, smiling as she took the baby.

The nurse firmly laid Minka back onto the bed and changed some thick cloths that lay beneath her. Minka's eyes didn't leave the woman holding her baby. Her baby. *Hers.*

"Have you ever changed a diaper?" the nurse asked Minka. She motioned for the other woman to give the baby back to her young mother.

Minka shook her head, not wanting to set her baby down again. "I can do it though."

The nurse went back and forth around the curtain, bringing in supplies. Minka's arms cradled the sleeping child. She was so light, but Minka's arms trembled.

"Set her down on the bed and unwrap the blankets."

Minka moved with slow care until the nurse helped speed up the process.

"Look at that little foot, and her little toes and hands," Minka murmured as her newborn's body was revealed. Her skin felt incredibly soft, like nothing Minka had touched in all her life.

She remembered the jabs to her ribs and the rolls of little knees or elbows that had startled her so. These tender feet and knees and arms had made those movements. She wanted to study every inch of her baby. The tiny toenails, the dimples in her fingers, the soft pink in her fair skin. The wrinkles in her feet were lined in white.

"I've never seen anything like . . . oh, look at her tiny chin, and oh, her ears." The nurse brought a thin cotton hat and pulled it over the baby's head.

"Undo the pins on the diaper," the nurse said with a sigh. But Minka's obvious joy softened her terse words.

Of course Minka had known that a baby was inside her. And she had felt the movement. She had known that it would come out and had expected that part to be painful. But nothing had prepared her for this. This . . . *connection*. It was as though this tiny other person shared Minka's soul.

Suddenly, Minka wanted her own mother. For of course Jennie understood. Now Minka did as well. Tears burned her eyes. She had never imagined she could feel this depth of love for a person she'd just met—like she would throw herself in front of a train to save her, with no hesitation.

Minka could see that she'd made a mistake. The thought of adoption was suddenly unbearable. She was never going to be able to part with this wondrous gift.

Midway through the changing, the baby stirred and burst into a soft protest. Minka's lips parted at the sound, such a sweet and beautiful cry. She quickly changed the diaper as the nurse instructed her. Then the older woman demonstrated how to wrap the baby and bounce her until her cries softened and she returned to sleep.

"You must change this often," the nurse said, patting the baby's bottom. "Any time it is wet or soiled. If you do not, she will get a rash or an infection."

Minka nodded with a sense of urgency. She would do everything the nurse told her. She couldn't allow anything to harm this perfect little human.

"Your name is Betty Jane," Minka whispered when the nurse left them alone. "En je bent zo mooi." *And you are so beautiful.* She didn't understand how the nurses could be so workaday about Betty Jane. Minka held her baby against her chest, smelling the fuzzy, pale hair. When Betty Jane awoke—staring at Minka with deep-blue eyes—the girl stared back in utter wonder at this miracle alive in her arms.

Then Minka saw her own twisted fingers against the soft fabric. She moved one hand farther under Betty Jane and let an open end of the blanket fall over the other one. As she held her newborn in the quiet, clean room, Minka had the sense that she and Betty Jane were the only two beings on earth.

* * *

Wrapped up in her own pressing events, Minka had no idea how momentous this year of her baby's birth would be. Infamous for the Wall Street Crash, also known as "Black Tuesday," 1929 marked the beginning of the decadelong Great Depression in the United States.

The year was also notable for the births of people who would shape the world in diverse ways: actress and future princess of Monaco, Grace Kelly; the man who would usher in each New Year for four decades, television entertainer Dick Clark; actress and humanitarian Audrey Hepburn; American civil rights leader and Nobel laureate Martin Luther King Jr.; the future first lady of the United States, Jacqueline Lee Bouvier, later Jacqueline Kennedy; and Anne Frank, whose life would be cut short at the age of fifteen but whose words written in an attic in Holland would reach around the world.

The year 1929 also saw the first flight over the South Pole

completed, Hemingway's *A Farewell to Arms* published, and the first Academy Awards ceremony hosted at the Hollywood Roosevelt Hotel in California.

But to a seventeen-year-old girl in a hospital in Sioux Falls, South Dakota, this year would be remembered as the one that irrevocably changed her life. Forever after, there would be a split.

Her life before May 22, 1929.

And her life after.

Little did she know that, just a few weeks before, Miss Bragstad had received the letter that would help set the course of Betty Jane's life.

Jewell, Iowa, May 8, 1929

Dear Miss Bragstad,

Nine years ago, while we lived in Irene, S. Dakota, we adopted a little baby boy which was born at the House of Mercy. . . . The boy has given us much satisfaction. We have talked it over considerably of late, Mrs. Nordsletten and I, of adopting a little baby girl.

We have namely 3 boys but lack a girl. We hearby ask you if you are in a position to place a little infant in our home? It was through the Home Finding Work of our church that we obtained our boy, and it is then the same channel that we desire a child this time, too, if possible. May we soon hear from you?

Sincerely yours,
Rev. & Mrs. Peder Nordsletten

❋ ❋ ❋

Several days later Minka returned to the House of Mercy with little outward fanfare, but inside her, it was as if the sky had cracked open, unveiling the universe. She could hardly believe that other mothers felt as she did. She could hardly believe that she *was* a mother. And she never wanted to be without this feeling of wonder again.

Minka longed to see her family. A letter from her mother waited in her room. Miss Bragstad had passed the news of Betty Jane's birth to Reverend Kraushaar and to Jennie. Minka's mother sounded anxious to know if Minka was well and expressed her regrets that she couldn't be with her.

Minka no longer felt the shadow of uncertainty and dread that had followed her for months. And she didn't want to keep her baby a secret. She wanted her mother and sister to marvel over every inch of Betty Jane's tiny body, to ooh and aah over the flutter of her eyes as she woke, to laugh with her as Betty Jane squirmed with her hungry mouth, seeking food and then suckling a bottle as if starving.

Feeding Betty Jane was heaven, watching her soft cheeks pucker as she drank, giving her the nourishment she so urgently wanted and needed. Minka wished she could have nursed her baby, though she understood why this experience was denied her. Instead, she learned to heat evaporated milk in a saucepan to the perfect warm temperature, then stir in just the right amount of powdered formula, a fattening mixture of sugar and starches.

In the beginning, Betty Jane always fell asleep while drinking. As her mouth went slack, a thread of milk would trickle from one corner. Minka would wipe it away with her thumb, as gently as if stroking a thin-shelled robin's egg.

"She is a beauty," Miss Bragstad said one day, taking in the perfect face of the baby, as well as the beaming expression on Minka's face. "Don't tell the other girls, but I've rarely seen a baby as beautiful as that one."

The duties of motherhood came instinctively for Minka. Her breasts ached in the week after Betty Jane's birth, then eventually soothed as her milk dried up. Her stitches failed to heal properly—*perforated* was the term the doctor used—but Minka's years of demanding physical labor, mixed with the new wonder and joy of her baby, reduced her pain to little more than an annoying grating in the background.

Everything was a miracle. The baby's deep-blue eyes stared up at Minka as if they knew her. As she slept, Betty Jane's mouth worked at an imaginary bottle. One time when Betty Jane smiled in her sleep, Minka laughed so delightedly that the baby woke up and began crying. But her baby easily soothed, and Miss Questad told Minka that Betty Jane was one of the best and sweetest babies she'd ever seen at the house.

Each day, Minka's heart became more tightly bound to the little newborn. Nothing else mattered now.

The first week passed, and another. Minka's confused thoughts swung wildly as her new emotions burrowed deep. She couldn't put a stop to either of them.

There were days when she knew she'd never part with her precious daughter. Somehow they'd make it. Her mother had been alone with three children when she was only a few years older than Minka.

But then a glance at her own hands would remind Minka. As Betty Jane slept, Minka pictured her child growing up on the dairy farm. She imagined her wearing overalls, her hands growing callused from chores and her little fingers bending until they would no longer straighten.

How could Minka provide for her child in the way she wished? Her own mother had been blessed by meeting Uncle. Would she be as lucky, especially since it was her own selfishness that made her want to keep the baby?

Not selfishness, her aching heart screamed, *this is love*. A mother's love. Her love. The greatest love she'd ever known.

Minka longed to give her little girl all that she'd never had—a closet stuffed with beautiful dresses and hats in the latest style.

Necklaces and strands of pearls. Betty Jane should have piano lessons at a young age and sing in the church choir.

But how would they walk through town without everyone believing the worst of Minka, and of Betty Jane? Minka would not allow this precious girl to work as she had. But what could they do?

Wrecked hands, callused fingers, stains on her teeth from Uncle's well water, no education, no skills beyond milking cows and twisting sausages . . .

Minka would give her life for this girl—she would not hesitate. She wanted the very best in the world for her daughter.

But was she the best for little Betty Jane?

✸　✸　✸

Minka was watching Betty Jane, asleep in her bassinet, when she heard the gentle knock. She already knew it was Miss Bragstad by the rhythm of her footsteps down the hall and her usual four raps on the door.

"Minnie? Is this a good time to talk?"

Minka wanted to decline. Talking with Miss Bragstad before the baby's birth had opened up a new world of possibilities and a window to self-confidence. But today, Minka did not want to discuss the subject that the older woman had delayed raising— the subject that had been waiting in the shadows, haunting her through restless nights ever since she'd returned from the hospital.

But Minka's manners won out.

"Yes, ma'am," she said.

Miss Bragstad entered, smiling at the bassinet. She laid a hand lightly on the baby's stomach, then turned to Minka. The smile didn't waver.

"We must talk about your plans."

Minka nodded her head, but her eyes jumped to the baby. She reached into the tiny bed and gathered up her infant. Betty Jane groaned and grunted as she was jostled from her deep slumber, then settled back to sleep at the sound of Minka's heartbeat and the feel of her warm arms.

"What have you been thinking, Minnie?"

Miss Bragstad believed in the benefits of their policy. Young women were expected to tend to their own babies for up to six weeks after the children's births. The staff could not care for the infants, and the young women needed to be at the House of Mercy to heal after their deliveries. After a month, the babies had adapted to a nursing bottle. Any illnesses or problems had been identified. The mothers were physically ready to return to their homes.

But many were also attached to their babies, and that was when this most difficult decision could be made with full awareness.

"I don't . . . I can't." Minka fought back tears. She did not feel strong, but panicked.

"All right," Miss Bragstad said in a gentle voice. She placed her hand on Minka's back.

"Mom said it is best that Betty Jane have a home with a mother and a father. She . . . I have no education. I'm just a milkmaid."

Miss Bragstad already knew this.

Minka did not say the other thing they both knew—that the child would grow up with the shame of not having a father. Her perfect little girl would be called names. And what would Minka say when Betty Jane began to ask questions about her father?

"This is your decision, Minnie. Only you can make it."

Minka wanted to say that she *had* made it. That there was no way she'd ever leave her baby girl. But she envisioned her own gnarled fingers pointing at her, taunting her. *Those perfect baby fingers will look like yours if you keep her. What kind of life will she have with you? You have not one thing of your own.*

"What do you think I should do?" Minka whispered.

Miss Bragstad didn't answer for so long that Minka looked up to be sure she was still there.

"I will never be a mother," Miss Bragstad said.

"You could; someday you . . . "

"No," Miss Bragstad said with a shake of her head that didn't convey self-pity, only acceptance. "Motherhood is not in the divine plan for my life. I can only observe and imagine what you feel for Betty Jane."

Minka listened. With Miss Bragstad, she'd grown accustomed to the nourishment of conversing on equal terms with another person, someone she respected. Now, as Minka watched the proper and disciplined matron pace the floor, she realized Miss Bragstad struggled with the dilemma. This wasn't easy for her, either.

"When I consider what is best for you, I have many hopes for your future. Raising a child as an unmarried mother . . . though that wasn't your fault, you will be judged. It is the way things are. I also consider what is best for your Betty Jane."

"And she would be better off with someone else." Grief tore at Minka's voice.

"That is not true. Look at you. You are a natural with her. But she, too, will be judged, all of her life." She paused. "But I do not believe anyone could love her any better than you do, Minnie."

For Miss Bragstad, every word of this conversation was painful. Minka had become a favorite of hers. From the first moment she saw Minka holding little Betty Jane, Miss Bragstad knew that the girl was smitten with motherhood. The days ahead would be terribly difficult, devastating even.

Miss Bragstad also knew that a baby would prevent Minka from making a fresh start, and what would become of both mother and daughter if Minka kept her? Who would marry Minka with an illegitimate child, even if the pregnancy hadn't been her fault?

"You have more to offer the world than just milking cows. I'm going to talk with your mother about your work. Perhaps she will get you music lessons, or you can go to college."

The words were empty comfort. Miss Bragstad would indeed impress upon Minka's mother the importance of giving the girl a different life after she returned home. But for Minka, music and education were nothing now, in comparison to the baby in her arms. Miss Bragstad realized that Minka's entire disposition had changed. Some girls experienced a cold detachment after their babies were born and didn't want to hold them. Others bonded deeply with them.

Minka was completely in love.

Miss Bragstad excused herself after a few more minutes.

"I will pray that you will make the right decision, whatever that might be."

They discussed it on other occasions, in hesitant pieces of conversation. In the light of day, Minka settled on the belief that Betty Jane would have a better life with a respectable family. She made the decision, certain that she could be Betty Jane's selfless champion, sacrificing her own wants for her daughter's future.

At night, when the moon cast a lonely glow across her bedroom floor, Minka wanted to clutch her daughter in her arms and flee to points unknown.

But finally the daytime prevailed. Minka went to Miss Bragstad, carrying the child in her arms down the creaking stairs and through the hall to the matron's office. She didn't wait until Miss Bragstad made her rounds to check on the girls or until they sat together at a meal—Minka had to speak her decision before she took it back.

"You'll find a very good family?" she asked after the dreaded words, the worst words she'd ever spoken. "A mother and a father for her? The best mother and father?"

Miss Bragstad wished she could share the letter she'd received from Reverend and Mrs. Nordsletten. A better home for Betty Jane could not be imagined; this family was like an answer to a prayer that no one had yet prayed. Miss Bragstad could not violate privacy rules. But she wanted to offer Minka a bit of comfort.

"Yes, Minnie. I promise you. In fact . . . I have a family in mind. One that is looking for a little girl. It is a minister and his wife."

Minka looked up. "A minister?" The anxious hope that filled her eyes made Miss Bragstad's heart ache. "Are they from here? Around here?"

"I can't tell you any more than that, Minnie. But it's a very good home. I couldn't hope for a better one."

Minka bent close to Betty Jane.

"Did you hear that, sweet girl? You're going to grow up in a minister's family." A flush of pride swept through her, followed by a fresh wave of hurt. Betty Jane's future was arranged.

Already, strangers were waiting to bear her away.

❊   ❊   ❊

Another baby cried from a room down the hall, wailing all through the night. "Colic," Miss Bragstad told the girls at breakfast.

Minka had been taught all her life that pride was a sin, but she couldn't help feeling proud of her daughter. It seemed there had never been a more perfect baby. She couldn't stop staring at Betty Jane and rarely set her down. Now that she'd made her decision, she further drank in the sweet face, storing up every detail for the time to come.

"Today, Margaret is leaving us," Miss Bragstad announced one day. Minka knew this meant that the girl was leaving, not the baby.

That night, Minka heard the baby crying from the other room. The child had been colicky before Margaret's departure, but somehow his cries sounded more lonely now.

Minka didn't leave her room the next day except to use the bathroom and to prepare bottles. She spent the hours with Betty Jane, holding her close, smelling her hair, her skin.

A dozen times, her resolve faltered. She did not know how she would do it when the time came. How could she leave her baby here? How could she hand her over and actually walk away?

Betty Jane stared up at her with those blue eyes. One of the girls had told her that all babies' eyes were blue and that they'd change in color over time. Minka didn't want to think of this. She didn't want to consider all the things she'd never know about her sweet Betty Jane. For now, this was her baby. Hers alone.

Minka thought of Jane and the dairy. It seemed like another life now. She'd been a child then. Now she was a woman. Not just a woman—a mother. Nothing would take that away, no amount of pretending or returning to the dairy as if nothing had occurred. *Everything* had occurred. She'd awoken from a dream, and she could never fall back into her former sleep again.

Although Minka knew that Betty Jane would never remember her, she lavished affection on her. She wanted her daughter to know her love, to never feel that Minka had abandoned her. Somehow, maybe, she could convey that.

✳ ✳ ✳

Miss Bragstad had already gently explained that she would not be at the House of Mercy when Minka left on June 27 to return home to Aberdeen. The matron had planned a trip East long before she'd even met the DeYoung girl. The conflict in dates saddened her—she felt a sense of failing Minka by not being with her on her most difficult day.

Over the years, Bertha Bragstad had said good-bye to more young girls than she could count, but she had a feeling that she would not be able to conceal her own emotions when it came time to bid farewell to the strong yet sensitive Minka.

At least before she left, she could secure the best possible home for Minka's daughter.

June 17, 1929

Rev. and Mrs. Peder Nordsletten,

Dear friends:
*Referring to your inquiry for a baby girl, I beg to state we
now have a very fine baby girl, born on May the 22nd,
who will be ready for a home by the 28th of this month. We
require our mothers to stay with their babies a certain length
of time, and this time will be up the 29th of this month.*

*This child is a very normal baby, blue eyes and brown
hair. The mother is of Holland descent. Comes from a very
good family and was referred by Rev. Kraushaar of Aberdeen,
who spoke very highly of the girl and her family. . . . Very
little is known about the father of the child.*

*We feel this is a very desirable child, and it certainly would
be a comfort to the mother and people of this girl if they could
know the baby went into a good Lutheran home. They think
a great deal of the child, but realize it would be much better
for her to live in a foster home and so are willing to have her
placed now. The mother is seventeen years of age. . . .*

Sincerely yours,
Miss Bragstad

❋ ❋ ❋

On the morning of June 27, the Sunnyside Dairy truck returned
once more to the House of Mercy. As Jennie stepped down onto
the driveway, she saw Minka sitting on the porch, holding a
bundle wrapped in a blanket. Jennie wasn't aware of closing the
truck's door. She didn't hear the hinges squeal. Her eyes were large
as she came up the porch steps toward her daughter.

"This is Betty Jane," Minka said. Her voice was as proud and
awed as a courtier announcing the presence of royalty.

As Minka passed the newborn into Jennie's arms, Jennie

glanced at her daughter with a flash of panic in her expression. Then she looked at the baby.

A soft gasp escaped from her lips. Her vision blurred until she blinked.

"Zo mooi," she whispered. *So beautiful.* The baby wore a white baptismal dress. One chubby arm batted at the air.

"We're waiting for the minister to come," Minka explained. "They said we could . . . we could have her baptized before we . . . before we go." The last words trailed off.

Honus had come up beside Jennie. All three of them stood staring at the baby.

When Minka spoke again, it was more firmly.

"We will baptize her, and then say good-bye."

Minka was wearing a pretty black dress that Jennie had never seen, and she had a strand of white beads around her neck. Her hair had been cut in a bob and was now curled into perfect waves. She looked sophisticated and smart. Her voice held an authority Jennie had never heard before.

And her dear face was so ravaged that Jennie had to look away.

Honus nodded at Minka's words. His hair was matted down from the hat he now held in his hands. He stepped away to gaze out from the porch toward Miss Bragstad's flower garden.

The local minister arrived. Minka had witnessed baptisms at church, where babies often cried from the sprinkle of water. Betty Jane just kicked her legs. Minka could not focus on any of the words the reverend uttered. Her heart raced; her stomach churned. She wished these moments with her baby would never end. She wanted to stay here forever.

Honus took a photograph in the garden. Betty Jane lay on a wicker chair, propped up by bunches of thick blankets. Minka knelt beside her, facing away from the camera. She couldn't bear to take her eyes off her infant daughter for one moment. Minka didn't know it at the time, but this picture would become her physical link to this day, to her child. She would carry the photograph with her for the rest of her life.

Her mind raced frantically with all the private words she wished to say.

I love you so much, my sweetest darling. I am only doing this for you. Please don't think that I've abandoned you. I wish I could be with you every day of your life. But you will have a better life without me. How I wish I could be the mother you deserve. But you will have a happy life and a happy home. You won't have to work so hard. You will wear pretty dresses and bows in your hair and necklaces. No overalls—I hope never overalls for you. I will love you every day of my entire life. I promise you that.

Minka carefully lifted Betty Jane again. She could say a hundred things more. She could hold the small bundle for the rest of her life, if only time would stop.

She felt the back of her baby's soft neck, her velvety cheek. Minka slipped a finger into one tiny palm and felt Betty Jane's fingers wrap and squeeze her crooked one. Her head pounded, and she closed her eyes. She'd never fainted in her life but was in danger of doing so now.

The small group walked along the dirt drive of the House of Mercy toward Honus's truck, Minka cradling her daughter in her arms. The scent of cut grass lay sharp around them, and when Jennie glanced at the house, she saw faces floating in two upper windows, hands holding back the lace curtains. Other pregnant girls, witnessing their own futures.

Minka bent and kissed Betty Jane's cheek once, then a desperate second time. When she handed the small bundle to Miss Questad, one end of the white blanket slipped down, exposing skin mottled pink and cream. Minka tucked the blanket back around the baby, patting it with her twisted fingers. A tear dripped onto the soft yarn, and she patted at that, too. Then one explosive sob escaped her trembling mouth.

Jennie's own vision blurred. Never before had she felt so incapable. There wasn't a thing her hands could do to smooth this moment out, to shape it into something that worked. She would never see her first grandchild again. Suddenly, that knowledge seemed unbearable.

Miss Questad wrapped one arm around Minka, holding her tight with closed eyes. Minka finally stepped back. She turned away from Betty Jane, faltered once, then straightened her body and walked toward the truck. Honus nodded to Miss Questad, whose arms were now too full for a handshake. Jennie helped Minka climb in.

And then somehow they were in the truck and driving away. Minka could not look back, or she would scream. Ordinary trees flashed by the windows, ordinary sunshine glinted off the glass, and meanwhile Minka's insides were breaking apart and crumbling to dust. This must be what dying felt like. To know that the life created inside of her, the life she had held in her arms—that life was better off without her. To leave the most important part of her behind, forever.

No. Death would probably be kinder than this.

Chapter Eight

Hours later, Jennie and Minka stepped out of the truck at Riverside Park in Tante's hometown. Instantly they were enveloped by sounds and smells: organ music pumped up and down, mixing with happy screams and the aroma of grease, meat, and sugary treats. Electric lights hung from tree branches and wooden signs. Booths with striped skirts offered sales of Coca-Cola, Kewpie dolls, and fairy floss, a spun-sugar confection that some people called "cotton candy." The combined effect was so startling that the pressure on Minka's heart loosened. She'd never seen or heard such commotion.

Jennie's instinct had been a good one. At the end of this terrible day, the thing they needed was distraction, and this place certainly provided it. After leaving the House of Mercy, they had made the two-hour drive to Iowa, where they were spending the night with Tante Hogerhide. On the way, Jennie had sat in the front of the truck, every muscle in her body clenched. Although only a few muffled sounds came from the back, Minka's grief was like a damp fog pushing into every inch of the vehicle. Jennie didn't know what to say and therefore said little, even to Honus.

When they arrived at Tante's house, there was a spread of food waiting. Tante had prepared enough for a banquet, as if the varied dishes might soothe the pain. Honus mumbled something about needing to look at a sag in the roof eaves before dark and escaped to the yard. Minka tried to be polite but couldn't swallow more than a couple of bites. Then Tante mentioned nearby Riverside Park. Jennie jumped at the chance to get her daughter out of the too-quiet house, where a missing baby girl seemed to fill every room.

A breeze pushed off the lazy Big Sioux River. The sun hung low in the sky, drawing away the day's heat and casting a soft light over trees and water. There had been a trace of warm rain earlier in the day, but it had passed and the ground was now dry. Mosquitoes dipped and jabbed while pedestrians slapped at arms and necks.

"Look at that," Minka murmured, pointing to a wooden roller coaster carrying a compact train of screaming people into the air. Her voice wasn't joyful, but the note of curiosity belonged to the old Minnie. It was the first unprompted thing she'd said since leaving the House of Mercy. Jennie was quick to reply.

"I haf never seen such a thing," she said. "So high in sky . . . so fast . . . I would fear to fall off." They stood and watched the passengers swooping around. Crowds of people moved along the pathways. Every several yards there was a new spectacle: a merry-go-round, an enclosure with people driving miniature cars around in a circle, something called a Tilt-A-Whirl.

They were standing near a giant wooden wheel carrying swinging carts into the air when Jennie noticed Minka staring at a young woman holding a small bundle, a bundle just like the one Minka had held only that morning. A baby. Two small children wiggled around the woman's legs. The woman patted her baby's back as she listened to a barker calling from a small booth.

Minka's eyes shone with tears. Her jaw was tight. Jennie sifted through words in three different languages but couldn't find any that meant anything useful.

Still, Jennie's plan was working as well as it could. Jennie and Minka wove between the performers and crowds lined up for rides, their eyes sweeping around the sights. Minka looked at everything, although little seemed to truly captivate her. When Jennie bought some fairy floss, Minka ate from the paper cone with mechanical movements, as if unaware that she was pulling at the pieces of fluffy confection and putting them into her mouth.

In the fading light, Minka moved like a ghost. Jennie half-wondered if her daughter would start passing through walls and trees, if people would soon walk right through her.

Minka spoke.

"Miss Bragstad said they'd come for her soon—within a couple of days." They'd wandered near the Big Sioux River, away from the crowds. Electric lights reflected in the black, mirrored surface of the water.

"Ja." Jennie's mind snatched at scraps of phrases. "Dat will be good. Dey will take good care of her, you know."

"I know, Mom." Minka stood perfectly still, a pale statue wearing a fabric dress. Only her lips moved. "It will be a good home."

Jennie didn't know if they should talk about the baby. She wanted to connect with this wounded part of her daughter, which right now seemed to be *all* of her, but she didn't want to cause more pain. Surely a compliment wouldn't hurt?

"I remember how she look at me, her eyes," Jennie said. "She is smart baby, ja? She will do well." Two boys ran past them, headed toward the merry-go-round. Their excited voices broke the quiet, then faded out again.

Jennie pressed on. "She had ears like you, I think. You had ears dat stuck out from your head. I will never forget."

Minka's reply was quiet, but there was granite in her voice. Her words were a benediction. A promise.

"I'll never forget anything about her, Mom."

Jennie gazed at her daughter, filled with worry. How was Minka supposed to heal if she couldn't forget about Betty Jane?

※ ※ ※

Once they had hugged Tante good-bye the following morning, Honus turned the truck northward again. The more miles that separated Minka from her little girl, the more she felt her absence, and the more the silence seemed to settle in the truck like a heavy burden.

Honus drove all that day, while Minka slept in the back on a blanket—numb, exhausted, and sweaty. That night, in the middle of South Dakota, they stayed with more Vander Zee kin. These people knew nothing of Minka's ordeal, and Jennie excused her daughter by murmuring, "Ze voelt zich ziek": *She isn't feeling well.* Minka fell into a guest bed early in the evening. The room was stuffy, and the sheets were as warm as though freshly ironed. She lay watching the summer sun's last light fade across the bedroom walls and cried herself into the welcome oblivion of sleep.

The following day they started the final leg of their return. Minka's fatigue seemed to consume her. She curled up on the blanket and had just about fallen asleep again when Jennie cried out from the front seat. Minka sat up with a start and looked in the direction her mother was pointing. Honus was already pulling over to the side of the road.

The roof of the farmhouse to their right was engulfed in flames.

Her heart pounding, Minka jumped from the truck, one thought echoing through her mind: *Are there children in there?* Panic sliced through her, and she raced to the front door. When no one responded to her frantic knocks, Minka rushed inside ahead of Jennie and Honus.

Seeing no one and hearing no cries, the threesome began carrying furnishings and other items out of the house. They even managed to remove an upright piano from the parlor. A few neighbors arrived and helped to salvage everything they could. In the end, they saved everything except the stove. Finally, the lady of the house pulled up, frantically crying out as she held on to the hands of her children.

Though the house couldn't be saved, the woman thanked Honus, Jennie, and Minka for rescuing so many of her family's things. A neighbor offered lodging to the distraught homeowner and led her and her children away. Shaken but relieved, Honus, Jennie, and Minka got back into their truck and drove the final hours home.

At last the trio turned into the driveway of the dairy. The truck's headlights swept across the house, then onto the barn. Honus's bulldog, which had been lying panting near the shop, ran out to greet them. The sky had gone fully dark thirty minutes ago, but the air was stifling. Earlier that day, across town, a volunteer observer had penciled the day's high temperature in a weather bureau log: 103 degrees.

It was long past dairy bedtime. The travelers stepped from the truck and stretched out sweaty arms and legs. Honus lifted the lantern from its hook near the kitchen door, scratched a match, raised the wick. Jennie entered the kitchen, holding her carpetbag and leftovers from dinner.

Minka carried her luggage bag. Its contents were a poor representation of her momentous journey. Three pairs of underwear. A loose nightgown. Two long-sleeved dresses. She'd taken these with her months before, when snow lay on the ground.

The huge dress she'd worn every day near the end of her pregnancy had been left with Miss Bragstad, for another girl to use.

Jane emerged from the darkened hallway.

She'd been dozing and hadn't heard the engine turn into the drive, but the dog's bark and the shutting car doors had roused her. Her eyes went first to her sister, whom she hadn't seen in nearly half a year. The lantern light revealed softer planes on Minka's face—softer than when she'd left. She looked bedraggled. All three of them did.

"Well, hello," Jane said. "Welcome home."

"You are nog wakker, Jane?" Jennie said. *You are still up?* When she was tired, her Dutch and English blurred together. "I thought you would sleep."

"I knew you'd be back today," Jane said, stepping closer and looking at Jennie, then Minka. "I thought it would be earlier. It was too hot upstairs, so I was in the spare room down here." Noticing their red faces, she asked, "Jeepers, were you in the sun?"

"We had an avontuur." *Adventure.* Jennie chuckled. "Did you eat, Jane? I haf some ham and bread." She set the dinner basket on the table.

Honus picked up the lantern from the sideboard. "I want to look in de barn," he said and stepped back into the night.

"Did you miss us, Minnie?" Jane asked. She sat down on a kitchen chair. "You were gone forever. What did you do there?"

"Yes, it was . . . yes," Minka said. After hours in a car, her limbs were stiff. She remained standing. "I, uh, I helped Tante around the house. She needed some help."

"Did you get to travel anywhere? What did you see?"

"No, I just . . . I didn't get out too much—"

Jennie interrupted.

"Minnie, tell Jane what happen today. Wit de fire." She placed a plate in front of Jane, with slices of ham and a biscuit smeared with strawberry preserves. "You want something too, Minnie?" She pulled out three glasses and filled them under the faucet.

Minka shook her head. "No, thank you."

"Fire? Did you catch on fire?" Jane took a bite of biscuit.

"No, not us. We were near Mitchell . . . ," Minka began.

"Oh. Did you see the Corn Palace?" Jane had heard of the

elaborate meeting hall established in the last century and heralded as "The World's Only Corn Palace"—but of course she had never been as far away as Mitchell.

"Well, we drove by it. It's really big, and it has all these paintings on the outside and flags all around the top. There were people lined up alongside it."

"But you didn't go in? I wish you would've gone in."

"We were late because of de fire, Jane." Jennie handed water to the girls and sat down with her own glass. She would have tidied up the kitchen, but it wasn't necessary. Jane had kept things immaculate.

"Was the fire in Mitchell?" Jane asked.

"No, just before it." Minka took a drink of water. "We saw a farmhouse by the road, and there was smoke just pouring out of it."

"From de top," Jennie said. "A big gray . . . *poof.*" She lifted her arms.

"Was anyone in it?" Jane asked.

"No, I went to the door and knocked," Minka said. "But no one was home. I went in to check. The fire was up in the attic, so we started carrying stuff out."

"Dat is why our skin is sunburned," Jennie said. "And dirty. Was so hot!"

"Goodness," Jane said. "Did the people ever come back?"

Minka was staring at the cookstove, her face as empty as blank paper. The silence stretched a few beats too long.

Jennie jumped into the gap.

"Ja, de lady came back wit her children when we had almost everything out. A cow had got loose . . . she went to put it back inside de fence. And so . . . everything was burned inside, while dey were gone. But at least we save her things."

Jane finished her snack. She rose and went to the sink, turned on the faucet, scrubbed her plate clean.

"Well, girls," Jennie said with a small sigh, "you haf better sleep now. Tomorrow is de good-bye sermon of Reverend, and we haf to get up early to bake pies for de dinner."

Minka pushed back from the table. "I'll be there in a minute," she said to Jane. "I need to go to the bathroom, clean up a little." More than anything, she craved a few moments of solitude. There was pressure building in her chest and around her eyes, a sensation that was quickly becoming familiar.

Once behind the bathroom door, Minka sank to the floor as broken sobs ripped through her. She clutched the bottom of the sink to balance the tilting room, clapped her other hand over her mouth. She was finally back home, the place she'd desperately longed for over the past six months. Yet it wasn't the same and never would be. There was no solace here. She'd left her true home behind, in an upstairs room, in a bassinet, in the soft bundle she'd never hold again.

❋   ❋   ❋

The following morning, the Vander Zee family were in their places at Zion Lutheran as Reverend Kraushaar said good-bye to his tearful congregation. Everyone was sad to see the beloved Reverend go. After the service, he welcomed Minka back privately. She told him all about her sweet baby, and he reassured her that the Lord had helped her make this decision.

"You will not be sorry for this, Minnie," he said gently.

Monday night, after Jane went up to bed alone, Minka sat down at the kitchen table. The room was dark, and the kerosene lantern cast a ringed light onto a small stack of white paper. She'd pared the end of a pencil, making a nice point of the lead. Her hands were weak with eagerness. She was about to compose a letter to the House of Mercy, her sole link to her daughter.

Minka knew her baby may have already gone home with her new parents, but she could still *feel* Betty Jane's presence at the other end of the letter.

This first missive covered six pages.

. . . But first of all I want to know how little Betty Jane is getting along? And did Reverend come after her all ready and how did they like her and just what did they say about her. And did you dress her up nice? You don't know how good we all feel about it that she is getting such a nice home. I just can't feel bad about it when I stop & think it over.

I also got a nice Baby book for my self so I could keep little Betty's record. . . .

Everybody says I sure look good and they don't seem to know a thing. I sure feel good about it to. . . .

I will never forget what a good home I had and I surely appreciated what you folks have done for me and little Betty Jane. I'm going to make all of you something as I think you will appreciate that more than gitting it out of the store. . . .

. . . I wish you would write me back a big fat letter & tell me all about Betty & her new parents. That is, what they said. And did you ask them if they would receive gifts from me?

. . . Please over looks all the errors and write and let me know all about little Betty. If she is there yet kiss her for me. . . .

. . . Will you put 'personal' on my mail? Please.

Minka slipped the envelope into the mail. Every day for a week, she ran out to greet the mailman first, her heart thumping. Then, a reply came.

July 5, 1929

My Dear Minnie:
. . . No, there surely is no need of you worrying about Betty Jane, because she will be taken well care of. The people came to get her Monday afternoon. When they came I went up

*and told Ella she should dress her up in her new togs, and she
did look so cute. I put Betty in her new Mother's arms, and
the mother seemed she was so overtaken with joy, both the
mother and father said she was far beyond their expectations
and said to greet you and tell you they were some proud
parents. . . . In regards to sending her things later they would
rather you would remember other unfortunates that needed
it. As she would always have all she needed. . . .*

*Ella did so well in taking care of two babies, and I'm
sure she made no preferences, yours got as good care as her
own. . . . Yes it was so hard for Ella to leave her baby, but it
too gets a good home. . . .*

Grateful to have those few details, Minka wrote again.

July 15, 1929

Dear Miss Bragstad & Questad . . .
*I received your letter a number of days ago and sure was glad
to hear from you and to know that little Betty Jane pleased
them so. I know that was a great gift to them. I sure hated to
give her up. But I know it was for the best. I miss her so every
night because they keep me busy in the day time.*

*I got me a little Baby Book and I wonder if you would
write to them and ask them if I could get a lock of hair from
Betty for it? That is later on—as I don't think she has much
hair now.*

*I got me a big doll and put the same clothes on it like
Betty had. It sounds foolish doesn't it?*

*. . . I am sending you folks each a little gift to show you
my appreciation and I hope you like it. I made a little pillow
slip for the bed Betty slept in as I had a little cloth left.*

*. . . Did you hear from Betty's folks since they got her? For
I'm so anxious to know how she is getting along.*

> *. . . I am making Door Stops now out of oil cloth you*
> *have probably seen them. And selling them for a Dollar so*
> *am making a little money.*

Minka continued to write letters as the hot months of summer passed, but even she couldn't have guessed how faithful her correspondence would be. Minka would eventually compose exactly sixty such letters. She always inquired after Miss Bragstad and other girls from the home. She shared news of her own life. But the desperate thread running through each letter would always be a plea for news, any news, about a silky-haired baby girl.

And although she rarely received information about her daughter, and never was granted the lock of hair or any other mementos, Minka would continue to write, to ask, for almost two decades.

✳ ✳ ✳

In August, the one-year anniversary of Scatterwood Lake, and Mack, and *It*, passed unnoticed by Minka. That girl she'd been before the sewing circle picnic seemed like someone she barely knew.

Her absent baby was now at the center of Minka's entire being. She sensed how disastrous it would be to succumb to the powerful emotions that pushed up inside her. At every moment, she was conscious of holding her feelings back, the way she'd seen Uncle pull the reins on his big, gentle workhorses, Dick and Doc, when she was a child.

Relief came only in solitude. During afternoon dusting, Minka could lose herself in memories, knowing the hot air upstairs would dry the tears from her cheeks quickly. And during the nighttime hours, after Jane went to sleep beside her, Minka could silently soak her own pillow as her arms and chest ached for her child.

The pain was astonishing in its relentlessness.

At least Minka's days of milking cows were over. Miss Bragstad had indeed spoken to Jennie about Minka's need to lead a more normal young girl's life. Honus hired a couple of men as dairy workers, and Minka and Jane returned to the tasks they'd done at Uncle's, household and garden chores only. As autumn nights turned chilly, they canned pears and tended to baby turkeys and dug potatoes from the ground, picking 125 bushels in three days and earning strained muscles in the process.

In late October, just as the stock market was crashing in far-away New York, Minka was hired by an Aberdeen couple to clean their house. She earned a dollar a day. She was talented at such work, disciplined and thorough. On Sundays, Minka brought her employer's two toddlers home with her for a few hours, to give their mother a break. One of the children was a two-year-old girl, and every time Minka held her, she imagined that it was Betty Jane's warm heaviness filling her lap.

At any moment, Minka could have said how old her own daughter was, down to the month, week, and day. But no one was asking. Nobody knew to ask.

As Minka lost weight, deep hollows appeared under her cheekbones, dark smudges under her eyes. Jennie skirted the edges of her daughter's sorrow. Only late at night did they speak of the child, the granddaughter Jennie couldn't admit to longing for as well. Jennie sought ways to lighten the pain. Although paying for dentistry seemed extravagant, she took Minka to the dentist, since the brownish stains left by artesian well water bothered Minka. The doctor lightened the spots by rubbing her teeth with heated hydrogen peroxide. Jennie made a point to celebrate Minka's birthday in November and gave her eighteen dollars, "one for every year."

The childhood that had actually ended years before was now officially over.

In mid-November, as Betty Jane was turning six months old, Miss Bragstad wrote to Minka. The House of Mercy, she mentioned, would have to make do with a chicken dinner for Thanksgiving, as she couldn't get a turkey. She also included a few of the lines that Minka lived for: news about Betty Jane. Miss Bragstad rarely had direct information to share—whenever she did, Minka would unfold and read the letter over and over again until the paper grew soft in her hands.

Little Betty is getting along just fine. They give us such good reports, and some of their friends are writing in for babies, if they can get one as nice as she is. She certainly is fortunate to have the home she has.

Minka was so thankful for the news, she promptly crated up one of her mother's turkeys and mailed it to Miss Bragstad. For years to come, she would send Thanksgiving turkeys when they were available, a few dollars if they weren't.

Christmas was especially hard for Minka. Although they'd never decorated a tree or exchanged gifts at Honus's, Christmastime had always meant special music at church and lights strung around town. On Christmas Day, in between regular chores, she and Jane would gather around the warm stove, eating turkey and slices of pie and listening to carols on the radio.

Now everything was different. Minka seemed to see babies everywhere, bundled in blankets against the cold. Their harried mothers scurried along sidewalks, sending steamy puffs of breath into the frosty air, shopping for food or presents. Minka was too shy to ask to hold one of these babies, but her arms felt profoundly empty. She tried to imagine Betty Jane enjoying her first Christmas.

She wrapped a package of gifts for the House of Mercy and wrote to Miss Bragstad.

. . . I wonder how she liked her first Christmas. I could see her sitting in her little high chair looking at all the bright

lights. You let me know what [she] got & how she liked her tree.

But there was one thing lacking and I bet you know what that is don't you. It never seemed like Christmas to me & suppose it never will after this. It will in Spirit but not other wise. . . .

With Love to all, Minnie

P.S. Be sure & ask how Betty liked her Christmas.

✳ ✳ ✳

One evening Minka sat at home, listening to the family's new Atwater Kent radio with Honus. Jennie and Jane had left on an errand. Over a crackly background, a newscaster on the radio wrapped up a sober piece on local crop prices and the national stock market, both of which were in free fall. Minka found it hard to be as interested in other people's suffering as she once had been. Her own heart ached too much.

There was a static-filled pause after the news program, and then music began, strings and piano. A woman started to sing, her voice as soft as a rain shower and filled with regret.

Without Jane's presence to ensure Minka's composure, her emotions spilled over. Hot tears slid down her face. Sobs escaped her throat and shook her shoulders. She sat helpless, alternately clasping her fingers and wiping her cheeks.

Honus's palms rubbed the legs of his work pants. For a few moments he wondered if Jennie would walk through the door, returning early to rescue him, but there was no rattling engine in the driveway. He'd seen such displays of grief only at grave sites, and he was filled with uncertainty. Would the kindest thing be to ignore Minka's tears?

But there sat the closest thing to a daughter he'd ever have, a sturdy but slight girl, now nearly gaunt with grief, and that grief was like a sinkhole, drawing the whole room in. He rose, crossed the floor, then hesitated another moment. He sat down next to Minka. Raising his left arm, he placed it around her thin shoulders, careful not to apply too much pressure.

They sat quietly, the worn farmer and the weeping girl. They kept watch together over a ghost, a baby who would never be there.

✳ ✳ ✳

The snowy winter passed. As the new year of 1930 unfolded, a brainy young Kansan named Clyde Tombaugh discovered a new planet called Pluto, but there were few bright spots closer to home. Every day brought more bank failures, more gloomy reports on the radio. Men were "riding the rails" now, hopping onto moving trains in hopes of finding work somewhere down the line.

With the switching yard just across the street from the dairy, hungry men came knocking on the Vander Zees' door, looking for a meal—"Anything you can spare, ma'am, anything at all." Minka and Jane dished up potatoes and biscuits, set out plate after plate, carrying out the legacy pressed into their blood and bones: a person must do what needs to be done. They fed as many as they could, but there were always more knocking on the door.

Minka's emotions seesawed. Mixed in with the despondency were times when she felt energetic, bursting with plans for a future that would count for something, for Betty Jane's sake. Most of these dreams would remain unrealized, thanks to the Depression and a lack of funds, but hoping for them helped to push Minka's sorrow away. Since colleges did not yet require a high school diploma for admission, Minka sent away for a brochure to Augustana Academy. The Academy was near Sioux Falls, not far from the House of Mercy and Miss Bragstad—and Minka's memories of her baby.

She joined the choir at church and began taking piano lessons, even though she didn't have an instrument to practice on. Hoping to join Jennie on a trip later that year to Holland, Minka began saving her housekeeping dollars in a dresser drawer. She dreamed of sailing across the ocean, having an adventure, taking risks.

She had nothing to lose anymore—nothing as important as what had already been lost.

Betty Jane's first birthday approached. More than anything, Minka wanted to send gifts to her baby, even anonymously, but Miss Bragstad wrote and gently explained that this wasn't possible. Disappointed but undeterred, Minka decided to make things for other babies at the House of Mercy.

Honus gave Minka money to buy fabric and thread and lace, and each evening, after Jane went to bed, Jennie and Minka worked late into the night. They made eight tiny gowns. Eleven cloths for burping. Four small blankets. Three little shirts, the hardest to make. Three bands of ribbon to tie around newborn heads.

As Minka sewed, she imagined Betty Jane toddling around her home unsteadily, grabbing at everything with soft, chubby fingers. She wondered if her hair had come in yet, and if it was curly.

Just after Betty Jane's first birthday, Jennie left for Holland, her first trip back since leaving as a twenty-one-year-old mother. Her two-month visit would be a surprise for her Dutch relatives—even her own father didn't know she was coming.

In the end, Minka wasn't able to go along, but she saw Jennie off at the train station. As she hugged her mother good-bye, Minka pressed her photograph of Betty Jane into Jennie's hand.

"Take this with you," she murmured, "for luck." And then she blurted out, "Look at her all the time, Mom!" Maybe it was foolish, but Minka wanted her little girl to see her ancestors' homeland, even if it was only Betty Jane's likeness that could make the trip.

Back home, Minka was tired of keeping the secret. After a year of crying into her pillow, and staying up late to prepare gifts for

Miss Bragstad, and waiting until Jane was out of the house to write letters, Minka was ready to tell her sister. Jane had distanced herself, aware that something was wrong, knowing there were secrets wafting through the house. Finally, Jennie had agreed. It was time.

✳ ✳ ✳

"A baby." Jane stared at Minka as if she'd told her the cows in the barn were really elephants.

"Yes. A little girl."

"You. You had a baby?"

They were alone in their bedroom. The talk began after Jane had asked in the irritated tone she often used now, "Why aren't you changing for bed?"

Minka had prepared for this, earlier retrieving her treasured photograph from its hiding place. With two hands, she presented it to her sister.

Jane's astonishment deepened. She took the snapshot and sat on the edge of the bed, leaning toward the lamp to view the image. She didn't move or speak for so long that Minka wanted to shake her.

"That is why you've never worn the dress again," Jane stated without looking up.

Minka glanced at the closet, surprised at Jane's words. She realized that her sister was correct. The green dress with the apple appliqué she'd been so proud of sewing had hung in the closet ever since that August day when Betty Jane had been conceived. Jane had borrowed it without asking when Minka was gone, but Minka would never wear it again.

In the nearly two years since that day, Jennie had told Jane the basics of conception and childbirth. The girls no longer spent the majority of their lives secluded on the dairy. No matter how much the dairy needed Minka and Jane, especially during these times of economic hardship, Honus and Jennie realized that the girls also needed a life apart from work. Miss Bragstad's directives had brought that message home.

Jane continued to work at home with Jennie, but she enjoyed more freedoms now, visiting friends and attending socials and other well-chaperoned events. Jane knew about the world now, about courtship and marriage. She knew that babies most certainly did not arrive by stork. But she had never guessed *this*.

"You were not at Tante Hogerhide's?" Jane asked. Her eyes remained on the photograph.

"I was for a few months. Then I went to the Lutheran House of Mercy. It was this beautiful house in Sioux Falls for other girls like me . . . well, kind of like me. Most of them hadn't been, you know, unwilling in their circumstances." Minka had kept every word connected to her child stuffed deep inside, lest she slip around her sister. Now it all spewed out, like water from a broken dam.

"There was this flower garden, and I didn't work while I was there—can you imagine not working for weeks and weeks?—but I was as big as a house. I had the baby at the hospital. Then I took care of her for five weeks. It was just the two of us every day and every night."

"Mom wouldn't let me retrieve the mail. It made no sense."

"She is the sweetest baby in all the world. Even Miss Bragstad and Miss Questad, the women at the house, said this. And the family—her new mother and father—said that she far exceeded their expectations. Their friends want to adopt a baby just like her."

"I cannot believe this," Jane said, not seeming to hear Minka now.

Minka sat beside her sister to offer comfort. It didn't cross Minka's mind that Jane should be comforting her instead.

"I am sorry we lied to you. Mom and Reverend Kraushaar told me it had to be that way. It was best for you, too, they said. No one could know."

Jane snapped her eyes to Minka. "Reverend Kraushaar knew this also?"

"He helped arrange everything. He was very kind. But what did you think was happening? Sometimes I thought you must know."

Jane shook her head, leaning close to view the photograph near the light again.

"Never. I never thought this. I believed it was about Tante, but I could not figure out what was so bad to be kept such a secret, even from me. I have been so angry that you wouldn't tell me."

"What did you think Tante had done?" Minka smiled at the thought of the dowdy woman doing anything scandalous.

"I thought up a hundred ideas. Maybe someone was in jail, or her son robbed a train or a bank or was smuggling alcohol. I have not been able to figure it out. I knew it had to be something terrible for you to keep it from me."

"Yes. And it has been very hard not talking to you about my baby. You just don't know how hard. I love her more than anything. I was so shocked by how much I loved her. See how beautiful she is." A tear surprised Minka, rolling down her cheek before she could stop it. She reached for the photograph.

"I didn't want to ever be away from my baby. Not ever. They said it would get easier. They said that I would forget. But it is not easier. I will never forget. I still don't want to be away from her."

Jane stared at her sister as if Minka had completely transformed before her eyes.

"I named her," Minka said softly. "I wanted to name her before . . . before I . . . " The words *gave her up* always clawed at her throat, made her feel like she was going to sob. They always would. Everything in her resisted saying them.

" . . . before I left." Minka savored her next revelation. "I named her Betty Jane."

There was a pause while it sank in. Then Jane looked up.

"Jane? Like . . . me?"

"Yes. Her middle name is for you."

They looked at each other. Jane's mouth curved into a tender smile. In that moment, Minka thought that her pretty sister had never looked more beautiful.

✳ ✳ ✳

During the rest of that year, and for several more after that, Minka and Jane remained on the dairy farm. They entered their twenties. Talking with her sister about Betty Jane relieved a bit of the pressure on Minka, even as it exposed her raw, unhealed wounds. The truth brought the girls close again. Jane listened. She heard stories she would have never imagined, coming from her quiet sister. The pieces fit now, and the sisters had each other again.

Minka no longer hid her letters to Miss Bragstad. Jane could retrieve the mail.

Before long, Minka's little Betty Jane would turn five. And by that time, Jennie, Minka, and Jane would find their lives transformed yet again.

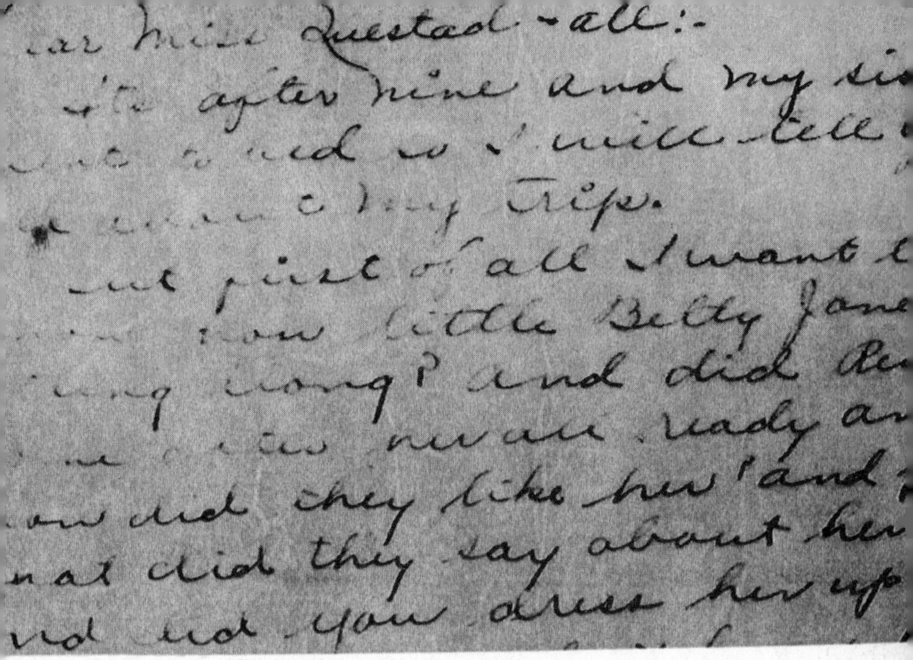

ar Miss Questad - all:-
te after nine and my si
to bed so I will tell
of my trip.
first of all I want t
how little Betty Jane
and did
all ready an
ow did they like her? and
hat did they say about her
nd did you dress her up

PART TWO

Longing

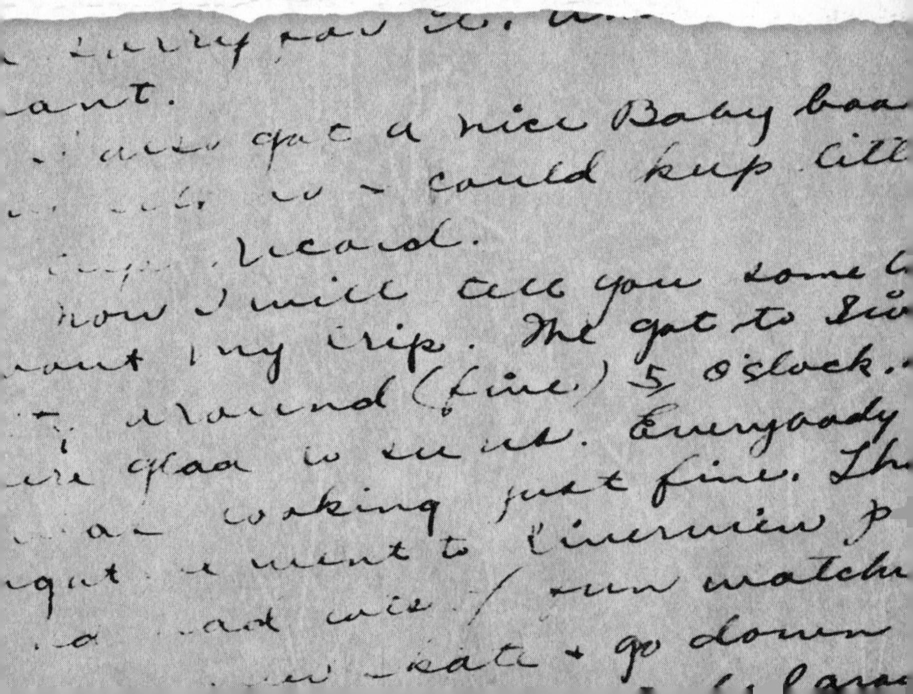

ant.
also got a nice Baby boo
could keep all
record.
Now I will tell you some
out my trip. We got to
(fine) 5 o'clock.
Everybody
glad to see us.
looking just fine.
went to Riverview
watch
skate + go down

February 26, 1935

Dear Miss Bragstad:

My stepfather passed away the 28th of January, after being sick only five days with pneumonia.

We miss him more than we can ever say. He was such a kind & honest man. Always aiming to do the right thing. He had thought so much of little Betty Jane. He never forgot her birthday. Nor at Christmas time. We miss him more each day.

Have you heard anything from Betty Jane lately? Can hardly believe she will be six years old in three months. It hurts me terribly to think she never could of seen her grandfather who thought so very much of her. And was so thankful to know she had such a fine home and bringing up.

Lovingly, Minnie

Chapter Nine

1935–1944

THE FIRST TIME Minka saw him, shouldering his way through the door with a box of apples and a wry smile, her heart thumped so wildly that she was sure the front of her dress must have rippled.

Minka had moved behind the grocery counter when he walked in. She was trying to appear comfortable with customers and experienced in the practice of running a store, even if both were quite new and exciting for her.

He was the handsomest man she'd ever laid eyes on—slim with dark hair and perfect cheekbones. He wasn't tall, but he carried himself precisely. He wore a fine suit, and a fedora tilted stylishly over dark, soulful eyes. Heavens, if he didn't look exactly like a movie star. He walked up to Minka's counter and set the box down. He looked into her eyes.

"Well, hello," he said.

Minka's fingers gripped the edge of the wooden counter. She reminded herself to smile. Her brain had completely drained. Cecil spoke from the meat counter behind her.

"Hi, Roy. Keeping cool out there?"

The visitor's steady eyes moved to Cecil. Minka glanced over, grateful to have someone else take charge of the interaction. Cecil himself was practically a stranger, but at least he didn't inspire such a foolish reaction in her.

"Can't complain." Roy's voice was polite and even. He looked back at Minka. His eyes were almost level with hers. She found herself wishing she were a couple of inches shorter. He tilted his head and pinched the brim of his hat with a finger and thumb. "My name is Eugene LeRoy Disbrow, but everybody calls me Roy."

Minka's throat felt dry. "My name is Minnie," she said. "Well, Minka. But most people call me Minnie. Pleased to meet you."

Cecil chimed in behind them. "Minnie's mom is the one who bought the store. They moved into the back yesterday. They're still getting the lay of the land." He looked at Minka. "Roy here is the salesman for Jewett Brothers. He'll be bringing your fruit around every day. We go way back—went to school together."

"Your family is new in town?" Roy asked her.

Minka shook her head, tried and failed to gather an explanation. "No."

"I don't remember you from Central High."

The old shame twisted in Minka's stomach. She raised her chin. "I didn't go to Central," she said. "I've lived in the area my whole life though. We ran Sunnyside Dairy, but sold it this summer . . . 'cause my stepfather died in January. My mom and sister are on errands right now." If Jane were here, she would be breezily flirting by now, but Jane had gone with Jennie to pick up fabric for new curtains.

Minka hadn't the slightest idea how to flirt.

Roy pointed a thumb behind him. "I've got a few more boxes in the car. I'll be right back." He turned and stepped through the doorway. The room felt suddenly empty.

Cecil whacked a piece of beef with a cleaver. He was wrapping roasts for customers who'd soon be coming in to prepare for week-end suppers. "Good ole Roy," he murmured.

Roy returned twice, setting boxes on the floor, plums and apricots and cherries. Minka came around the counter and stooped beside the boxes.

"These look good," she said, pointing to the apples. "The plums are small."

Why did she have to sound so businesslike? She should have engaged in some small talk with him, but Minka was no good at it; and now they'd moved right into the haggling. Maybe Jane was right—Minka was hopeless when it came to men.

"You're right," Roy said. "They're small. We're lucky to get any at all. Plums have done about the worst, lately. These had to come from up north. What about these?" He lifted a handful of cherries and held them out to Minka.

There was no way to avoid displaying her hands. Minka took the cherries, poked at them with a finger. "These look good. Nice color, and firm. These would make a wonderful pie."

"I'll bet you can bake a delicious pie," Roy said. Minka glanced at him. He looked amused about something.

"Well, yes," Minka said. "I learned when I was a little girl. There's a trick to a nice crust. If you put a little vinegar in the dough, and make sure the oven is hot enough before you put it in, it'll be nice and flaky."

Roy chuckled and glanced at Cecil. "Well, I'll be sure to come to you when I need to know how to make a pie."

"Oh . . . uh, I'm sure you could do well . . . " This conversation felt absurd to Minka. The chitchat stuck in her throat, and it seemed like she was missing something.

Roy got back to business.

"They're cheap, too," he said, gesturing to the cherries. "About the cheapest thing I have. The price has dropped even faster than the supply."

"Yes, things have certainly been hard on the poor farmers," Minka said. "I feel so badly for them. Some have lost everything."

"So what'll it be?" Roy asked. He'd shifted his weight to one foot, stuck his left hand in his pocket.

Minka glanced at Cecil, then back to Roy. "Well, uh, I'm not sure what they usually . . . or what they used to need. Or what we'll need . . ."

Roy snapped his fingers. "Tell you what. How's about I give you a few things, the same amount as usual, and then you can decide over the next few days if it's too much or too little."

"That sounds very good." Minka felt the uncertainty lift.

She loved this store already, loved its cleanliness and order and the lack of barn animals. She couldn't wait to feel at home in it.

Roy placed the fruit in the store's baskets, gave Cecil some news about a mutual acquaintance, then touched his hat again.

"I'll be seeing you tomorrow, ma'am," he said to Minnie.

It wasn't the first time she'd been called ma'am, but it was the first time since becoming a real professional woman. Minka felt buoyant. This was the new life she'd been dreaming of, the fresh beginning. And it was starting off well.

"Bye, Roy. Nice to meet you."

He turned and left. The door scraped shut behind him.

"Good ole Roy," Cecil said again. His tone was indecipherable.

❊ ❊ ❊

When Honus had died suddenly of pneumonia early that year, Minka was surprised by the depth of her sorrow. Honus had ended her education and limited her life in many ways. But he'd been kind about Betty Jane, and he was the only father figure she would ever know.

Her brother, John, had moved back to Aberdeen several years before, after leaving the navy, and he had married a sweet girl named Dorothy, with whom Minka had especially bonded. When

Dorothy became pregnant, Minka confided what she'd never told her own brother—that she'd had a baby of her own. Dorothy gave birth to a little girl and named her Betty Joanne, in tribute to the niece she'd never meet. Minka adored her brother's child, who was just two years younger than her namesake, and playing with her had both eased and pricked the ache in Minka's heart. Then John and Dorothy moved to faraway Rhode Island, and Minka had to say good-bye to another little girl.

Now, more than five long years into it, the Great Depression still had a choke hold on the country. In the early 1930s, people who'd managed to hang on to their farms had resorted to burning corn they couldn't sell, in order to have fuel for cookstoves and furnaces. Plague-like swarms of grasshoppers had ruined millions of acres of crops. Massive dust storms, whipped up from land that had been too quickly cleared of prairie grasses, buried entire farms, decimating plants, blacking out sunlight, and killing whatever didn't move out of the way.

Many farmers who'd escaped all other disasters were crushed by years of drought. Fields were so dry that sparks from passing trains set them on fire. Embers from a train's smokestack had once ignited and burned all of Jennie's apple and plum trees, and almost consumed Honus's alfalfa crop.

Yet thanks to his and Jennie's frugality—the very quality that had pinned Minka to the dairy during her teenaged years—the Vander Zees were not only surviving the Depression, they'd even managed to save some money. After Honus's death in January of 1935, Jennie wore black dresses and grieved. But she was soon making practical plans to sell the dairy and provide for her daughters.

She found a corner grocery store for sale in Aberdeen, a stone's throw from the towering brick walls of St. Luke's 159-bed hospital. A grocery was a smart business choice, and this one included a butcher counter staffed with a skilled meat cutter. People weren't buying luxuries, but they still had to eat. Recent poor weather had made it difficult for people to grow their own food. Jennie made an offer on the place. Twenty-two years after she'd been stranded in a foreign country with three babies and a smattering of English, the Dutch widow became a property and business owner.

The store had comfortable living quarters attached: a bedroom for Jane and Jennie to share and a closed-in porch where Minka could sleep. It would take Minka a while to get used to sleeping alone, but she was the most independent of the three women. At nearly twenty-four years old, she relished the thought of finally having her own bed, her own quiet space.

On only the rarest occasions was Minka jarred back to the memory of *It* and Scatterwood Lake. The loss of Betty Jane had pushed out all other trauma. Despite her prolonged suffering, she could never regret having had Betty Jane, and so she made an effort to not think about Mack at all. In the end, she tried to simply forget the details of that August day when her baby was conceived.

In the years since Betty Jane's birth, Minka had continued to write to Miss Bragstad.

March 10, 1931

How is she getting along? Mother brought two little wooden shoes home [from Holland] for her. Possibly they would just about fit her. How we would love to see her patter in them just for a second. . . .

May 6, 1931

. . . Have you heard or seen anything of my baby girl? She must be a big girl by now. The older she gets the more I miss her. But know she has a lovely home & parents so there is nothing to worry about, but comes natural for a Mother I

guess. Hope she has a happy birthday & will have many many more. . . .

Sunday is Mother's Day and may the Lord bless them all. . . .

May 20, 1931

Just a few lines before I mail this pkg for my little girl. Hope she is well & happy & that her folks enjoy her birthday as she does. . . .

Hoping to hear from you soon & if possible give me some news of my Betty Jane.

August 6, 1931

I'm sure my little girl is growing like a weed. And getting into mischief at this age. I try & picture her in my mind all the time, but I wonder if she's anything like I have her pictured? . . . Hope I may receive some good news for I'm getting lonesome for her.

October 1931

. . . Have you heard anything from Betty Jane? She'll be 2 yrs & 5 mo tomorrow . . .

September 1932

I can't believe my Betty Jane will soon be 4 yrs old. . . . Please write me about her if you have seen and talked with her as she is quite a girl and should be able to tell a big story. . . .

November 1933

Well Miss Bragstad I suppose it tires you to answer the thousands of questions similar to mine, but I would like to know how my big baby girl is getting along. Is she still a happy little girl and does she have good faith?

If you would only give me an answer on these if possible it would help me so much in carrying on. Some times the hills are hard to climb, and if I could only hear of her once in awhile it means so much. The sun shines much brighter, seems I can hardly endure it at times.

Next Fall she starts to kindergarten and soon a young lady. But seems she's only a baby yet.

December 1934

. . . know Betty Jane's folks must be busy also preparing for Christmas programs etc. She must be quite a girl by now. How is she getting along with her school work?

Minka's thoughts of Betty Jane had scarcely diminished with the passage of time. She tried to picture her daughter growing. It was hard for Minka to believe that her "baby" would be in school now, wearing hair ribbons and making friends. Minka wondered if Betty Jane was plagued by the same shyness that Minka had battled. She hoped it wasn't so. She prayed everything good for her child. Although her personal faith was still in its fledgling stages, she'd never prayed as much as she did after the House of Mercy.

When she wrote to Miss Bragstad, she imagined Betty Jane writing out the letters of the alphabet in perfect script. Minka was sure her little girl was smart. And pretty and kind.

She only ever envisioned the very best of her daughter.

✳ ✳ ✳

The day after Minka met Roy, he came back with more fruit and a little less flirty amusement. Minka guessed he'd realized that the plain shopkeeper with the ruined hands was an inadequate target for his charms. It was almost a relief. Now she could pretend that he was just another business acquaintance and try to ignore his dashing good looks.

They fell into an easy rapport. Roy came in every morning, and they looked at boxes of fruit together, generally agreeing as to its quality. As weeks and then months passed, Minka grew confident in her new job. She served customers when they came in, filled phone orders, and selected food from vendors.

Other than the constant ache of missing Betty Jane, Minka had never been so content. No longer was she a quiet observer. Now she was in charge of her own life and part of a business, and it was immensely satisfying. Miss Bragstad's kind attention at the House of Mercy, although it had been for only a short time, had helped Minka to blossom. She was pleased with her growing ability to chat with people, even strangers.

While housewives moved through the store placing food items in baskets, their children came straight to the counter, where penny candies gleamed from inside glass jars. They filled bags for a nickel: so many Boston Baked Beans, so many licorice Snaps, so many Tootsie Rolls. Minka treated the children like valued customers, bending down to help with their painstaking selections.

Almost always, the dainty little girls made Minka think of Betty Jane. One such girl, who had dark curls and a sweet tooth for lemon drops, told Minka that she was six years old. For a moment, Minka held her breath at the possibility that this might be her Betty Jane. But then Minka glanced at the girl's older sister and mother and noticed that all three had the same dark-brown eyes and thick eyebrows—they were clearly related. She exhaled and politely filled their order.

The store was open six days a week, although if desperate customers came by on Sundays before or after church, Jennie would answer the door and get what they needed. Jane kept the books, sending out monthly invoices. Jennie purchased a car, her daughters bravely learned to drive it, and they all took turns making deliveries. Evenings were spent sewing, listening to new radio programs like *Fibber McGee and Molly*, and visiting with neighbors. Jennie befriended nurses from St. Luke's, and when they needed to rest between shifts, they came to the store, went through to the family bedrooms, and lay down for a nap.

Roy and Minka's conversations expanded to cover more than just fruit, and she now often voiced her opinions. With Cecil joining in, they talked about national news, like devastating tornadoes in the spring of 1936 or the businessman Howard Hughes, who was setting exciting aviation records in an industry that had not even existed when the three friends were born. They discussed the Berlin Olympics, where a black athlete named Jesse Owens was embarrassing Nazi Germany. Minka listened to the radio every night and read newspapers when she could, and she remembered everything she took in.

Events in the wider world were capable of affecting her daughter, and that knowledge added importance to news items both great and small.

Talking to Roy and Cecil was fun, and they seemed to enjoy it too. Minka was a good companion. Maybe, she thought as she inched toward spinsterhood, that's all she was ever destined to be.

And then one day, two years after Minka had come to the grocery store and started her new life, Cecil stepped out for a sandwich, and in the quiet space that followed his departure, Roy asked Minka for a date.

✳ ✳ ✳

Eight years had passed with Minka thinking desperately of someone she could never have, the baby she'd released in the flesh but never in the soul. What a change—and even an odd relief—to have someone new in her life who wanted her attention.

Roy took Minka to the Capitol Theatre, where they saw the wonder of a full-length animated film, *Snow White and the Seven*

Dwarfs. Two months later, the movie *Test Pilot* set both their hearts racing. Roy thrilled to the daredevil antics of the lead character, an aviator, while Minka lost part of her heart forever to the actor who portrayed him, a dashing Clark Gable.

Other times they went dancing at the pavilion in Wylie Park. This familiar place, home to Lake Minne-Eho, had always made her a little sad. Her young father had drowned here, just yards away from where a band now played and couples swung, sweating and laughing, beneath strings of lights. But to be here with a beau, to be an ordinary girl in a pretty dress at last, made Minka's spirits soar. After so much sadness, being happy and falling in love was like being reborn.

Minka had only ever danced with a shuffling Honus and didn't know the real steps. Roy was an excellent dancer and a patient teacher. According to him, the trick of being a good dancer was keeping your knees flexible.

"Honey," he said easily, "now, you'll have to let me lead." His warm hand on her back was an anchor, a thrilling promise.

He was so sure of himself, so worldly, so capable and smart! Being in Roy's presence made Minka nearly dizzy after years of sitting in the background with her awkward manners, her big hands and feet, watching girls from church get married and start families. Now, half-educated, damaged-goods *Minka* was on the arm of the handsomest man in town.

Their dating was casual at first—weekend outings to a park or a show. Seasons came and went. The biggest news was no longer the economy, but the way the angry little German chancellor named Hitler was devouring whole sections of Europe. It seemed that Roy and Minka could talk about everything. They had matched minds, quick and curious. And if Roy never exactly told his girlfriend she was pretty, his attentions made her feel like she almost was.

Things were perfect, until the day Cecil brought up Roy's wife.

❋ ❋ ❋

Roy handed over the previous day's orders, then leaned an elbow on the counter and lit a cigarette with a match. His schedule now included extra time at the grocery each day so he and Minka could chat.

Today their conversation turned to foreign affairs. Japan was at war with China. Spain was at war with itself. Germany was headed toward war with everybody.

"You know they're gonna call us up," Roy said, not for the first time. The prospect was on every young man's mind. "This thing in Germany—it's bad news. That guy is not going to stop."

"No, doesn't look like it." Cecil sat on a wooden stool, wiping his hands with a rag. He'd been slicing up chickens.

Minka spoke up. "Maybe we won't have to get into it. I mean, what if it ends before we get there?" She'd been a child during the last war, the Great War. Uncle had been too old for conscription, and the whole thing had seemed scarcely to touch their isolated farm. Honus had fought in Italy, but that had been before Jennie met him.

Now that Minka was old enough to really imagine it, the idea of war seemed terrifying.

"No," Roy said, "this one's turning bad. Dad says he's seen this before. America's gonna have to get on board, sooner or later, and when we do, all hell is gonna break loose. Sorry, honey." He glanced at Minka.

"They'll send us somewhere first," said Cecil. "Somewhere for training. Otherwise they'd have green young fellas shooting their own feet off."

"I know how to handle a gun, but I don't wanna be a foot soldier," Roy said, slapping his pants with one hand. "I've been thinking about it. If I have to go, I wanna be up in a plane. One of those fighter planes."

"Goodness," said Minka. "A pilot? Roy, you don't know how to fly a plane." She was rubbing apples with a towel, making the rosy skins glow.

"No, but they teach ya. They give you all the training and then ship you over."

"How do you get in?" Cecil asked. "Do you have to take tests? Do you need classes first?"

"You just have to pass the physical, same as the regular army," said Roy. He turned his head and blew smoke to the side, away from Minka. "The problem is my age. They don't want anyone over twenty-eight. Not for pilots."

"Aren't you thirty, like me?" asked Cecil.

"Next birthday he will be," said Minka. "September fifth," she couldn't resist adding proudly. Girlfriends knew such details.

"Yeah, but I thought of a way around that." Roy leaned forward intently. "A friend told me you just need a birth certificate to enlist. I can use my little brother's."

"Which one?" asked Cecil.

"Well, Robert's, probably," said Roy. "I've got eight years on him. I'd just have to use his name."

"What if you get caught?" Minka asked. She didn't like bending rules.

"Shoot, honey, when push comes to shove, they're gonna be happy for every poor ole sap they can get." He watched as Minka fanned out apples in a basket until they looked like a bouquet. He'd never seen anyone take such care with the way things looked, from the displays in her store to her slim, perfectly ironed skirts. A neat man himself, he appreciated that quality in others.

"Roosevelt doesn't seem like he wants to send our boys over there," Cecil said.

"Oh, it'll happen eventually," Roy said. "But I may not wait around to see. If Canada gets in first, I'll go up there and join the Royal Canadian Air Force."

"If it comes to that, it's gonna be hard on everyone," said Cecil. "The women left at home, the families . . ."

"It'll be hard not to know what's happening," Minka agreed. "But we will all just have to square our shoulders and do what needs to be done. It's the only thing you can do. And anyway," she continued more shyly, "I can write letters."

Cecil looked at her. He looked at Roy.

"Sure, honey. You can write to me," Roy said.

There was a pause as Roy took a drag. Then Cecil cleared his throat.

"Have you, uh, heard from your wife lately?" he asked Roy.

Roy looked at him.

"Not lately, no."

"Your what?" Minka said. She was straightening tin cans of applesauce on a shelf. The words were so utterly ludicrous, they simply failed to register with her.

There was another pause.

"His, uh, wife," Cecil said, his voice strained with casualness.

For a moment, Minka thought, *It's a joke.* She saw Roy staring at Cecil; he wasn't smiling. Then a hot flash cut through her, and she had to grab the edge of the counter to keep her legs straight. Her mouth wouldn't work.

"We're divorcing," Roy said, his voice cool.

"Wife?" Minka found her voice, but not a normal volume. "You're married?"

He looked at her. All of a sudden, she desperately wanted the warmth to return to his eyes.

"Was," Roy said. "It's over."

"Wha . . . Where is she?" Minka asked.

Roy stubbed out his cigarette, straightened his suit jacket.

"She's in the Black Hills," he said. "She's got tuberculosis. She's divorcing me."

Minka couldn't think of a thing to say.

Roy stared at Cecil. Cecil held his gaze.

"We got married right after high school," Roy said as he looked back at Minka. "She's been gone a long time. It wasn't working. It's over, honey."

Cecil stood up, untied his apron, laid it over the counter. He grabbed his hat.

"I'm going for a walk, Minnie," he said. "Roy."

Roy didn't respond.

Cecil shut the door. There was silence.

"It's been over, I promise," Roy repeated. "I haven't got the papers yet, but—"

"When did you meet her?" Minka usually didn't interrupt Roy, but her world was spinning.

"In school. We got married too young, and then she got sick and had to go away, and it just . . ." He shrugged. "Faded away."

"Do you still love her?"

"No, honey. I guess I did a long time ago, but . . . not now."

Minka held herself still.

"I'll get it taken care of before I go away," Roy said.

Then he changed the subject. Effortlessly, the way he guided her on the dance floor.

* * *

Minka didn't know what to do. She wondered how many other people knew about this absent wife. What would her mother say? Minka's life, save for one particular incident over which she'd had no control, had been one of rock-solid propriety. She never missed a Sunday service; she knew what the Scriptures said about divorce. What would the other women at church say? What did Roy's parents and brothers think of her?

She wanted to grab Roy's arm and get answers. But her body went into automatic mode, serving a customer who came into the store.

What should I do? Why has he treated me like his girlfriend? Does Roy care about me at all?

She realized what a fool she'd been. Of course he wasn't serious about her. How could someone like Roy be interested in someone like her? Yet, Roy's attention continued, even intensified over the following days.

And behind the panicked doubts and questions swirling in Minka's mind, there was an unavoidable truth, which became more insistent in the days to come. She didn't want to lose Roy. She'd already lost so much.

Once the initial shock passed, Minka worked at the problem like a ball of dough, pounding it down, kneading it in her thoughts. How could he have kept the truth from her? But then, who was she to say anything about dark pasts, about secrets?

Yet . . . *married?*

As Roy returned day after day, his charms dismantled her. Newly emboldened, Minka told him about Betty Jane, and of course he couldn't raise an eyebrow at the revelation. Not now. Roy was deliberately tender and kind about her loss. His reaction sealed the bond between them.

Meanwhile, life rushed willingly to distract from personal complications. Rumors of war continued. Hitler had already defied the Treaty of Versailles and remilitarized the Rhineland, then annexed Austria and the Sudetenland. By March of 1939, Germans goose-stepped down the streets of Prague after an invasion of Czechoslovakia that nobody stopped. Britain and France simply looked away.

"If Germany invades Poland, they have to fight," Roy told Minka. The prospect of losing Roy in the skies over Europe kept her awake at night. Minka prayed fervently for her sweetheart's safety, but praying for God's guidance in her own life—and her decision about whether to marry Roy—never occurred to her. God was powerful, true, but Minka thought of Him as distant, removed, and formal. And she may not have prayed for His answer anyway: her heart wanted Roy for its own.

Perhaps Minka looked away too. She never again brought up the subject of the weak-lunged young woman in the Black Hills.

✳ ✳ ✳

As the grueling thirties drew to a close, war eclipsed all other subjects, personal or collective. The years at the grocery had been the most satisfying of Minka's life, but it was clear that everyone's daily routines would soon be drastically altered. Minka felt the winds of risk blowing and decided to upend her own life.

John and Dorothy now lived in Rhode Island, where Dorothy worked the night shift at a cannery. She sent a letter—would Minka be willing to move there to help watch their daughter in the evenings?

Roy, busy with his own military plans, told her to go.

In July 1939 she packed her clothes in a valise, hugged Jennie and Jane tightly, and reveled in Roy's departing endearments. Then she boarded a train bound for the East Coast. Her stomach churned with nervous exhilaration.

Providence was a noisy city bursting with nearly fifteen times the population of Aberdeen. Almost immediately, Minka found a job at a Jewish dressmaker's shop, measuring and cutting wool and silk fabrics, selling buttons and notions. Each morning, she rode a bus into the city, dodging trackless trolleys, sturdy black cars, and a startling number of pedestrians. Her evenings were sweetly filled with games and conversation with her eight-year-old niece. They went shopping together and sat among the flowers at beautiful Roger Williams Park.

Minka missed Jane's familiar presence, although Dorothy was a dear companion. Minka mostly longed for Roy—his male strength, his charm, their dynamic conversations, the grounding that came from being a couple.

On September 1, two months after Minka left Aberdeen, Hitler's Third Reich invaded Poland. After years of aggression, it was the last straw. Two days later, France and Britain declared war on Germany. Shortly thereafter, in the Canadian parliament's first independent declaration of war, Canada joined the fight.

Roy could not imagine continuing to peddle fruit while battles raged. He boarded a northbound train with Robert's birth certificate folded carefully in his pocket. Six months after arriving in Montreal, he was accepted into the Royal Canadian Air Force. The letters that flew between him and Minka only deepened their affection.

The following spring, German forces invaded Holland, and personal news from the region ceased. Jennie would have to wait through five agonizing years, until the end of the war, to learn that her family had survived.

When Roy finished his yearlong pilot training, Minka traveled to Montreal for a visit. Her suitcase was packed with her best clothes, most of them sewn herself with help from her aged Italian neighbor lady. The dreaded dairy overalls were a memory from the far-distant past.

This was Minka's first trip outside the United States, and she dressed beautifully for it, in tailored suits with slim jackets, with belts or ribbons tied around her waist. She fastened brooches to her chest, pins on her collars. Her hair was neatly curled and pinned behind her ears. Her Italian friend had made her a pretty, feminine soldier's cap, and Minka wore it proudly for her pilot beau, tilted to the right just like his. She tried to keep her hands covered up with soft gloves, although Roy never teased her about her big, twisted fingers. To the day he died, he never would.

Roy and Minka walked through green Montreal parks under a warm summer sun. They were no longer starry-eyed children—Minka would be thirty in a few months—but the war had covered everything with an exhilarating tension. Roy was headed to England, to fly bombers alongside members of the Royal Air Force. There was no way of knowing whether he would ever come back. Perhaps they would have only this day, this moment.

It felt almost like the end of time.

Using a camera borrowed from Dorothy, Minka snapped photo after photo of Roy in uniform. And though she usually preferred to stay behind the camera, she posed for several snapshots. Roy said he wanted something to remember her by. Like millions of women around the world, Minka promised to wait faithfully for her man.

And then, after receiving a final vaccination against smallpox, Roy was gone. Minka returned to Rhode Island. Four months later, on December 7, 1941, the Empire of Japan bombed a naval base at Pearl Harbor. America was at war. Men who'd fought and bled in the First World War now sent their sons to fight in the second.

Newspapers were filled with updates on troop movements, and American citizens who could not fight were eager to help in any way they could. In Rhode Island, mills and plants churned out bayonets and uniforms and parachute cases, and a shipyard was rapidly built to supply cargo vessels under the new Emergency Shipbuilding Program. A navy base packed freshly minted sailors onto newly christened vessels before sending them across the water to fight for all of their survival. Theaters broadcast the news of the war in film reels before featured movies, giving anxious citizens an additional reason to take in a show.

Minka's own life, against such a dramatic background, remained largely quiet. She kept selling buttons and fabric, tending to her niece, Betty, and sending letters. Minka wrote to Miss Bragstad at Thanksgiving and Christmas, including a dollar in each letter to be used "towards your turkey." And she sent a letter each May, with presents for the babies at the home, to commemorate Betty Jane's birthday.

She also wrote to Roy in England. Occasionally she received a note or picture from him. He mailed her black-and-white photos of himself, each marked with the same signature across the bottom: *Always, Roy.* He wasn't allowed to give details of his sorties, so his letters were short.

Long after the war was over, Minka would find Roy's little black book, filled in with the names of British girls he'd courted during those desperate days in England. But such possibilities never crossed her mind while she sat at home, waiting.

Roy transferred to the US Army Air Forces early in 1943, still using the false name of Robert Disbrow. He flew back and forth across the Atlantic, delivering bombers to the war effort, until stress began to lash his stomach with painful ulcers. In May 1944, Minka got a surprise phone call from New York—it was Roy, who'd just been shipped back under medical leave. Military doctors did surgery but couldn't fully repair the damage to his digestive system. During a brief army hearing, Roy asked for permission to keep flying planes, but in the end, he was honorably discharged.

He came home, for good. He came back to Minka.

But he didn't come back the same.

Chapter Ten

1944–1947

IN OCTOBER OF 1944, just before Minka's thirty-third birthday, she and Roy married quietly in an empty church in Providence. It was a wartime wedding, modest and simple. The bride wore an everyday dress she'd sewn herself. The couple skipped a honeymoon, and Roy went immediately back to his job working the night shift at the shipyards, a position he'd obtained that spring, after his discharge from the Army Air Forces. For a while Minka juggled overlapping schedules, cooking midnight dinners for her new husband, then rising a few hours later for her shift at the fabric store.

When she wrote to Miss Bragstad that Christmas, for the first time she signed her letter as a grown-up: "Minka" instead of "Minnie."

> I'm wondering how my little Betty is. I know I should be very proud of her now. She must be a young lady, nearly sixteen. I think of her so often, and hope so much she'll always be a credit & joy to her parents. You will write me in your letter, a bit about her won't you?

> . . . *I'm enclosing a bit towards your Xmas dinner at the*
> *home. I sincerely hope it will be a merry one for all. The*
> *home must be a blessing for many a girl today—I only wish I*
> *could find a little boy & girl under my Xmas tree. You haven't*
> *a pr of twins, have you?*

When Germany surrendered the following May, in 1945, America was nearly overcome with giddy relief as sons and brothers and husbands came home. Eager to take advantage of the new GI Bill, Roy decided to move to Minneapolis, where he could take drafting classes at the Dunwoody Institute. The renowned Mayo Clinic was nearby, too, in case he needed treatment for his recurring stomach problems.

For the rest of her life, Minka would consider Minneapolis, with its acres of glittering lakes and clusters of bushy green trees, the most beautiful city she had ever seen. The mighty Mississippi River flowed right through it, like something from a fairy-tale kingdom. The downtown district was crowded with grand cathedrals and skyscrapers, cultural institutes, and fancy hotels. Block after block, a glorious, giddy mess of honking cars filled the streets, and a person could go dizzy looking at all the signs and advertisements lining the sidewalks. Half a million people called this city home—and when they went out in public, everyone seemed to dress to the nines.

Minka had spent time here before, briefly, a few years after Betty Jane's birth. A businessman from Aberdeen had a home here, and when jobs dried up in South Dakota during the Depression, she'd come here to be his housekeeper. She'd been lonely and heartbroken then, but her life was different now.

Now her name was on the deed to a tall, narrow house on a tree-lined street just two blocks from the beaches of Lake Calhoun, a popular spot for boaters and sunbathers. Jennie had given her the money for a down payment—recompense for all the years of milking cows and twisting sausages and working in the store.

Although the house was already a half-century old and in need of fresh paint and a good cleaning, it was roomy enough to take in renters, and Minka envisioned it becoming a beautiful home under her loving care.

Most satisfying, the last name printed on that deed was Disbrow.

Two months after they arrived in the City of Lakes, the girl who'd once marveled at the novelty of an icebox watched as something called an atomic bomb put a horrifying coda on the Second World War.

In the booming economy they both found work, Roy on a production line and Minka at another yard goods store. Each morning, the couple had coffee and oatmeal together in their new kitchen, then set out into a city that seemed to sweep residents along the sidewalks with postwar energy. In the evenings, Minka cooked dinners that were easy on Roy's sensitive stomach, often a simple pot of navy beans, his favorite. Then the couple changed into old clothes and worked on the bottom half of their house, readying it for renters.

They painted walls and fixed plumbing and hung cheerful green-and-white-striped awnings outside. Roy installed window boxes and built decorative shelves around the bulky radiators. Minka cleaned house and spent hours in the basement with a washboard and wringer, doing laundry by hand as she always had. She sewed dresses for herself and wool coats for them both.

The newlyweds' days were filled with brisk work. Their nights were filled with something else—a dark legacy of the war.

Roy had spent some six hundred hours in bomber cockpits, and in the unguarded moments of sleep, those hours returned to lay claim. It all came flooding back: terse instructions and prayers in cramped rooms. Exhilarating dread during liftoff. The incessant, maddening blare of a straining engine. Explosions and flames and smoke popping beyond a rain-spattered windshield. The static that cut into the voices of friends on the intercom. Sandwiches and scotch in London afterward, for those who'd survived that run.

As the endless loop played, the darkened bedroom in Minneapolis would be pierced by Roy's hoarse cries.

"Minka! Minka, they didn't come back."

His wife tried to soothe him, but he'd flail.

"Don't you understand? They didn't come back!"

"Yes, Roy," Minka would say. "I understand." But it took him a long time to settle after a nightmare.

Still, the couple was blessed in the ways that mattered. Bad dreams could be outgrown, Minka thought. They had a marriage, a home of their own, a new life.

And Minka was determined to have another baby, even though Roy expressed no interest in having children. Betty Jane's absence was a hole that never filled.

What Minka could not guess was that the very month she moved to Minneapolis, if she'd left her new house and gone just two miles down 31st Street, past Powderhorn Park where the next Olympic speed-skating trials were to be held, and if she'd turned right on Longfellow Avenue, she would have seen a brown-haired teenager named Ruth Nordsletten helping pack her family's belongings into a borrowed truck. The Nordslettens had lived in Minneapolis for two years, but Ruth's father had just accepted a pastorate in Wisconsin. They were moving on.

Ruth was a pretty, sensible, outgoing girl who, for the first five weeks of her life, had been known by another name. Sixteen years earlier, a new mother with a broken heart had called her Betty Jane.

✳ ✳ ✳

Minka waited until Roy had finished the last of his grasshopper pie and had lit a cigarette. She sat down in the chair next to his, hands clasped on the fabric of her dress—one of his favorites—watching his face as smoke drifted in front of it. The windows were open, filtering some of the day's heat out into the evening air.

"I went to the doctor today," she said, trying to keep her voice steady. "He gave me a test . . . and I've got some news."

She fervently wanted this to be good news for him. A year after moving to Minneapolis, Roy had new creases at the corners of his eyes, and he didn't smile much these days. Canadian officials had recorded his wartime weight as a slight 130 pounds, but he was even thinner now—his elegant suits seemed to hang on him. He'd begun stopping at bars to drink before coming home, a wasteful habit that baffled Minka.

He needed a distraction, something good and hopeful to pull him from his memories. Something other than the drinking, which put a nasty bite in his attitude. Surely *this* was the thing to do it.

Roy leaned back, resting his right arm on the table. "What's your news, honey?" he said.

"Well . . ." It was difficult to remain casual. "How would you feel about being called 'Daddy'?"

Roy looked at her. He seemed to be waiting for something else.

"I'm . . . I'm pregnant. We're going to have a baby."

Roy did not leap up and sweep her into his arms. He didn't start humming, as he used to do when he was happy. He didn't even smile.

Instead, he squinted at her.

"Are you sure?"

"Yes. The doctor said so. And I can tell because . . . well, you know I've felt this before. A long time ago. With . . . with Betty Jane."

Minka waited, nearly bursting with all she *wanted* to say. That she needed to hold her own baby in her arms again. That on the bus home from the doctor's office, her eyes had filled with happy tears. That she was secretly hoping for another little girl, although she'd be just as happy with a boy, or twins, or whatever would come.

She didn't say any of this. She waited for Roy to speak.

"Shoot, honey."

Minka didn't realize that she was holding her breath.

"You know I wasn't planning for us to have kids."

Minka felt a hot pressure behind her eyes. She resisted it.

"I know. But Roy, I think you'll . . . I think you'll love the baby. Once it comes. Once you see it, and hold it, it just . . . it changes everything. You can't help it."

Roy stared at her. Minka looked down at his plate, where a bit of piecrust lay on a smear of chocolate. Outside, she heard a car door slam, an engine cough.

"Well. Okay."

Disappointment welled in Minka, searing and rough. She tamped it down. There was enough love in her heart, enough longing, for the both of them. And once the baby was here, everything would change. She knew that firsthand. He'd see.

✳ ✳ ✳

On a dark Saturday evening in mid-December, as a light snowfall frosted the frozen grass in their small yard, Minka's labor came on strong. Roy drove her into the heart of Minneapolis, past streets hung with Christmas lights and green garlands, to St. Barnabas, a pretty hospital that looked like a brick castle. Roy handed her over to the staff, then sat in the lobby smoking and looking at that morning's newspaper.

Minka was grateful when Dr. Robbins pushed a needle into her spine and injected her with medicine to block sensation in her lower body. The contractions were strong enough to take her breath away.

A few minutes before 3:00 the following morning, Minka's baby was born. The doctor and nurse busied themselves near the end of the table, slapping, rubbing, wrapping, murmuring to each other. The doctor raised his head, glanced at Minka.

"It's a girl, Mrs. Disbrow."

And Minka felt she could fly.

She craned her neck for a closer look, but the nurse hurried the baby out of the room.

"She's, ah, just going to take the baby to the nursery," said the doctor from between Minka's legs. "I'm just sewing you up. She was a very big baby."

"Is she all right?" Fear sliced through Minka.

"Um, yes . . . well, she was a little blue. But she's breathing. So . . . we'll see what's going on."

As it turned out, the baby, whom they named Dianna Dace Disbrow, had a closed valve between her heart and lung, a condition that resolved after eight days in the hospital. Minka stayed with her, happily breast-feeding for the first time and staring into her daughter's big, blue eyes. Here was all the sweetness and joy of cuddling a newborn, and none of the wrenching pain of saying good-bye. This one, she got to keep.

Roy brought Minka a single red rose. His brother Robert sent a telegram from Aberdeen, gently ribbing Roy, who'd been sure the baby was a boy: *HEARTIEST CONGRATULATIONS AND DEEPEST SYMPATHY. TRY AGAIN.*

Minka wrote to Miss Bragstad on Christmas Eve, using a single sheet of paper torn from a hospital notepad. Mother and baby were to be released from the hospital that day. Minka shared the good news. She wrote how happy she was, how darling the baby was. And, as always, she brought up her first daughter.

Hope you have a very merry holiday season. And that your getting good news from Betty Jane. She'll be a young lady of 18 in May. Bless her heart. . . .

Before Dianna's birth, Jennie had driven the nearly three hundred miles from Aberdeen to provide help for the expectant parents. When Minka carried the baby home, the place was warm and glowing with candles and filled with the smell of fresh-baked bread. The proud grandmother had prepared enough food to feed an army. A pot of buttermilk-barley soup simmered on the stove, waiting to be topped with butter and maple syrup. It was a perfect homecoming.

And Minka had been right about the baby. From the beginning, Roy was besotted.

* * *

The minute he walked through the doorway each evening, Roy laid his hat on the sideboard and held out his arms for the child he called "Dolly." He'd settle her on his lap and sing little tunes made up on the spot, or waltz across the floor while Dianna watched his face. Within months, she'd begun to grunt along to his music.

Minka had never been so happy. Instead of writing letters begging for scraps of news about her baby, asking questions that rarely received answers, now Minka could fill a pretty baby book with all the information she wanted. She recorded every detail about her daughter: each new tooth, every new pound, new skills, favorite toys. Dianna didn't like to be laid down, so Minka learned to dust and tidy with one hand while cradling her baby in the other.

Unwilling to give her daughter up to a sitter, Minka became one herself, quitting her job at the fabric store and taking in children during the day. Her new life took some getting used to. Caring for little ones involved an astonishing amount of work, with diapers to be changed and washed, meals to be fixed, tempers to be soothed.

It was hard to adjust to the constant clamor, but she managed, even holding to her old Dutch standards in housekeeping. She scrubbed everything, every day. After meals, dishes were washed and put away immediately. Clothes were hung up, never tossed on beds or chairs. Such was Minka's aversion to clutter that she discarded almost anything she wasn't using, including letters. She didn't keep a single page of her correspondence with Miss Bragstad or a single wartime letter from Roy.

The only thing she held on to was a small collection of photos, neatly stacked in boxes. And tucked away in a drawer where no one could find it, Minka kept the picture of baby Betty Jane. From time to time when she had a few moments alone, and always on Betty's birthday, she pulled it out and savored the memory of her very first love. Her prayers became like a mantra: *Please let her be healthy. Please let her be happy. Please let her be loved.*

In March the Disbrows drove back to Aberdeen to christen Dianna at Zion Lutheran, Minka's childhood church. The baby wore a long, white gown that Minka had sewn. Grandparents, as well as aunts and uncles from both sides, doted on the gorgeous baby. Dianna had her mother's high cheekbones and her father's olive skin, dark hair, and bright eyes.

It was a festive occasion, offering barely a hint of the trouble to come.

After the christening Roy posed for a picture with his three handsome brothers, all of whom had also served in the recent war. In the photo, taken in their mother's living room, two of the brothers are smiling, but the other two wear the recently coined "thousand-yard stare." The suffering of veterans, once called "nostalgia" but now referred to as "shell shock," had been observed for centuries yet was little understood.

One of the blank-faced Disbrow brothers would soon be dead by his own hand.

The other one, the brand-new father, would live longer but in no less pain. Roy's post-traumatic stress disorder, as the condition would later be known, was a catalyst that was already propelling him toward alcoholism. And it would soon awaken something that rested deep within and would eclipse all else—a disease that would one day ruin his life and devastate his young family.

✳ ✳ ✳

The Disbrows returned home to Minneapolis, leaving South Dakota behind again. Even with rent coming in from the downstairs neighbors and Minka's child-care wages, there didn't seem to be enough money. Minka took a second job at a drugstore, working evenings and weekends. Her constitution was as strong as ever. She never missed work, even when her nights were broken by her daughter's hungry cries or her husband's nightmares.

For the Christmas of 1947, Jennie and Jane came to visit. Although money was tight, conditions had improved far beyond the frugality of the farm years and the Depression, and the three women created a feast. They stuffed a turkey, mixed Jell-O salads, layered marshmallows over yams, assembled pecan and apple pies. Minka draped garlands and pinecones in the little-used dining room and set the table with china and a perfectly ironed tablecloth.

A steam radiator hissed, keeping the bitter cold out of the small rooms. Roy put up a tree, everyone decorated it, and Dianna stared in wonder. Jane, who doted on the baby, taught her to scrunch up her nose on command.

Late that night, Minka composed a letter to Miss Bragstad.

The superintendent of the Lutheran House of Mercy was in her final two years before retirement. In nearly three decades, Bertha Bragstad had encountered more young women than she could remember, heard every story and excuse, and witnessed innumerable tears. But no girl stood out like the Dutch milkmaid who'd conceived through rape and then fallen in love with her baby girl. For almost nineteen years, far longer and more often than Miss Bragstad could have predicted, Minka had kept up a correspondence. The girl had donated money, handmade clothing, gifts, and turkeys, even through a depression and a war.

She had been unable to forget her baby, even after all this time. But this would be Minka's final letter. Her second daughter had

Uncle's house, where Minka grew up (Jennie on left, Uncle on right)

Growing up

ABOVE ▲
Jane (L) and
Minka (R),
around 1917

Uncle at Scatterwood Lake—where,
years later, Minka would attend the
sewing class picnic

Board of Foreign Missions

Ev. Luth. Synod of Iowa
and Other States

OFFICE OF SECRETARY
REV. W. F. KRAUSHAAR, M.A.

Aberdeen, South Dakota
April 3. 1929.

uth. escue Home
ioux alls, . ak.

y dear adam:

    I have an unfortunate girl in my congregation
ex ects to give birth to a child about the end of this month.
ave investigated her case and am convinced that she was the
victim of a dastardly crime of assault. She comes of a good fam
and has been staying with relatives at Sioux City. Could you
take her in and help her when her time comes? Her family is no
sealthy, but they will pay whatever your regular fees are.
I must mention too, that her people want her to give her baby
away since the father is a fugitive criminal, but the girl seem
rather inclined to keep it. Possibly you can give them the best
advice. o you find good homes for such children? Of course, the
would prefer a lutheran home.
    I would greatly appreciate an early reply.

    Faithfully yours,

        W. F. Kraushaar.

Reverend Kraushaar's letter to
the Lutheran House of Mercy
on Minka's behalf (1929)

Betty Jane

The only picture that
exists of seventeen-
year-old Minka and
Betty Jane

BELOW
Minka's
inscription
on the back of the
photo: "Sweetest
little girl in the
world—Betty J"

Sweetest little girl
in the world—Betty J.

One of the many letters Minka
wrote asking after Betty Jane

ABOVE ▲
Minka in Victoriaville, Canada,
on a 1941 visit to Roy

RIGHT ▶
Roy mailed this photo to Minka in 1943,
after he'd transferred from the RAF to the
US Army Air Force.

Jennie and her grandchildren
Dianna and Donnie (1951)

Roy, Minka, and their daughter,
Dianna (1947)

Time marches on

Ruth on a parade float for "Hospital Days" in Viroqua, Wisconsin (1948)

Love,
Ruthie

The lost daughter

ABOVE ▲
Ruth at age twelve

BELOW ▼
Ruth and Charles on their wedding day: September 24, 1948

Ruth ("Betty Jane") with her adoptive parents, Olava and Peder Nordsletten

Mark Lee floating above Earth during NASA's Space Shuttle *Discovery* STS-64 mission, September 1994

◄ RIGHT ▶
Ruth and Charles with son Brian (center) at his West Point graduation in 1981

An unexpected legacy

The Lee family gathers for Charles's eightieth birthday party in 2008.

Minka at the Portland, Oregon, rose gardens with (L to R) grandson Gary; sister, Jane; daughter Dianna; and grandson Grant (1993)

Family

RIGHT ▶
Minka with the flowers she tends at her apartment building; taken in March 2006, just two months before she would pray to see Betty Jane again

Minka and granddaughter Cathy (author of *The Waiting*) in 1995

ABOVE ▲
The last photo taken of Minka and her sister, Jane, together (1999)

❧ Reunited ☙

On August 18, 2006, Minka and her long-lost daughter were reunited
—after nearly eight decades of waiting.

Minka with her two daughters
(Ruth and Dianna), together for
the first time

Minka and Ruth today

Together

ABOVE ▲
Celebrating birthdays . . .
together at last

◄ LE
Four generations united for t[
college graduation and Arm[
commission of Taylor L[
(Ruth's grandson): (L to F[
Taylor, Minka, Ruth, ar[
Brian Lee (Ruth's sor[

just learned to walk—her first was now a college-aged adult. She would have kept writing forever if her letters had prompted news about Betty Jane. But Miss Bragstad's letters were always gently vague. She passed along very little information, other than to say that Betty Jane was "a fine girl" who was "happy in her home."

Minka didn't know that Betty Jane's adoptive parents had renamed her Ruth. She didn't know that the girl would be married within a year to her high school sweetheart.

As much as Minka longed for news, she didn't really know anything.

> . . . we are all fine here. My mother is with me, has been since Nov. My little girl is a year old, and needless to say we all love her dearly. She has brought so much joy into all our lives. She has big blue eyes & medium dark hair, looks a lot like Betty Jane did, although Betty was fairer. . . .
>
> Would appreciate a line from you & if you have any news about Betty, I'd surely love to hear how she is. . . .
>
> Please write me if you have word Miss Bragstad, will make my Xmas happier just to know she is fine and happy. . . .

Minka enclosed a Christmas stocking with the letter—a gift from her baby, Dianna, to whatever babies were now at the home. She would write no longer. From this time forward, Minka would hold on to just one photograph, a handful of memories, and a promise she'd made the day she said good-bye to her first child.

She would *never* forget Betty Jane.

Chapter Eleven

1947–1955

MONTHS PASSED. Roy continued to drink, and Minka's disappointment deepened. As his absences grew more frequent, arguments began to fracture their lives. But the couple was in perfect unity on one point: their enchanting daughter. Dianna was proving to be as smart as she was beautiful. She seemed to do everything early: by her first birthday, her rosebud mouth sparkled with twelve perfect teeth. Two months later she learned to put her shoe straps through her buckles. At eighteen months she memorized her first of many poems, "I Had a Little Pony."

Determined to give her daughter the affection that her own mother had not known to give, Minka held Dianna, cuddled her, kissed her. She wrote a wistful note in her baby book: *As I write this you are sound asleep in your little bed. You've had a busy morning creeping all around & exploring rooms & drawers, mostly Mommy's cupboard, where pots & pans are pulled out & banged over & over again. . . . Mommy hopes you won't grow too fast, & that you'll always be as happy as you are today. Sometimes we can't always be, but Mommy's hoping & praying her little girl will.*

By the next summer Minka was pregnant again. Her last child, a son they called Donnie, was born on the third day of 1949, giving Minka the matched set she'd dreamed of. Donnie was another pretty baby, with big eyes, curly blond hair and, within months, a winning smile.

Roy enrolled at the Dunwoody Institute to study mechanical drafting. He would take classes on and off for two years, producing beautiful drawings and earning good grades but accruing frequent absences for health problems. His stomach continued to bother him, and he worked so deliberately that his teachers marked him down as being "slow" to complete tasks. In reality, his mind often raced, making it difficult for him to concentrate. He complained, "When they've gone around the broomstick once, I've gone ten times."

He was obviously intelligent. His wife found his challenges puzzling.

There was sweetness in their lives, at times. On Sundays, Roy read the comic strips out loud to the children while Minka made waffles for breakfast and pot roast for dinner. Refusing to yield to polio fears, which kept many people away from public places in the early 1950s, Minka took the children swimming and fishing at Lake Calhoun. On Sunday evenings the family went for rides around the lake in Roy's big Buick, stopping on the way back for tall ice cream cones. When snow piled up on city streets in winter, they went sledding.

Christmas was the most special time. The whole family went shopping at Dayton's department store, where Dianna and Donnie stood in long lines to ride the elevated North Pole train. Even sensible Minka played along with the legend of Santa. She baked cookies to leave out on Christmas Eve, while the children knelt by the window, watching fat flakes drift from a cloud-darkened sky. After reading *The Night Before Christmas* aloud and tucking the kids in bed, she and Roy stayed up late, wrapping presents and leaving behind a milk-stained glass and a plate of crumbs for Dianna and Donnie to find in the morning, while their parents pretended to sleep.

Since that first simple dress she'd sewn—the one that would forever be linked with Betty Jane—Minka had become an expert seamstress. Roy preferred to wear store-bought suits, but Minka made all her own clothes, and the children's as well, everything from overcoats to fancy dresses. She even sewed pretty clothes for Dianna's dolls, decorated with miniature trim and buttons and lace. When the family went out, all four got "dolled up." Roy and Donnie wore suits, hats, and shiny shoes; Minka and Dianna wore pretty dresses and hats, gloves, and jewelry.

Jennie eventually sold the grocery in Aberdeen, moved to Minneapolis, and bought a whole apartment building a few blocks from Minka's house. Jane, in her midthirties now but still unmarried, came with her. Although Minka was busy with work and her children, the women were thrilled to live close to each other again. Jennie retained her married name, Vander Zee, so Dianna and Donnie called her "Grandma Van." They loved to spend the night at her place. In the mornings she'd bake cinnamon rolls while ever-vivacious Aunt Janie cleaned house in her slip, dancing and teasing the kids, who adored her.

The family's joy was clouded by the darkness that seemed to follow Roy. By now, he stopped at the bar every night. At home he smoked cigarettes compulsively. His fingertips reeked of unfiltered smoke, and Dianna and Donnie would hold their breath in the haze around his chair. Sometimes he seemed to be another person, a cruel and cunning stranger. The children learned to be watchful of this other Daddy.

Minka began attending a Lutheran church in Minneapolis, where the rituals were familiar and comforting. The weekly reflection and prayers grounded her.

Roy would not go along, but he found some solace in gardening.

He spent hours in the yard, planting bright, puffy dahlias along the back fence, a fragrant lilac in one corner. He built a sandbox for the children. But Roy couldn't always remain with his hands in the rich soil and warm sunshine on his back. Other responsibilities tugged at him. Before long the seasons changed, and his garden spent months buried beneath the heavy snow. This outdoor therapy could not last.

The Disbrows' lives lurched between darkness and light. Sometimes Roy was the smart, charming man Minka had fallen in love with. The whole family would go "to town" for dinner, the children acting grown-up in their best clothes. They'd sit at the bar with their parents, dipping cherries in their Shirley Temples, smiling at the barkeep. In summer, Roy rented a small cabin on the lake, where they'd fish and swim and wake up from naps with sweaty hair plastered to their necks. Roy bought gifts for his wife and children—an engine for Donnie's ever-expanding train set, a fancy new doll for Dianna. He'd put a record on the player and sweep Minka around the living room, dancing as he'd taught her to do years before, while Dianna and Donnie giggled and grinned.

As hard as they all tried, it kept crashing down around them. It was as though the happiness was too heavy to prop up, for long.

✳ ✳ ✳

The first sign of a problem with Dianna came when she was three years old. She'd gone to the sink to get a drink of water before naptime. Minka heard the faucet splashing, splashing, and followed the sounds into the kitchen.

"Dianna? Honey? What are you doing?"

Dianna stared at the wall above the sink, her tiny fingers gripping a cup.

"Dianna? Come to bed."

There was no reply, no movement. After turning off the faucet,

Minka stroked Dianna's curls and tried to turn her chin up. The little face was as blank as a porcelain doll's.

No amount of shaking or talking got the slightest response.

Minka lifted Dianna and hurried into the living room. She picked up the clunky black phone and yelled into the receiver.

"Operator! I need a taxi! My little girl . . . she's . . . something's wrong . . . please, get me a taxi!"

Heart thumping, breath quick and sharp, Minka ran to get Donnie from his crib. Dianna lay against her shoulder, stiff and hot. Minka staggered to grab her purse, then inched her way down the stairs to wait at the curb. During the ride, she kept trying to rouse Dianna. In her hurry to propel herself into the hospital, she forgot to pay the taxi driver.

Dianna woke up the next day, seemingly undamaged, but the doctors had a sobering diagnosis: the pretty little girl had experienced a grand mal seizure. She had epilepsy. The doctors prescribed Phenobarbital and Dilantin in high dosages, which managed the seizures but temporarily dulled Dianna's lightning-quick mind. When she started school, she struggled to earn good grades, swimming through a fog of medication and fatigue until her doctor finally determined the proper dosage.

There was more trouble to come. One Sunday, two weeks before her seventh birthday, Dianna spent the night with Grandma Van. The next morning, Roy brought her home to see Minka before school. It was cold outside, so Minka watched from the screened upstairs porch, holding Donnie in her arms. He was almost five but small for his age, and Minka didn't mind carrying him—the gentle boy was her last baby.

She watched Roy park across the street. Dianna rounded the car. She was wearing a tan wool coat that Minka had sewn, the buttons fastened tight against the icy air. Her hair was pinned back. She looked up, saw Minka, waved. Her curls bobbed. She started running across the street, her breath trailing behind her.

The approaching car was a brand-new Buick sedan with a monstrous metal grille in front. There wasn't time to stop, and the street was slick. Brakes screeched, Roy hollered, Minka cried out helplessly from above. Dianna's dark curls disappeared under one whitewall tire.

By the time Minka lurched down the stairs, Dianna's blood was smeared across the rough pavement. A patch of her hair had been torn off, exposing a white square streaked with red. Roy yanked a wool army blanket from his trunk, spread it on the frozen pavement, and laid Dianna on it. Her eyes fluttered open.

A neighbor appeared with a cup of cocoa, a helpless gesture for a hurt little girl. An ambulance raced up, sirens blaring. Minka sat in the back, cradling Dianna in her arms as the driver sped to the hospital. Roy followed in their car.

After X-rays, lab tests, and a few nights in the hospital, Dianna was pronounced well enough to come home, minus some hair and with a permanent flat spot on the back of her skull. For years afterward, Minka watched her closely for signs of long-term damage. Dianna had nearly been killed. Minka had almost lost another daughter.

As tough as she was, Minka felt certain she couldn't have borne that.

✳ ✳ ✳

Minka found a new church within walking distance of her home, a Christian and Missionary Alliance congregation, and began nurturing her spiritual life in earnest. She was greatly intrigued by the CMA's outreach programs around the world. Visiting missionaries came to services and told spellbinding tales of remote tribes of cannibals, of angels standing guard around campsites. Such stories opened Minka's eyes to parts of the world that she hadn't had the opportunity to learn about in school.

After Dianna saw Minka baptized at the church, she asked to

follow suit. As mother and children attended each week, Minka began to view God as more of a heavenly Father—someone who was interested not just in mankind as a whole, but in her personal life as well. She began tentatively praying for wisdom and guidance in her chaotic relationship with Roy.

More and more, wisdom and guidance were desperately needed.

One morning when Dianna was still a toddler, Minka was at the kitchen sink, washing dishes. Roy came in, eyes glittering. He paced behind her. He spoke abruptly.

"Who is he? Did you see him last night?"

Minka's stomach clenched. The water on her hands was suddenly too hot. She adjusted the faucet, squeezed the rag, scrubbed at the tines of a fork. These absurd ramblings came out of nowhere these days.

"Roy. Stop it."

"Who is he? Who're you two-timing with?" He halted right behind her.

"Roy, I said stop it. I've never two-timed on you, and you know it." She slid a cup into the soapy water, jammed a washrag into it. "When on earth would I have time for such foolishness? After riding the bus home late at night? After working fourteen-hour days?"

He was a B-17 bomber, homing in.

"Are you gonna see him tonight, honey?" The familiar endearment held no lazy tenderness. "You gonna have some fun?"

She'd had enough.

"Oh Roy, be quiet. Why don't you clean up your *own* backyard?"

For two seconds the water ran, bubbles popped. Then Minka's right arm was jerked backward as Roy spun her around. The dishrag slapped against her dress. A blurry shape approached her face, too fast.

Roy's fist slammed into her nose, crunching the cartilage.

A warm gush of blood followed the shocking pain. Minka

staggered sideways, turned toward the sink. Tears ran, blending with blood and dripping onto her dress. She watched the mixture swirl in the dishwater, cloudy and dark.

The blow jarred loose a memory from long ago. She'd been perhaps seven years old, splitting wood for the cookstove. Her hand slipped as she was trying to wrench the ax free, and the wooden handle slammed squarely into her face. Blood poured and Minka cried and Jennie came running.

Accidents happened on a farm, and medical help was a long buggy ride away. Jennie used the edges of both her hands to force Minka's nose back into place, then taped it up and put her daughter to bed. *Lie very still*, she'd instructed gently.

This time, Jennie wasn't there to comfort her. Behind her, silence. Then Roy's hand was on her back. His other hand pushed a dish towel in front of her. They mopped at her face together.

Neither one of them noticed their young daughter, watching from an alcove in the hallway.

"I think it's broken," Minka cried. She had never felt so small, crumpled. "You broke my nose."

"Let's . . . uh . . . You need to go see a doctor. C'mon. I'll take you." The old Roy was back, and contrite.

Minka held the towel to her face. Roy fetched her shoes, the car keys, the children. He helped her to the car. He told her not to tell the doctor what had happened. And he made the timeless vow of a volatile man.

"It won't happen again, honey."

❊   ❊   ❊

Surprisingly, this man kept that promise. Although he continued to drink and the dark voices continued to scratch at his mind, Roy never hit his wife again. But the ugliness persisted, and became more frequent. Sometimes he slept under the outside stairs with a pair of brass knuckles, threatening to accost Minka's imaginary boyfriends when they showed up. Once he threw whiskey on his wife and took off down the street holding Dianna, with Minka running after him. When a policeman stopped him, Roy pointed to the alcohol stains on Minka's dress and accused *her* of drinking. Then the former soldier drew himself up and spit in the policeman's face, earning himself a whack from a billy club.

Roy's father had passed away, but his mother, Florence, still lived near Aberdeen. When she needed an operation for cancer, Roy and Minka invited her to stay with them in Minneapolis. Minka changed her bandages and cared for her during recovery. Florence loved her son but hated his drinking, hated what it was doing to his dependable wife, to their family. She dragged a cot near the front door and laid Roy's baseball bat next to it.

"Just let him come up here drunk," she said. "He'll have to deal with me."

Roy's mind clanged and clattered. He read newspaper articles about the American boys now fighting in Korea, and at night two different wars comingled in his dreams. He sought distraction at the cinema, watching black-and-white horror films that he found more manageable than his full-color nightmares. Alcohol brought a lessening, a loosening, so he drank. He didn't realize that the drinking also worsened his mania and hallucinations.

Talking relieved the pressure. Sometimes when Minka was working late, he told Dianna and Donnie macabre bedtime stories of buddies burning in their planes and begging him over the intercom to shoot them dead. Although he'd been nowhere near the Asian theater, he talked about Japanese soldiers putting splinters under the fingernails of POWs to torture them.

He seemed a million miles away, unaware that his horrified audience was a little girl in a lace nightgown and a little boy in footie pajamas.

Desperate for hope and help, Minka took a bus to Fort Snelling, which had become the site of the regional Veterans Administration after World War II. But harried officers there couldn't offer help, other than to suggest that she was fortunate—at least he wasn't beating the children. During one bad episode Roy threatened to divorce Minka, even hired a lawyer to draw up papers that accused his wife of outlandish wrongdoings. Florence came to visit again and went down to the lawyer's office with her daughter-in-law. "I am his mother," she declared. "And this," she said, stabbing a finger at Roy's papers, "is a bunch of lies."

Nobody knew how to help, how to fix a broken man.

Roy withdrew the papers. The couple would remain married for the rest of his life. But it was all too much for Minka. She couldn't take the stress and threats, the rages that made no sense. She couldn't stand her children's frightened eyes, the way they shrank into corners. Roy's drinking was the problem, she decided, and sobriety was the solution. It had to be.

John and Dorothy had moved to California, a place they assured her was bright and busy, a good spot for a new beginning. It was far away, near an ocean she'd never seen. Far enough away from Roy and the troubles that he would not, or could not, discard.

Minka made an agonizing decision. She would sell the house, the pretty place she'd been so proud of. She would leave the city she loved, her church, her mother and sister. She would uproot her children and issue an ultimatum to her husband.

He could come to them when he got sober.

And not a moment before.

Chapter Twelve
1955–1961

MINKA HUGGED her mother and sister good-bye at the airport. Jennie grasped Minka's arms, giving her a long, searching look that shared the words they didn't speak: *You can do this. You've faced adversity before. You are strong and are making the right decision.*

Jennie and Jane stood side by side, watching Minka and the two children cross the tarmac and walk up the steep stairs into the airplane.

"Good-bye!" Donnie called to them.

Minka held her children's hands, helping them board. She kept her sadness inside, as did Jane and Jennie. Tears were reserved for privacy.

The excitement of Donnie and Dianna's first flight was tempered by all they were leaving behind.

"Is Daddy coming too?" Donnie asked timidly. Minka couldn't offer a good explanation. Though she wanted her children to understand, how could she explain without speaking badly of their father? Her answers were vague and nondescript. "He has to stay and work." "He loves you but he can't come right now . . . he'll come later."

Dianna didn't ask. She'd witnessed more of the fighting, heard her mother crying behind closed doors, and felt her heart race at Roy's increasingly violent threats and manic behavior.

Inside the plane, the children stared out the small windows in amazement. For a moment, Minka wished Roy were there to tell his eight-year-old daughter and six-year-old son just how safe air travel had become—nothing like war, nothing like his nightmares. This flight was quite different from Roy's European sorties. Here, pretty ladies in starched caps and tailored uniforms passed out coffee and lunch. The children tried to ignore the sharp pain jabbing their ears, as thick cigarette smoke floated around the closed cabin.

California offered hope. That same summer of 1955, Walt Disney opened a theme park like no other in Anaheim, California, with the inviting words: *To all who come to this happy place: Welcome.*

Four hundred miles north in the same golden state, Minka hoped she'd brought her children to a happier place, that in this unfamiliar Bay Area they'd find safe, brand-new lives. She tried to bury the residual fears about leaving behind her husband and being away from her mother and sister, and the sense that the final tie to Betty Jane was being irrevocably broken by moving so far away.

After landing, Minka, Dianna, and Donnie were greeted at the gate by John and Dorothy. As they headed to John's car, Minka realized that she and her children had stepped into a California landscape that did not resemble her vision of tropical heat and warm beaches. This was a region of light and shadows. A cool summer breeze teased the sunshine outside the city of Oakland, while across the bay, San Francisco was hidden in fog so thick that every skyscraper had disappeared.

Jutting out from the gray mist were the massive towers and concrete pilings of the Bay Bridge, connecting Oakland to San

Francisco. Boats skimmed across the choppy waters of the bay, steering clear of massive cargo ships coming from all over the world to deliver and pick up supplies at the Port of Oakland.

"Where are the coconuts?" Donnie asked, resting his arms over the front seat of John and Dorothy's fancy car. John had become a successful car salesman after moving out West. His only child, Betty, was already an adult.

"No coconut trees around here," John said, reaching back to ruffle his nephew's hair. "But if you look far out that way on a clear day, you'll see the orange-colored arches of the Golden Gate Bridge and even the flash of light from the Rock."

John told his awed niece and nephew about the 250 federal prisoners who lived on Alcatraz Island, including Robert Stroud, the brainy, violent "Birdman of Alcatraz."

"You're going to scare them," Dorothy ventured.

"They need to know about the place they've moved to," he said with a laugh.

John and Dorothy would house them at first, but Minka liked having her own private space. And she knew her brother and his wife were well past the time of having little ones racing through their rooms.

Within a few months, with money from the sale of her Minneapolis home, Minka bought a small stucco house on Linwood Avenue, just four miles from the bay. The place had no basement, and Minka, who'd grown up under the threat of tornadoes, at first felt as if her house could easily be swept right off the earth.

There was no yard to speak of either, no garden bursting with dahlias. But the living room boasted a bay window, built-in bookshelves, and carpeting patterned in pretty pink roses. The kitchen was modern, with an oven built right into the wall. Minka soon had the house arranged to her old DeYoung perfection.

Just like Jennie so many years before, Minka was now a single mother. And just as Jennie had done, Minka squared her shoulders and got to work. When she took a bus to the district school office to enroll Dianna and Donnie, she asked the secretary if they had any available jobs.

"There's a position open in the cafeteria," the woman said.

"Perfect," Minka replied. She got the position and was grateful to know she'd be working near her children and during school hours.

School started that autumn without red and orange leaves carpeting the sidewalks. The shift of seasons was subtle in Oakland—autumn came a month or so later, and winters were mild. Minka missed the Midwest's fluctuating weather: snowdrifts and ice-covered lakes that glistened in winter, leafy trees robed in breathtaking colors in autumn, brilliantly hued tulips that boldly announced spring. She had always lived with defined seasons, and adjusting to the change was like living with an out-of-sync clock.

The atmosphere of the West Coast was different too—there was more liberal thinking than she'd ever encountered before, and communities brimmed with a sea of diverse cultures and nationalities: Chinese, Mexican, Middle Eastern, African, and other unfamiliar languages and peoples.

Minka sometimes felt overwhelmed by all the changes but was bolstered when she found a nearby church, Grand Avenue Alliance, that soon felt like home to her family. At night, when she sat at the bedsides of her sleeping children, who were now safe from the threat called *Daddy*, Minka felt reassured about her decision to come here.

Minka spent her days packaging sandwiches, fruit, and milk, and delivering bag lunches to the district elementary schools. She was never late, and nobody worked harder or faster than the former South Dakota farm girl. Still, money was tight.

She took a second job in the evenings, making phone calls for the American Cancer Society. Minka had no money for a baby-sitter, and John and Dorothy were too busy with their own jobs and schedules to help. Donnie and Dianna had to be left home alone. In between solicitation calls, Minka would phone her house, always saying the same thing when her daughter answered.

"Don't go to the door. Are you okay?"

Dianna would reassure her mother. And perhaps ten minutes later, Minka would call again.

"Are you okay? Don't answer the door for anyone."

She checked in with them over and over, until the children put themselves to bed. When Minka came in late at night, she'd straighten bedspreads, kiss soft cheeks, and listen to her children breathe, while racking her brain for a better plan.

A year after Minka moved to Oakland, Roy followed.

✳ ✳ ✳

He'd promised to stay sober, and he'd kept that promise, living the previous year in Jennie's basement so his mother-in-law could monitor his sobriety. But he felt unmoored without his children, without Minka's capable steadiness.

During sporadic phone calls, Roy made promises to Minka. Jennie confirmed that he hadn't been drinking and offered to move to California when he did. Minka believed that God could change anyone. The children longed for their father, and getting sober *had* been the agreement. In the summer of 1956, Minka said he could come.

Roy quit his job in Minneapolis, bought a brand-new Buick sedan, and drove to California. Jennie, who wasn't about to leave him unsupervised, rode shotgun, leaving behind forty-three-year-old Jane.

Though charming all her life, Jane had been so deeply attached to Jennie that it had crippled her ability to bond with anyone out-side the family. But recently she'd begun dating a fellow Aberdeen native, a former classmate of Roy's who now worked in management at a railroad company. Chris Froehlich wore expensive suits and smoked cigars, and Jane was smitten. For now, she decided to stay in Minneapolis.

That summer, President Eisenhower was preparing to sign the Federal-Aid Highway Act, and within a few decades the drive from Minneapolis to Oakland would be only a three-day trip. But Roy and Jennie had to stitch together a winding route on back roads and byways. Day after day, they puttered across plains and through towns and over the fearsome Rocky Mountains, the likes of which Jennie had never seen.

"If only I had one of my old planes," Roy mused to Jennie during one of their rest stops. "We could have been there in less than a day. It would have been something flying over those mountains." He would never fly again, and he'd never stop missing the sensation of escaping through the clouds.

Roy and Jennie both moved in with Minka. With her mother there, Minka no longer had to worry about her children in the evenings. Dianna and Donnie were ecstatic to have Daddy back. Minka was cautious. Roy's behavior had called for drastic measures, but families were meant to be together. Her thoughts were a roller coaster; she struggled to believe that Roy had really changed.

With his drafting skills, Roy found a job easily. Minka would dress the children in their Sunday best on the days she picked him up from work, and he enjoyed showing them off to his coworkers. The family resumed their weekend tradition of car rides, visiting Lake Merritt—a tidal lagoon in the heart of Oakland that reminded them, just a little, of their beloved City of Lakes and of their happiest times together.

For special treats, they drove to Playland, an amusement park on the beach in San Francisco, or ate at the Grand Lake Drive In, which everyone called Club 19 because hamburgers cost 19 cents each. Minka told her kids about the long-ago days when she'd shared a single milk shake with her stepfather, mother, and sister.

"I get to have my own milk shake," Donnie said proudly, and Minka was reminded that despite the hardships, her children were not struggling through childhood as she had. They had a better life.

There was an uneasy truce between the adults in their first months back together, one that Dianna and Donnie sensed and skirted.

And then one day, Roy stepped into a neighborhood bar. The dimly lit space enveloped him like an old friend.

Minka smelled the beer, threatened him, feared what was to come. She was more torn than ever. Her children were older, more attached to their father, yet there was little chance of hiding his drunken behavior. Roy made a few lukewarm promises, but alcohol was a controlling master that he couldn't seem to resist.

One weekend the whole family went for a drive. Jennie rode in the backseat with the kids. Roy drove while the women chatted over the seat.

Without warning, Roy veered toward the sidewalk.

Then up onto it.

Pedestrians stumbled back, against the front of a drugstore, shouting at Roy. Two of the car's tires bumped along the curb. Seat belts would not be mandatory for another dozen years, and little Donnie fell against the back of the front seat. Jennie caught Dianna around the waist.

"Roy!" Minka yelped. "What are you doing?"

He twirled the steering wheel. The car settled back onto the street. For a moment, it seemed like just a careless accident.

Then he jerked the wheel again, and the car jumped back onto the sidewalk.

"Roy!" Minka cried. She grabbed the dashboard and whipped her head toward her husband. "Stop it! Get back on the road."

There was a faint smile on Roy's face. Both hands gripped the steering wheel. His cigarette, clamped between his lips, dripped ash onto his trousers.

The car bumped along, half on the sidewalk. More pedestrians fled. One man hollered something, but nobody in the car could hear what he said. Finally, Jennie raised her voice.

"Roy. Stop this car *now*."

Roy pumped the brakes. The car stopped, flinging everyone forward.

Jennie collected her purse, opened the back door, and stepped onto the sidewalk. She pulled the children from the car, then turned to her daughter. Minka was trembling as she stared at Roy, her back pressed against the side window. "Kom maar hier, Minnie."

Minka fumbled at the handle, got the door open on the second try. She stepped out and slammed the door shut. All four of them stood staring at the car until Roy pulled forward and drove off. This time, he stayed on the street.

No one said a word. They walked to a bus stop and were soon on their way home. Minka sat with her back straight, her eyes damp, her mind far away. When they got home, Roy's car was in the driveway.

Dianna ran up the front steps first. Roy was sitting on a chair in the kitchen doorway with a rifle across his lap, a gun his daughter had never seen before. He stood up.

Instinct pushed Dianna back. She ran outside, shoved her brother and mother and grandmother toward the sidewalk. "Daddy's got a gun! Run!"

The women and children scrambled down the street to a neighbor's house while gunfire cracked behind them. As the neighbor dialed the police and Jennie stood at the doorway, Minka yanked her children against her, fighting back the emotion that caught painfully in her throat.

Officers came and arrested Roy. When his family returned to their house, they saw ragged holes where Roy had sprayed shells into the plaster ceiling, hunting some unfathomable prey.

✳ ✳ ✳

Roy was immediately transported nearly four hundred miles south, to the state psychiatric hospital in Camarillo. Minka waited a couple of weeks, then drove the children down the coast to the sprawling hospital campus, where patients stayed in mission-style buildings. Dianna and Donnie moved down pathways lined with palm trees, hearts thumping. Perhaps this place that looked like a tropical resort had fixed their daddy. They tried not to look at the bars bolted over the windows.

After they'd waited for a short time in a doctor's office, Roy was brought in. Dianna started eagerly toward her father before stopping and staring. Her eyes said it all: *That isn't Daddy.*

Roy's raven hair had turned snow-white. A pair of loose cotton pants and a shirt hung from his limbs. He'd become frail, turned old overnight. He was a sickly stranger.

"Please." His quiet voice held a desperation the children had not heard before. His dark eyes looked panicked as he pleaded with Minka. "Please take me home. I can't take this anymore."

Roy and Minka went for a walk while the children trailed behind. They heard only snippets of phrases. *Strapped down . . . wrapped me in wet sheets . . . electroshock . . .*

Roy's unpredictable, volatile behavior had been diagnosed, at long last. A doctor in a white coat explained to Minka how chemicals in the brain worked. He said that her husband's illness would not go away, and that for safety reasons, he could no longer live at home. And the doctor offered up a fittingly horrid name for Roy's disease.

Paranoid schizophrenia.

Minka didn't understand the terms. She only knew that she

wanted back the man she'd once known. And she wasn't going to get him.

Roy returned to Oakland, moved into a small apartment, and lived off his pension. From then on, he would visit his family only for holidays and the occasional birthday—the four of them would never again live under the same roof. Minka didn't consider divorcing him; she'd said *for better or worse, in sickness and in health*, and she would not break those vows.

Unable to handle the stress of a full-time job after his breakdown, Roy went on permanent disability. His spirit was fractured for good.

Still, it was a small blessing that he hadn't been confined closer to home for treatment. Two years earlier Dr. Walter Freeman, inventor and champion of the ghoulish "ice-pick lobotomy," which he was convinced offered a cure for schizophrenia, had set up shop just forty miles south of where Roy had sat that bleak afternoon, emptying a gun into his ceiling.

✳   ✳   ✳

Jennie had her own home in Oakland now. But she'd been feeling tired and feverish lately, so one afternoon she asked Minka if she could stay with her for a couple of days. Jennie's temperature kept climbing, and she couldn't shake her fatigue.

Not long after Jennie came, eleven-year-old Dianna walked home for lunch and found Grandma Van in bed, unconscious and foaming at the mouth. Dianna phoned her mother at work, and Minka hurried to the house. Minka was able to rouse her mother, but that night Jennie began calling her daughter's name over and over.

"Minka! Minnie! Min . . . Minnie . . . Minka! Min . . ."

"It's okay, Mom. Rest, just rest," Minka said, trying to calm Jennie while fighting her own panic. This weak and pale woman could not be her unshakable mother.

An ambulance arrived. A specialist at the hospital diagnosed Jennie with Bright's disease, an inflammation of the blood vessels in the kidneys. "If I'd treated her fifteen years earlier, I could have saved your mother," he told John and Minka. "But now . . ." He shook his head.

As soon as she got home, Minka called Jane. "You need to come immediately."

Jane didn't make it to California in time. The Dutch widow died on January 25, 1958, after almost a half century in her adopted country. She was beloved until the end. Even though she'd lived in Oakland for just a year and a half, twenty-four families honored her with beautiful flowers that filled the funeral home.

Minka performed the necessary tasks—making funeral arrangements, accepting food from church members, and providing for out-of-town guests—but inside, every inch of her felt empty and adrift.

It was the most jarring blow since losing Betty Jane. In quiet moments, a flood of unspoken questions came to Minka's mind: *I wish I'd asked how you were able to cope when Daddy died, if you ever wanted to give up and go back to Holland. Mom, I never asked how it felt when you saw Betty Jane. It was only a brief moment, but I know she captured your heart as much as she did mine. Did you think about her from time to time?*

Roy came to the service to pay tribute to the woman he'd always respected, the one he'd heeded even more than his own mother. He brought the prettiest bouquet in the room, a huge spray of red roses. The gesture touched Minka, made her wish once again that life didn't hold such sickness and loss that kept families apart and took loved ones away.

Jennie's savings, the money she'd worked so hard to accumulate, was dispersed among her children. John and Jane took the lion's share. Haggling over their mother's money seemed disrespectful to Minka. She asked for just a thousand dollars and used it to establish a scholarship in her mother's name at Simpson Bible College, at whose summer camps Minka would cook for many years.

Jennie and Minka had never been expressive in their relationship. They hadn't hugged or kissed when parting, nor had they poured on compliments or words of love. But now, after church on most Sundays, Minka would stop by a small flower shop near the cemetery to buy an arrangement of fresh flowers. The children sat silently as the scent of the blooms mixed with their mother's palpable sorrow, filling the car with a quiet reverence. They watched Minka approach Jennie's plot at the outdoor mausoleum, polish the nameplate, and slip the flowers into the holder.

Only after Jennie's death, witnessing their mother's gentle graveside vigils, did Dianna and Donnie realize how deeply their mother and Grandma Van had loved each other.

* * *

Minka had ample experience with pulling herself together and moving forward. But this time Dianna and Donnie were on the journey with her, and having children added a deeper layer of suffering to hard times. Now more than ever, Minka took to her knees in prayer. The practice became more than just a ritual; it was a lifeline amid daily challenges. No longer did Minka attend church simply because it was what good families did. Instead she looked forward to church as a place to serve others, to receive guidance for her own life, and to be encouraged by fellow believers.

In the midst of all the changes at home, Minka had found a career where she excelled. Cooking and organizing a kitchen were second nature to her. The Piedmont School District promoted her to cafeteria manager. Minka created meal plans a week in advance, coming up with recipes for chicken dishes with mashed potatoes, or macaroni-and-cheese casseroles. The teachers could choose a modified menu, with special desserts, colorful salads, and fat, buttery rolls.

During the summers Minka cooked at Camp Fire Girl camps and church camps as far away as Oregon. When she took a break from kitchen duties, she'd step outside where redwoods reached heavenward and the air was pungent with pine. Mountain peaks rose over the nearby forests, and lakes and streams were cold with glacial runoff. It was a drastic change in landscape and climate from sweltering summers in flat, open South Dakota.

Dianna and Donnie often accompanied their mother on these summer treks; Dianna would room with Minka at the girls' camp, while Donnie stayed across the street at the boys' camp. Minka saw him on weekends, when a new group of campers arrived.

"Mom, you have to see how good I can swim now," he'd say. The three of them would spend the afternoon at the deep mountain lake, where Minka's growing daughter and son would dive from the dock, shouting for her to watch and trying to coax her to join them. Minka had never learned to swim, but she enjoyed watching her children laugh and play.

"Watch this," Donnie shouted, attempting a new acrobatic move. She wished for Roy then—the Roy she'd first met so many years before. *You'd love it here, Roy, and you'd be showing off for them.*

He wasn't completely absent from the children's lives. Even when they weren't sure where their father lived or what he was doing, he rarely missed a school performance. One year when Dianna went off to a camp in Canada without Minka, Roy met her at the bus station to say good-bye. He sent care packages full of swimsuits, sweaters, and shorts to her that summer. Every piece of clothing was the latest style and fit Dianna perfectly.

His family found it impossible to resent Roy for his confusing disease, for the way his personality deteriorated when he drank. They loved him still. And Minka wouldn't allow regret to swallow her. She'd had enough losses, so she chose to cherish the now.

She loved those summer weeks—children's voices screaming with delight, their laughter cutting through the mountain hollows, and cozy nights spent around blazing campfires, singing or listening to a missionary's stories. Minka's room was decorated with Popsicle-stick crafts, beaded bracelets and necklaces. Week after week, Dianna and Donnie proudly gave her badges they'd earned for learning Scriptures.

Minka was grateful for the life she was able to give her children. They were safe from their father, but not shamed by a divorce. Best of all, they weren't milking cows, hauling water, cutting firewood, or performing other manual labor. Their summer days were filled with pulling back bowstrings and shooting arrows, riding horses, meeting kids from around the country, memorizing Bible verses, and hearing how much God loved them. It was a precious answer to prayer.

God had become the spouse she didn't have, an unwavering friend, and her refuge from loneliness and worry. When the ache for her mother, for Roy, for a view into Betty Jane's life became deep and threatening, Minka discovered an unexplainable peace. The divine comfort always came when it was needed most.

On many a summer's night, when Minka gazed at the moon, she wondered if Betty Jane had gone to camp as a child. She imagined her daughter winning all the awards for knowing Bible verses, and roasting marshmallows over a fire. So many years had gone by. Now her little girl was most likely married with children of her own.

In the cool evenings, Minka once again prayed for her firstborn. *God, I pray that Betty Jane found a wonderful man who loves her with all his heart and that they have been blessed with children and happiness. Most of all, Father, I pray that they all know Your love and grace every day, no matter where they are.*

Occasionally, when Minka helped with the food line during camp meals, she wondered if one of the adorable faces on the other side of the strawberry Jell-O or mashed potatoes might be her own grandchild looking back at her.

* * *

On May 5, 1961, astronaut Alan Shepard became the first American to travel into space, weeks after a Soviet cosmonaut had become the first human to do so. Like everyone else, Minka watched the event on television in awe. When she was born, the only option for crossing the ocean was via ship—now man flew beyond the bounds of earth. But Minka was too busy to do more than briefly marvel. The news did not take over her life.

It did, however, captivate a nine-year-old boy from rural Wisconsin, who was watching the launch, spellbound, on a fuzzy black-and-white TV at his one-room schoolhouse. At that moment he made a decision that would propel him through his childhood at the country school, through high school and the Air Force Academy, and eventually onto four space shuttle missions.

The boy with the dreams had a special connection to Minka, even though she did not yet know he existed. The future astronaut, who would one day float untethered in space, was Minka's grandson.

Chapter Thirteen

1961–1977

AFTER THE LOSS of their mother, Jane and Minka felt their own separation more keenly. Jane was no longer alone, having married Chris Froehlich in 1959, but she missed her sister. Eventually, Jane and Chris moved to Oakland, too, and juggled housing arrangements, first staying with Minka and the children and then moving out on their own.

Sometimes when the sisters met for coffee, they talked about how rapidly America was modernizing, in ways that often dismayed them. Men wore their hair scandalously long now. Women wore their dresses shockingly short. British fellows with bangs nearly covering their eyes took over the music scene, performing for hordes of fainting and screaming fans. A new magazine called *Playboy* had caused an initial uproar, but copies were selling out as fast as its young publisher could print them.

Then, the Friday before Thanksgiving week in 1963, the halls of Piedmont schools suddenly echoed with voices during class time.

"Something is up," one of the women in the cafeteria said as she came into the back room. Minka, focused on a food order, hadn't noticed anything amiss. Before they could investigate, a woman from the office burst into the kitchen.

"The president," she said, dissolving into tears.

"What? What is wrong?" Minka asked.

"Shot. Someone shot President Kennedy in Texas."

"Is he going to be okay? How bad is it? When did this happen?" The women in the cafeteria bombarded the secretary with questions.

"I don't know. We don't know anything yet."

By lunchtime, it was announced: JFK was dead.

Minka and the other ladies in the cafeteria stood together and cried. School was dismissed; children and staff were sent home. It was beyond comprehension. The Kennedys were the embodiment of a thriving country, with the president's winning smile and the fashion and sophistication of Jackie Kennedy. Minka had admired the couple.

She watched the president's televised funeral, joining the world in tears as cameras captured little John Jr. on the day of his third birthday saluting his father's casket on its path to Arlington National Cemetery. The country spun with grief, while fears and rumors ran rampant. Who had done such a thing? Was it the Russians, the Mob, Fidel Castro, or the man they arrested, Lee Harvey Oswald?

Camelot was no more, and within a few years trouble that had been rumbling in the background exploded. Another civil war seemed to rage in the South as protesters marched from Selma to Montgomery, and Dr. Martin Luther King Jr. spoke of his dream.

In her school kitchen, Minka discussed with the other women the civil rights demonstrations turning violent in nearby Berkeley, as groups of young people took over parks and business owners boarded up shops. Then came the murder of Reverend King and another Kennedy brother. It seemed the whole world was unraveling.

In this time of uncertainty, Minka's brother, John, died at the age of fifty-seven, shortly after being diagnosed with brain cancer. Minka had never grown much closer to John than they'd been as children, when he had impatiently teased her awkwardness. He'd been so different from her, with his quick boldness. But she had loved him and now grieved the slipping away of one more DeYoung.

Minka combated losses and fear with faith. She read her Bible and found strength in the Psalms, especially the first chapter, which declared that the person who delighted in the Lord would be "like a tree planted by the rivers of water," unbending and full of good fruits. She volunteered at church, teaching the children's "Lightbearers" program, making her own felt figures for the flannel-graph stories and even writing little songs to accompany the lessons.

If her faith was like blood in her veins, Minka's children were the beat of her heart.

Dianna, despite the challenges of her epilepsy and medication, excelled at everything. Minka paid for piano lessons, and soon Dianna could play difficult classical pieces beautifully. She was a superior student and shortly after turning seventeen was accepted to Westmont, a private college in Santa Barbara. The accomplishment thrilled her mother.

Donnie was following a different path. As a little boy, he'd prayed forcefully, like a preacher. When he was nine, Minka had taken him and Dianna to a Billy Graham crusade in San Francisco. When the charismatic evangelist gave the invitation to pray for a personal relationship with Christ, Donnie had run up to the front without hesitation.

But as Donnie got older, church interested him less, and

Minka, who had a good rapport with other children, struggled for the first time to connect with him. She knew her boy needed the male nurturing that Roy was unable to provide. Donnie began challenging his mother at every turn.

When Donnie started getting into trouble with a friend, Minka talked to the police behind her son's back, asking them to scare him good. Officers did just that, putting Donnie in a squad car and driving him to areas in town where drug dealers hung out and where addicts lived on the street.

He brushed off his mother's concerns as nonsense, but Minka met him head-on.

"Donnie-boy, you have to make a choice," she said. "There are two places to go: hell or heaven. You open the door either way. You have to live not only to *know* the Lord—you have to make Him Lord of your life. There's a big difference between just knowing Him and putting Him in charge."

Donnie's reply filled her with fear: "Don't worry about me, Mom. I'll always find a way."

Minka was frustrated with her teenaged son. She felt ill equipped to raise a young man in such a different environment from the one she'd grown up in. She spoke with a traveling evangelist who had three boys of his own. His advice was succinct. "I'll tell you the same thing I told my own wife: 'Get off his neck, but don't get off your knees.'"

Minka took the evangelist's advice and stopped hounding her son. She got down on her knees and prayed instead.

In 1967, Minka learned she was going to be a grandmother twice over. That spring Dianna, who had left college and married a coach, had a baby boy named Gary. A few months later, Donnie became a father to a little girl named Dawn.

Though still enrolled in high school, Donnie had married his girlfriend, and the couple lived with Minka for several months.

Nearly forty years had passed since Betty Jane's birth. Minka's "baby" Donnie was just seventeen. And yet the feel of Dawn in Minka's arms returned the flood of wonder she'd first felt so many years before.

Dawn's crib was in her grandmother's bedroom, and it was Minka who soothed her cries, gave her bottles. Even though Minka still worked full-time, she was the one who sat up with Dawn in a recliner all night when the baby was sick. The teenaged parents were not yet ready to take care of a child. It was exhausting work for a grandmother, but once again, for the third time in her life, Minka fell deeply in love with a baby girl. After Donnie and his wife got their own place, Minka still cared for Dawn each day after her work shift ended.

She understood that a new child was a gift, and ever would be.

❋ ❋ ❋

Minka and Roy had spent years apart, with only sporadic contact. He'd lived with another woman in the time he'd been away. But in the end, when he faced death, Roy wanted Minka. Only her.

He'd developed prostate cancer, which metastasized to his bones. He rang in the new year of 1972 during a two-month stay at the veterans hospital. His brain was hemorrhaging. Fluid clogged his lungs. He called Minka.

"Can you come? Come and spend the night?" he asked.

Minka barely recognized Roy when she entered the hospital room. He was only sixty-two years old but looked ages older, smaller and more worn than ever. But those piercing eyes that widened at her arrival told her that this was the Roy she'd known since 1935.

There was a Bible on his nightstand. He'd never had much use for church, for "religion," but he was reading the Bible now and accepting visits from the hospital chaplain. Knowing that brought Minka a measure of comfort.

He asked a nurse if they could bring a bed for Minka. But only a chair and a blanket were available.

"Oh, no," Roy said. "She works too hard for that." He turned to Minka. "You go on home, honey. You can come back in the morning."

Those were the last words he'd ever speak to his wife. When Minka returned the next day, Roy had slipped into a coma. Minka sat by his bed, listening to the breath rattling in his throat. She held his narrow hand in her larger one, squeezed and patted.

The good memories played in Minka's head now, only the good: Roy spinning her around the dance floor, patiently teaching her the steps. The red rose he'd bought when Dianna was born, still pressed into her baby book. The way he'd plotted with her to make Christmas morning a grand surprise for Donnie and Dianna.

She thought of Roy exclaiming over his favorite turkey with oyster dressing until the children laughed, and taking her off on long walks alone during family vacations. She remembered the way he'd grin when one of the children saw a new present lying on their bed.

And she would never forget the fact that this slight man, even when alcohol made him cruel, had never once made fun of her big feet or her large, twisted fingers that engulfed his own.

Tears ran down her cheeks. Regret squeezed her heart so much that she winced in pain. He'd had such talent, so many gifts, all smothered by illness and trauma. Maybe he hadn't fought hard enough against his demons. Maybe he had.

Roy was the only man Minka would ever marry, the only one she had ever wanted to. In the end, on February 6, 1972, death was a blessed release from the pain that had haunted him for so long.

❊ ❊ ❊

After Dianna and Donnie moved out, Minka sold the house on Linwood and downsized to an apartment. For years, motherhood had been her main focus, and it took time to let go of that all-consuming role. Other than a short period when Roy was away during the war, Minka had never lived alone. The rooms were awfully quiet at first, although she talked to her children regularly and visited her grandchildren. As time passed, she filled her days with new pursuits and grew to enjoy the silence, during which she could think and pray.

She began taking painting classes and discovered she had an artistic eye and skill with a brush. She created colorful landscapes and still lifes and gave them away to family or friends. She knitted and crocheted afghans and gave those away too. Friends taught her even more complicated stitches and patiently answered her questions.

Since her teenaged days in the Aberdeen sewing circle, she'd never lost her curiosity about the wider world. Current affairs amazed and bemused her in equal measure. A South African doctor named Barnard was transferring organs from one human to another. Nearly twelve thousand years after it first appeared, small-pox was about to be eradicated from humankind. A movie star had become California's governor, and a peanut farmer had been elected president.

People seemed consumed with monumental accomplishments, like constructing a twin set of ludicrously tall buildings in New York City, each 110 floors high, or preparing to launch a space-craft on a decades-long journey to the edge of Earth's solar system. Minka could only wonder at it all.

In 1977, after a twenty-two year career, Minka retired from the Piedmont School District. By now most of her family had relocated to Southern California. Jane and Chris, as well as Dianna and her husband and three small children, all resided in Orange County, nearly a day's drive away. Minka wanted to move near them, to be involved in their lives. Out of necessity, much of her life had been consumed with hard work, but nothing was more important to Minka than her family. Now she looked forward to spending her retirement doting on loved ones.

She decided to move one more time, to the small coastal town where Jane had settled, to live out the years the Lord had left for her. Her decades of hard work had provided her with financial security. In addition to a pension, the school district had made a special agreement to cover all her medical expenses for life.

Neither she nor they could have imagined just how long that would be.

Chapter Fourteen

1981–2000

MINKA SAT on a darkened airplane, listening to the great engines thrum, her shoulders hunched under a thin airline blanket. Her teenaged grandson Gary dozed beside her. On the other side of her, Jane's eyes were closed, too, but Minka couldn't tell if she was asleep. Here and there, dim reading lights dotted the cabin, which felt unnecessarily cold.

The sisters were both widows now. Jane's husband, Chris, had died in 1978, three years earlier. They needed something to look forward to, so Minka had proposed an adventure—she'd take each of her grandchildren on a lavish vacation. On this first trip, with Dianna's oldest child, the trio would spend three weeks exploring Europe. The journey would culminate in the country where Minka was conceived, her family's homeland, now called the Netherlands.

Everything had changed since Jennie had returned to Holland in 1930, carrying Minka's picture of Betty Jane with her. Minka now sat hurtling through the clouds, miles above the slow steamship route that Jennie had taken. And after all these years, the sharp pain of Betty Jane's absence had softened into a bittersweet hollow space, one that Minka accepted as part of her. Whenever she felt a deeper pang, triggered by memory or unexpected emotions, she simply prayed for her daughter.

Minka, Jane, and Gary landed in Germany and boarded a tour bus. They spent the next two weeks winding through the Alps. When they walked into the first enormous castle on the itinerary, Minka looked at Jane and asked, "Can you imagine how long it would take to clean this place? Once you were finished, you'd have to start all over again." They spent days on a boat, floating down the Rhine River, surrounded by mountains whose peaks were snowcapped all year round.

Every restaurant and hotel served delicious, fresh-baked bread. Gary teased Minka and Jane, who, unable to shake the frugality they'd had to practice as children, wrapped leftovers in napkins and stuffed them in their purses. Another legacy of their childhood proved useful on this trip. For the first time in decades they spoke German, the language they'd learned while running around Uncle's farm. Initially the sisters grasped for words, but they were soon speaking it with confidence.

They rode a cogwheel train up to a hamlet in Switzerland and woke the next morning to a foot of snow on the ground. Now it was the sisters' turn to tease Gary. During white winters in South Dakota they'd used a sleigh to get to church, but Gary had never seen such abundant snow. He kept pulling them to the windows to peer out.

The trip ended in Holland at the homes of Jennie's half sisters, Tante Jane and Tante Martha, who weren't much older than Minka. She'd kept in touch with them through letters, but now they were meeting for the first time. The aunts welcomed their nieces warmly in rapid-fire Dutch, and Minka and Jane fell into that language easily too, serving as translators for Gary.

The sisters were sad that they couldn't visit their paternal relatives. Years before, they'd discovered that most of Ben's family had been wiped out by the Spanish flu in 1918.

Minka and Jane toured the same windmills their parents had seen in the previous century, browsed gift shops whose windows and floors shone with the same thorough Dutch polishing they'd learned from Jennie. Among the goods for sale—towels and bells and watches—wooden shoes were the most popular items. Minka picked up a pair, running her fingers over the bright flowers painted on the yellow clogs.

It wasn't the first pair of wooden shoes she'd ever seen. Many decades before, when Jennie returned from her final visit here, she'd brought a dainty pair home for Betty Jane—a present for the granddaughter who would never wear them.

Visiting Europe was fun, and it helped Minka put together pieces of her heritage. But this wasn't her real home. *What if Bouche and Tjiske de Jong had not changed their names to Ben and Jennie, had never ventured to a new life in a faraway country?* she wondered. It was impossible to imagine.

Who would Minka be without South Dakota or Roy? Without Dianna or Donnie? Without Betty Jane?

✳ ✳ ✳

Soon after returning from that trip, Minka welcomed a new house-guest: Donnie's oldest daughter, Dawn, who'd lived with Minka as a baby. Dawn had spent the last several calming summers at her grandmother's apartment, leaving behind a chaotic home life in Oakland. When she turned fifteen, with Donnie's blessing, she chose to move in with Minka permanently.

Minka loved all her grandchildren but had bonded in a special way with Dawn. Through the years they'd shared everything from midnight bottle feedings to afternoons on the beach, where Minka had watched Dawn dig in the sand or ride bodyboards in the waves. Despite the decades between them, they had many things in common—both were practical and calm, and believed in working hard.

Other than the new address, not much had changed in her grandmother's home since Dawn had first lived with her. Minka had the same furniture and towels and dishes she'd had for ages. Whenever anyone mentioned that she should consider replacing her television—a grainy color set built into a low wooden cabinet—Minka would quip, "I'm certain it has at least a decade left in it." There was a basic answering machine in Minka's kitchen that did what it was supposed to do. She sewed her own plain slacks out of easy-care polyester, which she bought at the fabric store when it was on sale. She did her own repairs around the apartment.

Dawn found a job and enrolled in night classes to earn her high school diploma. Each evening, Minka drove her granddaughter to school, then waited in the parking lot until classes let out, reading devotional books until it grew too dark, then praying quietly. She taught Dawn to drive, to crochet, to bake. Together they watched and rewatched *Gone with the Wind*, which had first released in theaters when twenty-eight-year-old Minka was dating Roy. The movie starred Minka's old dreamboat, Clark Gable.

On Sundays, they went to the Lutheran church Minka had chosen when she'd moved to this town. She'd wanted Jane and Chris to attend with her, and her sister felt more comfortable with the familiar traditions of their childhood.

Minka managed comfortably on her pension for six years, but since her health was sound, she couldn't think of a single reason not to go back to work. She drove down to the local Kmart and landed a job stocking shelves. Minka enjoyed spending her paychecks on her extended family. She sent the rest of Dianna's family on a European vacation, like the one she'd taken Gary on. She took Dawn to Hawaii for her eighteenth birthday. When she heard that Dianna's daughter Cathy had cried over having only old and wrong-sized outfits to start the new school year, Minka bought boxes of clothing to send to her.

And she especially liked having money to put in the offering when missionaries visited her church and showed slideshows of children with less than any American child could imagine.

Minka would work at Kmart in a variety of positions for fifteen years, until the age of eighty-seven.

* * *

The world spun on. Minka had been eight years old when the Nineteenth Amendment gave American women the right to vote; in 1984, she watched a woman named Geraldine Ferraro campaign for the vice presidency. The following September, Minka read in the *Orange County Register* that researchers had finally found the wreck of the RMS *Titanic* on the ocean floor near Newfoundland. That great ship had set sail the year *after* Minka was born.

She'd outlasted a significant global political movement, too. In October of 1917, just before Minka celebrated her sixth birthday, a revolution in Russia brought Communism to power. Exactly seventy-two years later, crowds of East Germans with sledge-hammers laid waste to the Berlin Wall.

The world was nearly unrecognizable from the one she'd been born into. Scholars had their terms for the passage of time: Industrial Age, Space Age, Information Age. Minka had her memories, in most cases as vivid as the wrinkles on her hands.

Hauling bucket after bucket of water from the well to the kitchen, as the heavy wood and unyielding metal slowly pulled her soft finger bones apart.

Sitting in Uncle's outhouse with her teeth chattering, watching her foggy breath drift in the lantern light as snow piled up outside.

Bathing once a week in a metal tub in the kitchen, with five people using the same batch of well water, heated on the stove.

Lying in bed for days on end when measles coated her body or mumps puffed up her face, as Jennie came and went with spoon-fuls of molasses and damp cloths.

And then, in her memories, the world sped up, spinning like a carved horse on a carousel.

Her first peculiar glimpse of a lady's ankle peeping below a skirt, while sitting in the buggy waiting for her mother to sell jars of butter in town.

Seeing a machine called an airplane rise through the Aberdeen sky for the first time, as though pulled by a sorcerer's string.

And wars—so many wars! The first Great one, made real only afterward by the sight of limbless veterans in town; and the second one, the one that took her sweetheart away; and all those since, the ones that existed to her mainly as pages of newspaper print or television reports.

She'd watched the stock market crash in 1929 and a space shut-tle explode in 1986. During her lifetime, penicillin was discovered and genocide was inflicted. Babe Ruth set records and Bonnie and Clyde committed crimes and Neil Armstrong walked on the moon. She'd been around for the inventions of parachutes and particle accelerators, crossword puzzles and computers.

Life had carried her from one end of the century to the other. Now, with a new millennium drawing near, she kept as busy as ever. There was her full-time job at Kmart, where she'd been promoted to cashier. In the evenings she crocheted afghans, sewed frilly outfits for granddaughters, stayed up late doing word puzzles. She made crafts: table runners dotted with sequins, fabric clowns wearing pointed hats and ruffled costumes, and tabletop Christmas trees, fully decorated with lights and miniature baubles.

Minka had fashioned a life that suited her perfectly. She had a trim and tidy home, projects to nourish her creative mind, work and ministries that filled her need to be useful. She had a faithful God to serve, people to love, family to cherish.

And always, there was Jane.

✳   ✳   ✳

For nearly nine decades, the one constant in Minka's life was the vivacious little sister who ran ahead of her in so many ways but who also depended greatly on her older, steadier sister. They'd lived apart for just a handful of years, during the war and then after Minka fled with her children to Oakland. For the final twenty-three years of Jane's life, she lived just one-and-a-half blocks from Minka, and the two of them walked back and forth between each other's apartments several times a day.

Minka's grandchildren referred to them as one unit, "Gramma-and-Janie." The two women dressed alike, took vacations together, attended the same church, the same parties. Their immaculate apartments were decorated in the same bright colors—yellow and orange and white. When Minka had church committee meetings or parties to attend, Jane lent her clothes. When Jane was ill, Minka took her to the doctor.

In her eighties, Jane's health began to diminish. There was heart trouble, and then something else. The signs were subtle at first but soon became more obvious. Minka would come home after a long day at Kmart and find Jane sitting on Minka's front patio, dressed prettily, her bright lipstick slightly feathered.

"I wanna go out, Minka," she'd say.

Minka, who'd been looking forward to a quiet dinner, would tamp down a flash of impatience. "Where do you want to go, honey?"

Jane would name a restaurant or store, and Minka would drive her there. But after a few minutes, Jane would protest.

"I'm tired, Minka. Take me home."

Jane had always expected things to go her way, but this was different. Now she'd knock on Minka's door at six o'clock in the morning, complaining.

"You took my clothes, Minka."

"I didn't, Jane."

"Yes, you did. You took them."

"Jane, come in. Look and see if I've got your clothes. I don't have your clothes."

The changes escalated. Jane could no longer clean to the standards they'd both embraced since childhood, so Minka cleaned both their apartments. She took Jane to see doctors, again and again. They put her on medication, told Minka to keep an eye on her. Eventually Minka retired a final time, freeing her schedule for more diligent caretaking.

Things began disappearing from Jane's home. A large picture Minka had painted for her. Fancy silverware. Her husband's ashes. Jane couldn't remember where these things had gone, but Minka once caught her throwing good china plates into the garbage after lunch.

One day Minka watched while Jane worked in her kitchen. Jane leaned too close to the gas flame on her stove, nearly catching her sleeve on fire. There was another visit to the doctor. When he pressed Jane to tell him what her name was, she told him, "I oughta slap your face."

Before they left, the doctor took Minka aside. "Jane is succumbing to dementia. She can't live alone anymore. It isn't safe, and she needs more care than you can provide. I suggest you begin preparations to move her into a facility."

Minka went home and cried all night.

Not long after, Jane had a stroke, fell, and broke her hip. She was able to reach the phone, but she didn't call 911. She dialed the number she knew best: her big sister's.

Minka answered and heard incoherent sounds on the line. She didn't have a fancy phone that displayed which number had called, but she didn't need one. Minka knew Jane like she knew her own soul. She ran to her car and made the one-minute drive to her sister's apartment, where she found Jane on the floor, her mouth pulled to one side. Minka called the paramedics.

Jane never returned home. She went into one assisted care facility, then another newer one near Dawn's house. Jane was now an hour away, over the San Clemente foothills, but Minka drove back and forth as often as she could.

"Where's Mom?" Jane would ask, her eyes drifting over Minka's shoulder to the doorway.

Minka couldn't tell her sister that their mother was dead. Instead she smiled, picked up her little sister's hand, now bony thin and covered in age spots. She remembered Jane's small, delicate fingers; how she had felt envious that her own fingers weren't as lovely.

"Honey, Mom didn't come this time."

Jane closed her eyes and sighed. "Next time you come, bring Mom."

"I will try," Minka said, not wishing to lie. Then she told Jane about the weather that day, the sermon she'd heard preached on television, stories about people they knew from church. She urged her sister to eat, taking up the spoon herself to hand-feed Jane when her sister crossed her arms and stared at the window.

Minka maintained Jane's apartment back home, keeping it scrubbed clean and ready just in case, the curtains always open to let in the light and frame the beautiful view of the ocean. One day Minka offered to take Jane back to her apartment for a few hours, but her sister became alarmed. "Oh no, no, no!" Jane cried, shrinking against her pillows. She couldn't bear to see proof of what was happening, of what was disappearing.

On Jane's eighty-seventh birthday she fell again, broke her hip a second time. She was listless and sad.

In July of 2000, Minka received a call from the doctor. Jane was in hospice; the end was near. Minka packed her suitcase and drove to Dawn's to stay for however long was needed.

Jane wasn't speaking now, at least not words that anyone could understand. But on this last day, Jane reached out as if the weight of her hand was almost too much. Minka leaned closer, wondering if her sister wanted to touch her face. Instead Jane touched the shiny gold locket that hung at Minka's neck.

"Remember, you gave this to me," Minka said. Jane surely knew that; or was she only attracted to the gleam of gold? Jane held the locket between her fingers, let go, and reached again and again.

Before Minka left that night, she spoke to a nurse.

"Someone will call me right away if anything changes, right? Anything at all?"

"Yes, certainly," the nurse said.

But Minka was not called, and by the time she hurried to Jane's room the next morning, her sister's body was already cold. She reached for Jane's hand, then sank into a chair, weeping.

"I'm so sorry, Jane. I was supposed to be here."

Minka's companion of eighty-seven years was gone, taking a large piece of Minka's heart with her.

In the days to come, Minka would give away most of Jane's furniture to relatives, her nice clothes to missionaries. But she kept all of Jane's pretty jewelry in a huge cardboard box. When the loneliness made her especially sad, she'd pull the heavy box out and, with some effort, lift it onto her bed. She'd sit beside this treasure chest, taking out a few pieces. As her fingers ran over the beads, her mind ran through the memories. Minka couldn't bear to part with this last, intimate link to the baby sister who'd once called her "Gypsy" for her love of jewels.

Less than three weeks later, while Minka was still in deep mourning, she received a call from a relative who lived in the Bay Area. It was more bad news. The son she still called Donnie-boy was in the hospital. Minka's first instinct was to call Jane. As she reached for the phone, she remembered. Jane was gone.

* * *

Donnie, like his sister, Dianna, had been a sensitive, obedient child when he was younger. All Roy had to do was snap his fingers and say, "Straighten up and fly right," and both children would hop to. Roy had spanked Donnie only once, when his son and a neighbor boy set fire to some papers in the garage.

When they'd first moved to Oakland and Minka was working two jobs to make ends meet, six-year-old Donnie had walked to a nearby gas station. Although shy, he'd worked up the courage to ask an attendant if they had any jobs he could do, so he could take some money home to Mama. "Maybe I can pump gas?" The attendant took a long look at the skinny boy with the earnest, freckled face, then offered him a job cleaning the water fountain that customers used, in exchange for a few pennies a day.

Donnie had never left the Bay area. He'd fathered two more pretty daughters, Alexandria and Anastasia. In adulthood, he'd struggled to find his path in the world. There had been failed marriages, stops and starts in finding a career, but he'd been generally healthy. Minka had never stopped praying for and fussing over the sweet boy who still called her every week.

"Whatcha doing, Mom?" he'd ask in his soft voice when she answered the phone.

"Talking to you!" she'd say happily.

The news that Donnie was in the hospital came out of the blue. Minka called him, and as always he tried to downplay the trouble. "It's nothing to worry about, Mom. I'll be all right." But when Minka got Donnie's doctor on the phone, she was advised to come as soon as she could. Dawn made the long drive north with Minka, as her three small children slept in the backseat. By the time they reached the hospital, Donnie was unconscious. He'd had a brain aneurysm and had refused complicated treatments, which could have kept him alive but in a wheelchair.

As she looked at her son, the advice of the traveling evangelist from years ago replayed in her mind: "Get off his neck, but don't get off your knees." Minka sat at Donnie's bedside and began praying—fervently. She held his hand, her heart filled with both fear and boldness. Though he didn't open his eyes, Minka spoke to her son.

"Donnie-boy, remember what you always used to say when I told you that Jesus was the way? You said, 'Don't worry about me, Mom. I'll always find a way.' This time, you haven't got a choice. You come to the Lord. Remember? The Lord is the only way."

Minka felt Donnie's fingers squeeze around her own. Tears rolled down her cheeks. He'd heard her, she had no doubt.

"This isn't about what you can get yourself out of, Donnie-boy. Now you're wholly dependent upon Him. Your only hope is in Him." She knew how real, how alive her own faith was. God's ways transcended human understanding, human consciousness. She believed that Donnie would find comfort and connection with God, even if he could no longer speak to his mother.

On the evening of August 8, twenty-four days after losing her only sister, Minka said good-bye to her only son.

* * *

Three weeks later, Minka and Dawn stood on a hilltop in the Santa Ana Mountains. It was a perfect day, the temperature in the seventies with a clear sky. A light breeze ruffled their hair. Below them spread acres of sage scrub, wildflowers, and feathery bunchgrass. They each carefully held a box in their hands. Jane and Donnie had both chosen to be cremated.

Minka had picked this spot because Jane and Donnie had loved the mountains. Jane had been fond of all her nephews and nieces, and their children too. Now, in death, she would be together with her beloved Donnie.

Minka stood tall, the wind drying the tears on her cheeks and plastering her pants to her legs, and reflected. She was grateful for her long life, the many blessings she'd had. The Lord had helped her rise, time and again, no matter how heavy the burdens, no matter how great the losses. She'd now outlived her mother, her husband, her brother and sister, friends, nieces and nephews, even her baby boy. Minka knew that the Lord gave, and the Lord took.

On the cusp of her tenth decade of life, she reckoned she had reached the point where the taking far exceeded the giving.

Chapter Fifteen

THE DAY DAWNED beneath a gentle rain, uncharacteristic for a late spring day in the land of sunshine, palm trees, and warm ocean breezes. As the first dim light seeped through the plastic vertical blinds in Minka's bedroom, she lingered in bed a few extra minutes, underneath an old comforter patterned in yellow and white flowers. The pain of this special day had eased long ago. Now it was an annual event, like Thanksgiving or Christmas, that she marked with prayers and remembering. And gratefulness.

Today was Betty Jane's birthday. Impossible as it was to imagine, Minka's first child was now seventy-seven years old.

So many decades had gone by, but with perfect clarity Minka remembered the precious weeks spent with her newborn daughter. The warm weight of Betty Jane, her sweet scent, the wonder of her velvety skin, the pink in her cheeks, the pucker of her lips. Those weeks had been the best of Minka's life, and the worst. During that time, mother and daughter had existed apart from the outside world, with hardly an interruption.

Minka had grieved the end of that time, but she could not

regret her decision, not even now, when she'd spent a lifetime's worth of years longing for her daughter. Minka had given up her Betty Jane because of love. She had never stopped loving her.

And she'd never seen her again.

Today, somewhere, Betty Jane celebrated her birthday. Even as her own losses piled up, Minka did not doubt that Betty Jane was still alive—but she did wonder where on earth she was, what kind of cake she'd eat today, who would call her to give her a birthday greeting. Minka imagined children and grandchildren and a house full of love.

All the people to whom Minka had confided about Betty Jane were now gone. Honus and Jennie. Reverend Kraushaar. Miss Bragstad and Miss Questad. Jane. Her sister-in-law, Dorothy. Roy. No one else would ever guess that Minka had a secret history, a secret child.

The apartment complex was usually quiet, but even more so this morning. A unique quality fell over this moment, this day. Perhaps it was the rain.

Minka wasn't sure what it was exactly.

Even at ninety-four, Minka ordinarily was up early. First she'd make her bed, smoothing the flowered spread to remove every wrinkle. Then she'd pull on slacks and a sweater, hang her night-gown on a hook behind the door, and settle into a chair with her Bible. God always got the first portion of her day. And after that she was "off to the races," as busy as ever.

To keep her rent low, Minka did odd jobs around her stucco fourplex. She handled the rental paperwork when tenants came and went. She swept walkways and tended the landscaping, pull-ing weeds, planting hardy succulent plants and bright-red bego-nias. She watered the flower beds, early in the morning as this drought-prone region required, always careful not to leave any wasteful dribbles along the cement.

Minka's other activities depended on the day of the week. Each Tuesday, she hosted a ladies' Bible study in her home. She'd bake cookies and set out tea and coffee, and together she and her friends would study God's Word and pray for shared needs. On Fridays, she volunteered at her church, stuffing bulletins and praying. She was in church every Sunday, filling in wherever help was needed, whether playing with the tiny tots in Sunday school or providing snacks for a meeting. Other days held other tasks.

Keeping busy was more important to her than ever. A deafening silence had followed the losses of her sister and youngest child. Hundreds of times in the years afterward, she'd turned to tell Jane something or reached for the phone to call Donnie, only to be stopped cold by the truth.

To most people, Minka's hard-earned resilience appeared unshakable, but no one understood how it felt to outlive nearly everyone you knew. If not for her faithful God, the weight of loneliness might have dragged her into the grave too. In these recent years, Minka was convinced more than ever not only of the *fact* of God but of His absolute goodness.

She had practiced thankfulness for so long that it was a part of her. And today, as on every May 22, she would reflect on the blessing she'd kept locked in her heart for seventy-seven years.

Minka knew she needed to get going, to dress and eat a light breakfast before leaving the house. But she was enjoying these extra minutes of contemplation and memories. *Happy birthday, my dear Betty Jane. This is the day I feel closest to you, more than any other.*

Her thoughts turned into a prayer.

"God, wherever Betty Jane is celebrating today, I pray that she is happy and has had a good life. Although we only spent a few weeks of our lives together, I am thankful for those blessed moments. I hope she knows as much as I do how deeply You love her."

Minka opened her eyes as she finished praying.

She paused.

And then she added a new prayer. An impulsive prayer. An unreasonable prayer, one she'd never uttered before.

"Lord, I'd like to see Betty Jane again before I die. I won't bother her or interrupt her life. I just want to see what she looks like.

"Please, Lord."

* * *

Several hours later and two thousand miles away, a woman named Ruth Lee was going about her day. She'd already had coffee with her husband at the local McDonald's. Now it was time to do some work in the garden. The nearly ripe strawberries needed weeding, and it was time to plant the fruits and vegetables for their own table, as well as the pumpkins, squash, and gourds that filled their roadside stand each fall.

Ruth had lived in this pretty part of Wisconsin, a place of rolling land and dramatic seasons, for most of her life. In winters, snow piled up in great mounds until the Lees' back property looked like a postcard. And in spring it was idyllic, all blue skies and white clouds and fields of rich, black soil that would be knee-high in corn by the beginning of July.

She and her husband of nearly fifty-eight years had lived a good, satisfying life here, raising a large family in their trim white farmhouse. They had much to be proud of—every one of their children had earned a college degree and was leading a productive life. One of Ruth's sons had even become famous. A sign hung proudly from the family's barn: *Welcome to Viroqua, home of Astronaut Mark Lee.*

Ruth's phone rang. It was her third child, Brian. He'd already called her, as usual, on his way to work this morning. But now he had some news.

Today's mail had brought a special letter he'd requested recently on her behalf: a judge's order from a South Dakotan court, authorizing the release of Ruth's confidential adoption records.

As their conversation wound down, Brian asked if she'd had a good day, if she had any big plans for that evening.

Some celebrating was in order. It wasn't just any old day, after all. Today was Ruth's seventy-seventh birthday.

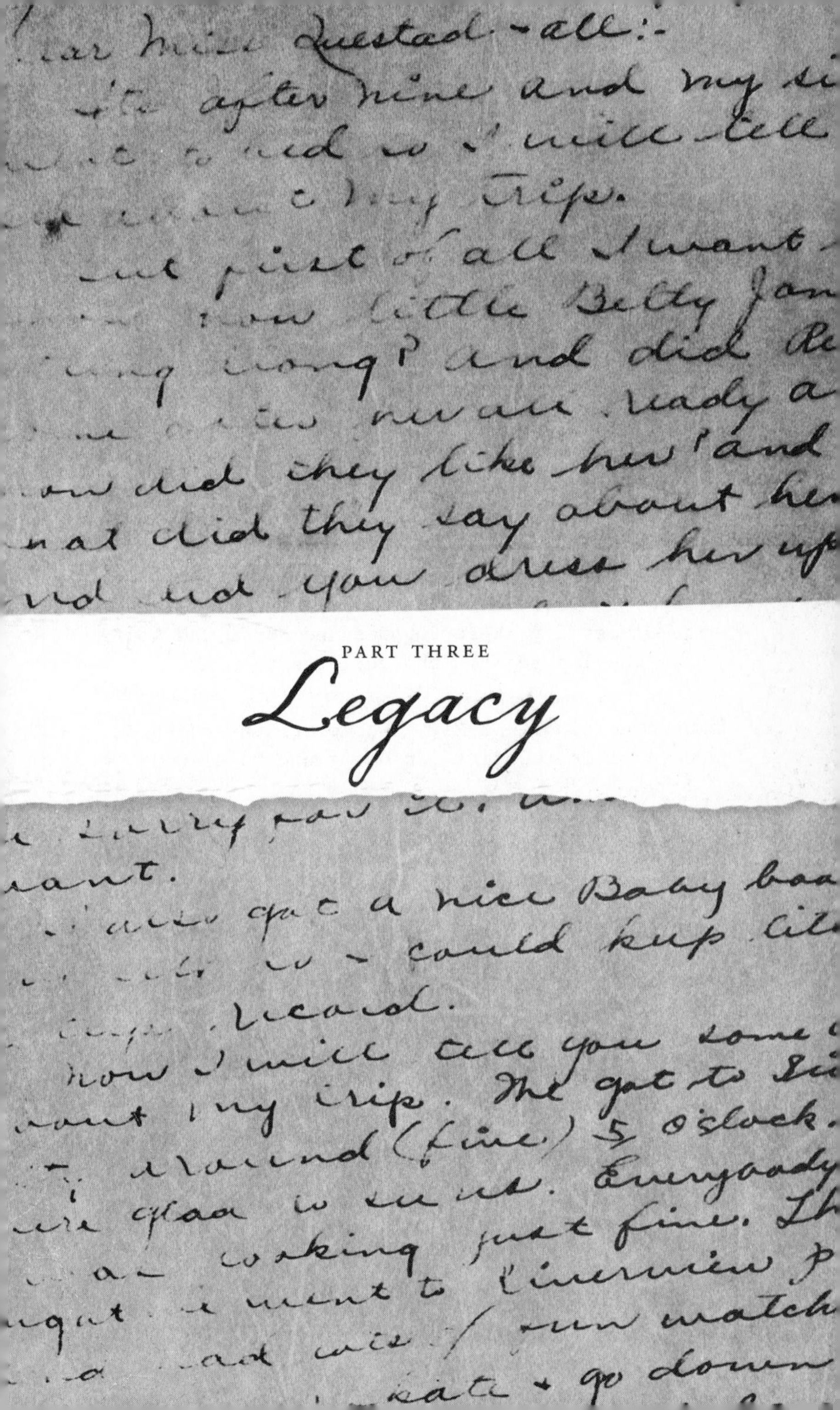

PART THREE

Legacy

Foster Home Follow-up
Re: Rev. Peder Nordsletten, Wallingford, Iowa
Betty Jane DeYoung (Ruth Priscilla)

4-11-30

Worker found the family at supper when she came to their home at Wallingford.... The entire family and congregation had become very much attached to the baby who was a sweet child growing and developing normally.

The house was a large parsonage, neatly and comfortably furnished; and both the pastor and his wife said they were quite satisfied and content with their new home. They had moved from Jewell, Iowa, October 31, 1929. A large well-kept yard—almost a park—surrounded the house and would be an ideal place for the children to play.

The family expect to go to South Dakota about the middle of May to complete the adoption and to visit relatives at Moe south of Canton.

—Harriet Mickelson

4-11-30

Worker spent the night in the home of Mr. and Mrs. G . . . who were members of Rev. Nordsletten's congregation. These people praised their pastor and his family highly. They said the congregation were very much pleased with the change and hoped the family would remain among them a long time. They too, loved the baby and were almost tempted to adopt one also if they could find one as sweet and lovable.

—Harriet Mickelson

Chapter Sixteen

RUTH ALWAYS KNEW she was adopted.

Her parents told her early on that her birth mother had been a young woman of Dutch heritage, with the last name of DeYoung or de Jong. She couldn't recall how old she was when she first heard the story; it was simply part of her, like her curly hair or the freckles on her nose. Ruth didn't consciously consider the story of her birth to be any different from those of her siblings. Her oldest brother had been adopted, the next two were not. They were all the same in her mind: the Nordsletten children.

At times, she'd think about the name her birth mother had called her: Betty Jane. It felt strange, like sliding her feet into someone else's wrong-sized shoes. Ruth didn't ask questions about her birth, but not because she feared knowing the truth or hurting her parents' feelings. There simply were no gaps that needed filling. She didn't think to ask for more details.

When her new parents had first seen Ruth at the Lutheran House of Mercy in Sioux Falls, South Dakota, on July 1, 1929, they'd fallen instantly in love with her.

"You were such a sweet, lovely baby," her mother would later say.

They'd arrived with a neatly pressed stack of cloth diapers, socks, and shirts, though little Ruth had already been dressed in a pretty outfit her birth mother had lovingly sewn, days before leaving the infant behind.

Ruth's new parents were Reverend Peder and Olava Nordsletten, of Norwegian heritage. Six-year-old Kenny, their youngest son, came with them to Sioux Falls. He couldn't wait to see his new sister and promised to watch over her in the backseat on the journey home.

After retrieving their baby girl, they returned to Jewell, Iowa, where Peder pastored a church. One of their first friends to visit was a Filipino missionary who was furthering his education in the United States. As the family discussed names, the visitor's suggestion was met with the most enthusiasm. From then on, she would be Ruth Priscilla.

After three boys, Ruth was the easiest infant the Nordslettens had held in their arms. Perhaps it was having a girl, they mused, but others confirmed what a pleasant child they'd brought home. Their sons filled the parsonage with masculine energy every waking moment. But even the boys froze in their tracks at the sight of their tiny sister. She softened them with her bright-eyed stares and sudden smiles, and soon enough she was responding with coos and erupting into giggles at their antics.

In years to come as Ruth grew up, sang at church, hung a Christmas stocking over her bed frame, lost teeth, made friends, and moved through childhood and adolescence, she never imagined that across the miles a woman was writing letters, asking for any scrap of information about her. Ruth didn't know that every May 22, while she was enjoying her birthday celebrations, this other woman was thinking of her and praying for her.

She didn't know that her birth mother carried a single treasured picture of Ruth as a baby, simply inscribed on the back: "Sweetest little girl in the world—Betty J."

* * *

By October of 1929, as Ruth was learning to sit up and grabbing at her brothers' hair with her soft fingers, the Nordslettens packed up and moved from Jewell, smack-dab in the center of Iowa, to a small farm town in the northwest corner of the state.

Peder was appointed to a trio of churches in the region, with the main one, Five Points Lutheran Church, several blocks from the town center. The family moved into the parsonage on 2nd Street, kitty-corner from the church. It was a spacious, two-story house with an indoor bathroom, a separate dining room, and plenty of bedrooms. The boys' eyes lit up at their first glimpse of the huge yard, with its wealth of garden space and a mature apple tree heavy with fruit. A weeping birch draped welcoming branches over the front walkway.

Before Ruth's adoption could be finalized, the family received a handful of unannounced visits from social workers. The reports glowed with praise: *The family impressed Worker very favorably. They seemed to her to be a wholesome, honest and sincere family.* There were no concerns about the adoption; a better family could not be hoped for.

In this Midwestern town, Ruth learned to crawl, then walk and run. She had three brothers to keep up with. The garden behind the parsonage was like a jungle to the children. It woke their imaginations as they explored and uncovered every hiding place.

Though she usually followed her parents' rules, Ruth had a secret vice.

She loved to climb trees.

They beckoned to her, branches waving in the breeze. While other young girls and boys considered professions that mirrored their parents'—homemakers, teachers, and farmers—Ruth decided she would live in a jungle, climbing trees and swinging from vines. But first, she would need to practice.

There were plenty of trees to choose from, and Ruth planned to conquer each one. She'd bunch up her skirt, reach around the smooth bark of the tree, and pull herself up. She knew how to test a limb's strength in her hand or beneath her foot before trusting her full weight to it. Ruth had figured out these skills on her own, without her brothers' help.

She climbed on and on with patches of sky encouraging her upward until the branches thinned out and the view opened around her. Ruth found a secure perch, her heart beating fast as she saw how high she'd reached. She spotted the tall steeple of the brick church, the roof of the post office, some kids chasing their dog, and—beyond the one square mile of her town—the wide, flat Iowa farmland that rolled out like piecrust all the way to the sky.

Getting down was the challenge. Her dress would catch on the branches and tangle around her legs as she descended. Several times she made it down before anyone noticed. But one day, she heard the screen door clap shut and her name called out.

"Ruth!" her mother said.

Ruth stared at the ground far below, wondering how she might slide down quickly. *If only there was a vine I could grab.* She spoke brightly, hoping her voice would drop like a weight and bounce up from the ground instead of reaching her mother like a tap on the head.

"Be right there, Mom!"

Then Ruth's eyes met her mother's through a break in the leaves. From her mother's open-mouthed gape, the wring of her hands, and the sudden bolt back toward the house, Ruth knew this wasn't going to turn out well.

Her mother called again, this time louder and directed indoors.

"Peder!" she screamed.

The porch door creaked and slammed. Through the open windows of the parsonage, Ruth heard her mother's frantic voice.

"What is wrong?" Hard footsteps came running from the second story and down the stairs.

"Peder, Peder, Ruth is at the top of the tree!"

Ruth slowly made her way to the ground, trying not to snag her dress and avoiding the stern expressions on her parents' faces. She was punished, but she would continue to climb trees for years to come. She couldn't help it. Eventually Olava tried ignoring her daughter's penchant for treetops, hoping she'd soon outgrow it.

When Ruth's feet were firmly on the ground, she worked in the garden with her father. With the double-fisted blows of the Dust Bowl and the Depression, a green thumb and gardening space within distance of a well were as valuable as gold. Ruth could soon identify the weeds that needed pulling and the plants that needed room to roam or a frame to climb. She learned to tell when the fruits and vegetables were ready for harvest. She picked peas, filling the skirt of her dress with them and flopping down at the edge of the garden to snap the sweet pearls from the pods and pop them into her mouth.

Olava dressed Ruth with ribbons and frills and sent her off to the two-room schoolhouse, where she learned to read and do figures, and where she'd get tricked by a boy into touching her tongue to the frozen chain of a swing.

One state away in South Dakota, Minka would have savored these images of Ruth's contented life. She had hoped Betty Jane's parents were attentive and loving. She would have loved knowing that her daughter had siblings to play with. But without detailed answers from Miss Bragstad, Ruth's first mother was left to imagine—and continue praying.

✳ ✳ ✳

By 1935, the year Minka would meet a handsome fruit salesman named Roy, America was in the grip of a financial catastrophe. But for many farmers throughout the Midwest, the trouble had begun many years earlier. The government was no longer guaranteeing top prices for livestock and crops, as it did during the First World War. Farmers were overextended, unable to pay bank loans or to sell, as land prices would not cover their debts. Banks closed their doors in ever-increasing numbers. In 1920, Iowa had 167 banks fail; the next year, the number was 505.

The tiny hamlet of Wallingford sat apart from the main routes west, which were miles north in Minnesota and farther south in Iowa. Along such roadways, caravans of desperate families who'd lost most everything drove trucks and jalopies with people, pets, farm animals, and precious belongings piled high or hanging off the sides. They mostly traveled west, to cities, towns, or lettuce fields, following rumors of a Promised Land, only to find that no place seemed untouched by calamity.

Peder listened to the grave news crackling from the radio beside his rocking chair.

"What are they talking about?" one of the boys asked his father, who had tuned in to one of President Franklin Roosevelt's "fireside chats."

"Quiet. We talk afterward," Peder said to the children. He leaned close to hear the president's assurances that change was coming, that there would be relief for the needy and financial reform for the country.

Parishioners and the occasional traveler needed hope, and Reverend Peder Nordsletten scoured God's Word looking for it. Bending his tall frame over his Bible and yellow pad of paper, he put together sermons that might offer comfort and, more importantly, reveal God's truths.

People wondered, *Why is God punishing us? Aren't we God-fearing people who attend church and give what we can?* They wanted to know how to bring the rain. How to bring back topsoil stolen by billowing dust storms. How to bring back their boys from far-away muddy trenches. They sought out the wise reverend, whose mind was a deep well of quotes and Scripture.

To Ruth, Peder was simply her father. Her relationship with him would always be woven together with her understanding of God.

On the inside flap of the English Bible he bought before her birth, Peder had written his name in a distinct script, recognizable from innumerable sermon outlines stacked on his desk and from the ledger where he kept a precise accounting of every purchase he made. Ruth watched him pore over the pages of that Bible until he knew where every Scripture and story was located.

Ruth would open the book as the years passed, even long after he was gone. She read his notes and records.

Peder Nordsletten
Aug. 5, 1923

After this, Peder had written the dates when his worn-out Bible was taken to a bookbinder and returned with a new cover.

Rebound Feb 1928
Rebound Feb 1938

On an inside page he kept track of how many times he read the Bible through from beginning to end. He'd learned English as a young man. As he'd struggled to perfect the language, it helped to read God's Word in the tongue he would mostly preach in.

Finished reading first time Sunday, May 1, 1927
Feb 17, 1929 - I started to read this Bible through a
    second time.
Finished Sun. Aug. 27, 1932
Started third time April 2, 1942
Lord, deepen my faith as I read it.
Completed third time, Sunday, March 19, 1944
Praise God

In addition to pointing parishioners to the Scriptures he knew so well, Peder had a repertoire of quotations he loved to trot out. While offering a hearty handshake he'd say, "A grip of steel to make you feel you're not in the world alone!" Another favorite admonition was from Sir Walter Scott: "Oh, what a tangled web we weave, when first we practice to deceive!"

Anchored in his deep heritage of faith, Peder appeared unbending as a man, unharmed by the storms of life. But his faith had been forged in the fire of loss.

It would be many years before Ruth would discover just how grievous that loss had been.

Chapter Seventeen

WHEN RUTH'S FATHER WROTE about his childhood toward the end of his life, he did so without complaint or bitterness. Yet Peder, the oldest of five siblings, was just ten years old when tragedy struck and changed his family forever.

Peder had been born in America on July 9, 1886, to recent Norwegian immigrants. They were blessed with one child after another, but earning a living was hard for the Nordslettens. Peder's father, Ole, worked for the George R. Newell Company in Minneapolis. His top wage while working for the grocery wholesaler was eleven dollars a week. He often walked the three miles to work to save a nickel on streetcar fare.

One night a lantern was knocked over in the kitchen. The flames quickly spread. There were five young children inside, and Peder's mother, Marie, desperately smothered the fire. But when her dress caught fire, she panicked and ran outside. The flames engulfed her. The children were saved, but seven agonizing hours later, Marie Nordsletten succumbed to death.

Peder's father was left with a broken heart. He did his best to care for small children who needed him but wanted their mother. His low wages made survival a struggle. The tragedy brought him to his knees, and his son later wrote that it was "the means of father's great conversion." Ole finally opened the Bible his parents had given him when he'd left Norway for America. The words within saved him. He later said that the hardest blow in his life had given him the biggest blessing—his faith.

Ole's parents wrote from Norway saying that they could take in two of the children. Eleven-year-old Peder and seven-year-old Anna were chosen because they were the quietest.

The children traveled with a neighbor by train to New York, then boarded a ship, where they took bunks in third-class quarters among the poorest passengers returning to Europe. They arrived just before Christmas, leaving behind a family in grief and a country fighting the Spanish-American War.

For the next four years, Peder and Anna lived with their aging grandparents. Peder described them as "very righteous; hence, religiously, we received a very good bringing up." They lived on a thriving farm in a large log home, which years later burned to the ground. The family seemed to be plagued by fire.

Peder was confirmed in the Lutheran church, and not long after, word came that his father had remarried. In 1902 the siblings returned to America, this time traveling alone. They arrived at a sod house, made from squares of compact dirt and constructed on the stark, empty flatlands of North Dakota, where Peder's father, stepmother, and siblings had settled.

Their new mother was not cruel, only unloving. The children would never become her own. She seemed to always be seeking something different—the greener grass or pot of gold, anything that wasn't where they were now. In the midst of such tension, Peder watched his father draw strength from his new faith, his connection to God.

One day while driving oxen, young Peder felt God's call. He decided to become a preacher. He worked hard, and by the age of twenty-three had saved enough money to enter Red Wing Seminary in southeastern Minnesota. His first year proved enormously difficult. With a limited English vocabulary, Peder understood little of what the teachers were saying. Since he had not completed eighth grade, he was required to take sub-classes.

But he studied diligently, steadied by prayer and the help of fellow students and faculty. On May 25, 1916, Peder Nordsletten "was deeply moved" when he held his diploma in his hand.

Two years later he graduated from the Lutheran Seminary in St. Paul, Minnesota, and the next day, he married his sweetheart, Olava, to whom he'd been engaged for a decade. During those years apart, Olava had been a nurse in a Catholic hospital in Canada and had attended the Moody Bible Institute in Chicago. The couple would be together for the next forty-two years.

✳ ✳ ✳

Ruth adored her family, her brothers included. She couldn't imagine a life without them.

Orville was the baby the Nordslettens had taken in right after the death of their firstborn, and he took the slot of oldest child as if made for it. According to the adoption home, he was of French descent, but as he grew, his frugality and attitude reminded his family of the attributes of a Scotchman. They nicknamed him Scotchy.

If Scotchy earned a dime, he saved it. Scotchy would shake his head at his younger brothers and their lack of restraint. He once told them, "I could paper my whole room with the dollars I've saved. But you two have nothing."

Born a year and a half after Scotchy, Olin was his brother's mirror opposite. Nicknamed Ole, pronounced O-lee, the boy saved his pennies only long enough to buy whatever had captured his fancy. Ole's antics kept Ruth in stitches but earned him the most punishment of all the children; it simply took more to straighten him up. But his mischievousness was softened by the generosity of his heart. On one occasion when he did manage to save some money, he used it to buy his father a radio.

Once while Ruth and her parents waited in the car to pick Ole up, they saw him bravely steal a kiss from a girl. They were all surprised, including the girl—though she didn't seem to mind.

When Ole was in his late teens, he interviewed for a position on a fishing boat. When asked if he could cook, Ole answered without a pause, "Oh yeah, I can cook." Ruth doubted that her older brother could even boil water at that time—she'd never seen him in the kitchen. But he got the job and was a quick study. Eventually Ole would become a minister, but he never lost his love of fishing.

The youngest brother was Kenneth. Kenny's hairstyle matched his father's, molded straight up and slicked back with thick pomade. He loved to roam the nearby gravel pit and swim in Lakes Spirit and Okoboji. Though he was youngest, his personality blended well with the other two boys—he was not as mischievous as Ole nor as focused as Scotchy.

With four active children of varied personalities, Olava never had a day without some kind of challenge. But the one place Olava would not tolerate misconduct was in God's house. Sometimes she doled out preemptive spankings to Ole and Kenny *before* church, with the promise of worse if they didn't control themselves during the service. Scotchy and Ruth were spared because of previous good behavior. They knew to sit like cherubs while their father preached.

For the Nordslettens, church and family life were knit together. There was no office in the church, so the living room was kept immaculate for parishioners who might stop in seeking counsel, issuing complaints, or requesting prayer. The humble room, furnished with a piano and plain furniture, was also used as the music and radio room. A local piano teacher used the instrument to provide lessons to children. In exchange, she taught Ruth for free.

Initially, the lessons made Ruth feel like she'd been corralled, forced to leave her beloved outdoors. The bench was too hard, and the steady tick of the metronome reminded her of a slow-moving clock. Eventually, though, playing piano evolved from a duty to a passion.

The parsonage was filled with music. Peder and Olava were accomplished singers. All of the children played instruments: Scotchy the trumpet, Ole the trombone, and Kenny the clarinet. Ruth played the piano and took singing lessons, and she later played the clarinet like Kenny.

In the evening, Peder would sit in his rocking chair beside the radio. The children gathered around to listen to the serial adventures of Jack Armstrong, and later Captain Midnight. Peder and Olava enjoyed *Fibber McGee and Molly*. The room was as quiet as a library except for the voices crackling through the speaker.

The dining room table was the family's hub, where everyone ate meals together. Olava used the table to spread out colored fabric squares to make quilts. It was the setting for family games like Rook, marbles, and Monopoly. Ruth especially loved it when her older siblings and their friends played Monopoly and allowed her to be banker. She enjoyed lining up the neat stacks of colored money and counting out $200 every time a player rounded the board and passed the giant "GO."

From the time she was a baby, Ruth was known for her pleasant disposition, but sometimes a deep stubborn streak emerged. One clear day Ruth packed her little brown suitcase, then marched up the street several blocks to the train depot. Peder held Olava back, picked up the phone, and told the operator to connect him to the depot's ticket office.

"My daughter should be showing up momentarily. Could you please keep an eye on her until I get there?"

After Ruth reached the two-story train depot, she fished in her pocket and sighed. *I should have asked Scotchy for a loan.* Shrugging her shoulders, she decided to explore. The long, rectangular building was one of the most ornate in town, with curved dormer windows that peeked out from a flat mansard roof. There was a central waiting room, a pavilion in each corner, and a canopied section for waiting passengers. The straight lines of the rails stretched tantalizingly to the horizon and seemed to pulse with the energy of faraway cities.

Ruth peered down the tracks from a safe distance away. She plopped onto a wooden bench and tried to picture the empty rows filled with travelers seeking adventure. Her stomach began to growl. *It must be time for lunch.*

Running away was more boring than she had expected, and when Peder and Olava arrived, she was ready to go home.

Ruth's childhood unfolded with mittens warmed on the grate in winter, bags of penny candy from the downtown store, a pretty Schwinn bicycle for her birthday. The years became imprinted with the smell of Olava's homemade donuts and soft molasses cookies fresh from the oven and with memories of summer Bible camps and hearing Big Band music over the radio.

Time pushed the family onward. The boys were nine, eight, and six years older than Ruth, and eventually they left home, one by one. Scotchy joined the navy. Ole became a fisherman and later went to seminary. Kenny went to Minneapolis to work for Braniff Airways. None of the boys were lost to World War II, which would begin and end as Ruth was coming of age.

At a time when hundreds of thousands of Americans were left homeless, the Nordslettens had a comfortable home, good food in their bellies, and a house full of love. Ruth's life wasn't free from challenges. There were the usual losses of youth and moments of tears and pain. But on the whole, Ruth Priscilla—once called Betty Jane—had a childhood filled with love and joy. A blessed childhood.

Almost as if someone she didn't know had been praying for the girl her entire life.

Chapter Eighteen

"I'VE ACCEPTED a new position as a traveling evangelist," Peder said to Ruth as they gathered at the dinner table.

"Your father has wanted to do this for a long time," Olava said, pulling up her chair. "He'll be reaching people in churches all around the country."

"But it means we'll be moving to Minnesota," Peder added. He studied his daughter's face, and as she asked questions, her parents assured her that the change was the right one for their family. They'd be settled in their new home before Ruth began seventh grade that fall.

She felt excitement and a thread of fear—Wallingford was the only home she could remember. Now, after eleven years, everything would be different.

They moved first to Fergus Falls, Minnesota. With 10,000 residents, the town seemed huge to Ruth—Wallingford had fewer than 250 citizens. On the north side of town stood the magnificent state hospital, one of the last insane asylums built in the

Kirkbride model. It resembled a towering castle and, at times, housed as many as two thousand patients.

Ruth spent seventh and eighth grade in Fergus Falls. She made friends quickly and loved to ice-skate on local ponds during the cold winters. But before Ruth's first year of high school, Peder and Olava decided the best home base for ministry was Minneapolis. As one of the largest cities in the country, it offered seemingly infinite resources and was a good central location for Peder's travels around the region.

Peder enjoyed his new position. He visited churches in twelve states and four Canadian provinces, staying in more than a hundred parsonages. He encouraged congregations with messages as a guest speaker, and he advised pastors as a veteran of the parish ministry.

Ruth and Olava appreciated the conveniences of Minneapolis. Ruth rode the streetcar to school every day, and it wasn't long before she could navigate the city with ease. Even on a tight minister's income she was able to dress well, and her cheerful and engaging disposition always drew people to her.

A few years later, a teacher of Ruth's would write in her yearbook: "You sure are filled with atomic energy—may it never burn out. However, be just a little more conscious of the serious side of life as well as the joyous."

Another remarked, "You really livened up my English class."

In the years that Peder traveled, Ruth and Olava grew closer than ever. They took the streetcar around the city to shop or sightsee, and attended church together. For a special treat they watched a movie at the cinema. Olava's favorite was *Lassie Come Home*.

These were war years, and ration cards were as normal as money to Ruth. Since her mother didn't drive, they at least weren't subject to gas rationing. At times, classmates or church friends told stories that related to the faraway war; of brothers, sons, husbands, and friends not coming home from places like Normandy and Iwo Jima. But as in the Depression years, Ruth was sheltered from tragedies taking place beyond the safe existence her parents built around her.

On rare occasions, Ruth was able to travel with her father. She was always welcomed with glowing compliments about how pretty she was, what a fine girl she seemed to be, how proud her daddy must be. Ruth, in turn, was proud of her father, and she missed him terribly when he was gone.

"How long until you come home this time?" Ruth asked her father on one of his visits. "You helped the boys prepare for confirmation, and now mine is coming soon."

Ruth had been studying hard for the ceremony that would be a public declaration of her faith. But she knew it would be easier to understand *Luther's Small Catechism* if she was sitting beside her father as he explained the lessons that he knew like the back of his hand.

Peder promised to be there to help his daughter prepare.

After her confirmation, Ruth continued to enjoy a full life in the city. Then suddenly, after only two years in Minneapolis, they were packing up again. Decades later, Ruth would be stunned to learn that as they were leaving Minneapolis, a woman named Minka Disbrow was moving in, just two miles from the cute bungalow house the Nordslettens occupied. Perhaps they'd walked the aisles of the same grocer, or brushed past each other on a streetcar, or sung hymns near one another at the same Lutheran church.

The Nordslettens were relocating to a small farming town in Wisconsin called Viroqua, where Peder had taken what would be his final pastorate. Ruth, now a junior in high school, was once again the new girl, but this would be her last time in that role. This town would take her in completely, and she would remain here for the rest of her life.

❊ ❊ ❊

After the grand city of Minneapolis, little Viroqua in southwestern Wisconsin was a throwback to Ruth's first tiny hometown in Iowa.

"What kind of hick place have we moved to?" she wanted to ask.

Ruth had grown accustomed lately to dressing well, in dresses or at least in pressed slacks and a blouse. But the girls in Viroqua wore rolled-up blue jeans, bobby socks, and saddle shoes, topped off with their fathers' white dress shirts. Ruth stared at the girls, feeling like she'd arrived in a foreign land.

At least Ruth had one relative at the small high school, and second cousin Anita was thrilled to show her around. With Ruth's quick smile and confidence, she didn't have any problem fitting in. She was a beautiful girl, the new pastor's daughter, and a fascinating newcomer to the students who'd known each other since playing in the church nursery.

To her own amazement, Ruth soon felt comfortable in the "hick" town. She even sported the local uniform of rolled-up blue jeans and bobby socks, although she had to settle for a T-shirt to complete the outfit. Her father's white button-down shirts were much too big for her petite frame.

Ruth met Charles Lee on one of her first days at school. She enjoyed talking to the handsome high schooler, although he sometimes acted strangely.

"What's up with Charles?" Ruth asked her cousin Anita.

"What do you mean?"

"Sometimes he acts really weird. I'll think we had a really good talk, then the next time I see him, he seems to be making fun of me or something."

A wide grin stretched across her cousin's face.

"What is it?" Ruth asked.

Anita couldn't contain herself. "It's not Charles."

"What? You're saying it's me?"

"No, I mean, you aren't talking to Charles."

Ruth squinted her eyes and felt a surge of annoyance. What was her cousin talking about?

"It's Chester, his brother. His identical twin brother."

"What!" Ruth said, crossing her arms at her chest. But a smile played at the edges of her mouth.

"Chester and Charles sometimes switch places. They've been doing pranks like that for years. They've tricked teachers, parents, anyone they can."

Ruth began plotting revenge in her mind, but bemusement wrestled with her anger—and won.

"At least now I know he's not stupid," she said with a laugh.

Ruth was never fooled by the brothers again. She and Charles continued to talk, and Chester liked to tease them. Before long, Ruth and Charles were going steady.

Through her junior and senior years of high school, Ruth and Charles were considered an *item*. Charles and his family belonged to the other Lutheran church in town, but later he began attending Reverend Nordsletten's parish.

During the summer months, Ruth went to Bible camps with many of the other Viroqua students, and she continued to sing and play the piano. Ruth's passion for music only grew during her high school years. She especially liked the Big Band music of Glenn Miller, Tommy Dorsey, and Sammy Nestico. As the family radio blared the music, even her parents grew to enjoy it.

Although separated in miles, the Nordsletten family remained closely connected. Scotchy was stationed in Corpus Christi, Texas, in the navy. Ruth loved wearing his peacoat when he visited. Kenny was in Minneapolis, and sometimes Ruth took the train back to the city to see him, as well as Ole and his wife. Ole was going to seminary and would become a minister like his father. Ruth's favorite times were when her brothers and their growing families visited. Olava seemed to glow when all her children were beneath her roof again, and Ruth adored the ruckus of voices—debating, discussing, or laughing.

To Ruth, a full house meant happiness.

✳ ✳ ✳

The morning of May 28, 1947, as Ruth dressed for her high school graduation, sunshine beamed through the windows. She wore a suit beneath her graduation gown, and white leather sandals, which she'd just purchased. Before walking to the school, Ruth posed on the parsonage's green lawn for a picture. The sky was the kind of blue that promised warmth and the coming of summer, although the temperature was making a surprising dip and a bunch of clouds crowded together on the horizon.

During the graduation service, the light coming through the windows softened, then faded. A freak snowstorm surprised everyone. Robed graduates hurried through the cold to their cars or raced home on foot, diplomas in hand.

Charles and Ruth walked together in the falling snow. By the time Ruth reached her house, her leather sandals were soaked through. The straps dried stiff and misshapen; Ruth could never wear them again. That night, eight inches of snow dropped on Viroqua. The storm set records across the Midwest, some holding firm until a May storm in 2013.

In Minneapolis, Minka Disbrow still thought of her older daughter, even as she held her infant, Dianna, in her arms. She'd continued to write letters to Miss Bragstad. She'd hoped that her Betty Jane would graduate from high school, an opportunity Minka never had. *Will she be going to college next fall? Has she fallen in love? Is she happy?* So many questions ran through Minka's mind.

Ruth was now older than Minka had been when she'd left the House of Mercy with a heart so broken it would never fully mend.

While Minka had spent her young adulthood grieving, Ruth was anticipating a bright future, full of promise.

*　*　*

In late summer of 1948, Charles took Ruth to a jewelry store. He'd been working at a local business and had saved for this day. After they chose an engagement ring, he asked if she wanted to wear it.

"No," Ruth said. Charles recognized her stubborn streak coming on.

"No?"

"I want you to put it on my finger proper-like, when we're alone," she said firmly.

Charles learned quickly that when Ruth dug in her heels about something, he'd better listen. This understanding would help him in the coming decades of life together. And once they were away from the curious eyes of the store clerks, Ruth welcomed the engagement ring onto her finger.

Ruth had her hope chest neatly packed with things for their new home: pot holders, doilies, dishes, aprons. She and her mother, Olava, had spent years making pieces for it and choosing items that would someday fill Ruth's own home. They'd purchased Jewel Tea dishes and cobalt-blue Depression glass for Ruth's future table, carefully wrapping first a platter and then a serving bowl. In the decades to come, Ruth added to the collection, which would survive countless holidays and years of small hands "helping out."

Ruth and her mother had bonded from the first day they'd met at the House of Mercy. They'd sung together, worked in the kitchen, and done housecleaning in Minneapolis for extra money when Peder was traveling. For several years, during the summer and autumn months, they'd canned fruits and vegetables side by side, waiting for the soft, popping sound of lids sealing over the boiling jars. Ruth would find this skill invaluable in the future, when she'd make canning and freezing an essential part of her family life.

Olava shared her cherished recipes with Ruth. Her beef vegetable soup had always been a family favorite, and the children couldn't get enough of her baked goods. Ole described them well: "They were out of this world and halfway into the next!"

Even with a houseful of children, Olava took bits of time to explore outside interests. Without any lessons, she had discovered a natural talent for oil painting. She could visualize a ship at sea or a mountain landscape—with no ocean or ranges for hundreds of miles—and her brush brought the image to life on canvas. Her children and grandchildren saved her paintings of a blacksmith's shop, a deer, a waterfall, a sailing vessel. The generations to come would have something to remember their grandmother by.

Since leaving Minneapolis, Olava had noticed a decline in her health. It was becoming difficult to open and close her hands from the effects of rheumatoid arthritis, which worsened as the years passed. She also suffered from asthma and struggled to catch her breath even when doing small tasks.

Still, she enjoyed every moment with her children, telling them stories about her life, such as her time working as a nurse during World War I. Or childhood stories like when she'd nearly drowned in the Two Rivers area at the age of fifteen.

She'd been delivering lunch and hot coffee to her father and brother-in-law as they worked in the hay fields on the other side of a river that divided their land. Two logs with their bark peeled back served as a little bridge. Olava's arms were full—coffee in one hand, food in another—and the logs were slippery. Halfway across, she lost her balance and fell into the river.

Frigid water filled her lungs, burning as it pushed out the air. She sank, but suddenly, "Jesus was beside me, the Lord in His white robes, as plain as day." He spoke to her. She asked His forgiveness. Together, they prayed the Lord's Prayer.

Olava's brother-in-law had heard a peculiar noise that roused his curiosity and drew him to the river. Instinct pushed him to run as he approached the water's edge. He dove into the water and pulled Olava out, putting her into a nearby wheelbarrow and running her across the log bridge and back to the house.

She later wrote of the event, ending her account this way: "When I hear of people here and there who meet death by drowning, I think of my own experience, when Jesus came so close to me as He did in the Two Rivers in Northern Minnesota. They too may have had similar experiences with the Lord, as I did, before death took them."

She had no idea that the story mirrored that of Ruth's maternal grandfather, Ben, who would perish beneath lake waters in the next state over, just thirteen years after Olava's near-death incident.

✳ ✳ ✳

Ruth and Charles's wedding took place on September 24, 1948. She was nineteen years old. It was a family affair: her father officiated, her brother Scotchy walked her down the aisle, her sister-in-law Arlett played the organ, Ole sang, and Kenny served as usher. The only shadow crossing the day was Olava's health. Scotchy and Kenny helped her get to the church to attend the ceremony, but she was quite ill.

After the wedding, Charles moved into the parsonage with Ruth, into the same house as her parents. The young couple was broke and wonderfully happy. And it had been such fun growing up in a house with four kids, Ruth decided a couple more would only increase the joy.

"I want six children!" she told Charles.

Charles looked at her and said, "If six come along, they will be welcome and loved."

Soon they were able to move into an apartment of their own. After bouncing around Viroqua a few times and saving diligently, they had their $1,000 down payment to build a small house on the south end of town. The payments were $48 a month.

By then, babies were arriving. Only a few months after their first anniversary, Ruth discovered she was pregnant. After a difficult labor, the couple welcomed a daughter, Deb, and Ruth happily immersed herself in homemaking and motherhood. Less than eighteen months later, Charles and Ruth celebrated the news that their second baby would arrive the following summer.

But the joy was short-lived, and Ruth's desire for six children was soon to be tested.

Chapter Nineteen

It was the longest month of Ruth's life.

She stared at the bedroom furnishings in a house that wasn't her own, listening to her toddler daughter and family members moving around in other rooms. She longed to feed eighteen-month-old Deb, to comfort her when she cried, to see every moment she was missing. She wanted to do anything but be alone in this room. But the doctor was emphatic: complete bed rest.

The problems had come almost immediately after Ruth found out she was pregnant again. The independent young woman was now at the mercy of everyone else for companionship, for snatches of time with her active daughter, even for meeting her most private needs. It took all her resolve to keep from hopping up to help. Ruth appreciated her mother-in-law's dedication to caring for her, but she wanted her own room, her own house, her normal life.

The doctor's words kept her in bed. More than all those other things, Ruth wanted a healthy baby.

Ruth missed her own mother, who was too sick to take on

caregiving or babysitting. She longed for Olava's beef vegetable soup, and the soft touch of her mother's hands on her forehead or shoulders as she tucked in the covers around her.

Ruth knew that Olava had once lost a newborn son, but now it was made real to her. How painful that must have been for Olava and Peder. She touched her stomach, and dread coursed through her. Would she know such pain as well?

The month finally ended, and Charles took her back to the doctor. The sky had never looked so bright nor the air smelled so clean. Ruth felt like an inmate released on good behavior, and her usual cheerful disposition returned. Surely her obedience of the strict orders would be rewarded with a positive report. But the doctor's words were hard to hear.

"I don't know if the fetus is still alive. But let's get you to the hospital and make sure you're okay."

Ruth put her hands over the slight round of her stomach. The baby just had to be alive. At the hospital, Charles called the family, asking them to get on their knees and pray for the child.

The doctor pronounced Ruth well enough to go off bed rest, but they would have to wait to find out about the baby. The Doppler fetal monitor wouldn't be invented for another six years, and it was still too early in the pregnancy to hear the baby's heartbeat on a regular stethoscope.

About a month later, Ruth finally felt the first sweet stirrings deep inside—proof that her child was still alive.

That August of 1952, Ruth delivered Mark Charles, a healthy 9 pound, 9 ounce baby boy. In later years, she'd remember those days in bed and think, *What we would've missed had we lost him.*

Motherhood had woken Ruth to a joy she'd guessed at, a love she'd only thought she knew. It was deeper and more marvelous than she could have imagined. But this was her second challenging pregnancy. The labor and delivery had been excruciating with both Deb and Mark, and Ruth's recovery was slow each time.

While she adored her children, Ruth was rethinking her dream of having six of them.

＊　＊　＊

In 1954, Charles took a job at a mink ranch, where thousands of the animals were raised in long rows of chicken-wire pens and sheds. The young family moved into a small farmhouse on the property, which they would later have to expand. Ruth's days were busy with caring for her brood, tending to her house, and going to church on Sundays at her father's parish. The Lees added a third child, Brian Michael, on a frozen day in late January 1957.

Although this pregnancy had also begun with a stay in the hospital, things swiftly turned around. It would prove to be her easiest pregnancy, and the delivery was quick, with no real labor pains at all. Ruth's spirit was renewed and along with it, her desire for a large family.

Sometimes Ruth believed her brother Ole had passed down the mischief gene to her children, even though her adoption meant that he wasn't a blood relative. Her little ones were full of imagination and pranks.

One afternoon Ruth paused in her cleaning and noticed a peculiar stillness to the house. Even with little Brian down for his nap, it was too quiet. That was a sure sign of trouble in a house with young children.

Ruth crept through the house, peering into rooms in search of Deb and Mark.

She went to the back room, where two-year-old Brian was asleep on a long davenport couch. His head was covered with his beloved football helmet, a plaything he wore so often that it wasn't unusual to find him napping in it.

But Brian wasn't safe from his siblings even with a helmet on his head. Bent over the toddler, eight-year-old Deb and six-year-old Mark were intent on their prey. First Deb, then Mark, took turns leaning in. They carefully lifted one of Brian's eyelids. When he twitched or his eye fluttered, they jumped back, curling up into fits of soundless laughter, openmouthed, while Deb motioned for quiet. Then they did it again. Random snickers slid out as they collapsed against the davenport.

Ruth struggled to keep her own chuckles silent, but she soon pushed the door open just enough to allow the creaking hinges to announce her arrival.

Deb and Mark jumped away from Brian, faces guilty as criminals'.

"What are you kids doing?" Ruth asked, as if she hadn't been watching them.

"Nothing," they said in unison, shrugging and glancing around the room.

"Were you lifting Brian's eyelids while he's sleeping?"

"Nooooo," Deb said.

"No, we didn't," Mark seconded.

"But I saw you." The smile she'd fought to hold back was now gone.

They denied it still.

The humor of their prank was destroyed with the lie. If Ruth hadn't seen their childish antics with her own eyes, she might have believed them. She knew she couldn't let it pass. One of her father's favorite quotes came to mind, "Oh, what a tangled web we weave, when first we practice to deceive."

"You two come with me. Now," she said, motioning them behind her, away from their sleeping brother. She took them to the bathroom for a lesson on how to clean the lie from their mouths with a touch of soap.

"Don't ever lie again," Ruth said firmly as Deb and Mark wiped their eyes. They glanced at one another, grimacing at the bitter slivers on their tongues.

"We won't," Deb said. Mark nodded his head in agreement.

Ruth knew they would probably lie again. They were children, after all, and children had to be encouraged toward good character—it didn't come without guidance.

* * *

Olava had been fighting it for years, but now she was sinking beneath disease. Her doctor would later reveal to the family that she'd had leukemia, in addition to her rheumatoid arthritis and asthma. By the time the doctor realized it, she was beyond treatment.

Her love of family kept her fighting so long. Olava's children and grandchildren brought joy to her pain-filled world. She cherished their visits, the sound of a full house, the stories and laughter and memories. Her grandchildren seemed to have limitless energy—it was hard to imagine she'd once been that strong.

For Deb, Mark, and Brian, trips to both sets of grandparents were always met with excitement. Grandma and Grandpa Lee, Charles's parents, lived on Main Street in Viroqua, across from Good Shepherd Lutheran Church. The house had a big porch, where the family would gather for the Memorial Day parade, watching for Charles's twin brother, Chester, a national guardsman, who almost always marched.

From the Lees' place, the children could go through backyards and a bit of woods and end up at their other grandparents' house.

At the Nordslettens', the children raced through the parsonage with its circular route of downstairs rooms. When they were too rambunctious, Olava and Ruth set the children at the table and strapped them into chairs. While the kids ate a snack, the women regained their energy before setting the youngsters loose again.

Ruth watched how her mother's face glowed when she brought her children over or when her brothers and their families came to town. They'd all laugh together, tell well-worn stories, try to catch up with new tales.

No wonder, then, that Olava didn't want to leave her family. But her failing body drew her ever closer to the other side of eternity, the side she'd approached when she'd almost drowned in a river so many years before.

When Ruth discovered she was pregnant a fourth time, she reluctantly kept it a secret from her mother. Why pain Olava with the knowledge of a new baby she'd never get to bounce on her lap, velvety cheeks she'd never get to kiss? Why remind her of all that she would miss in the years ahead? Even though Olava had been ill for more than a decade, Ruth could not yet imagine life without her mother.

In Olava's final days and hours, Ruth stayed at the hospital with her every moment she could. Her belly had not yet rounded out, but the tiny baby was there with them, growing inside. She felt torn between the two extremes: joy and grief, anticipation and dread, life and death.

Six months later, on December 2, 1960, when Ruth delivered Timothy James, it was with bittersweet wonder. She had a new life in her arms, but her own mother would never hold her newborn son. Olava had gone to be with Jesus.

✳ ✳ ✳

Ruth grieved her mother's death and worried about her father, now living in the parsonage alone. She wished to call Olava to share news about Tim's first tooth or tottering first steps, and every childhood marker that Deb, Mark, and Brian were passing: report cards, Christmas programs, and the funny stories that filled their home.

Ruth and Charles carried on her parents' values and traditions as if they were woven into their genes. God, family, and church shored up their lives. Ruth sang in the choir, and for fifty years she would be part of a women's quintet. She and Charles both taught Sunday school.

Five years after Tim, fifth baby Carrie Ann came along in February 1965, and then Jay Parker just over a year later. Jay arrived so close on Carrie's heels that people teased Ruth and Charles, asking if they'd figured out how pregnancy happened. There were fifteen and a half years between oldest Deb and youngest Jay. But true to Ruth's original plan, a total of six children filled their house.

For the first time, Ruth had two children in diapers. It seemed that if she wasn't changing diapers, then she was washing them, scrubbing the flannel fabric, hanging them to dry, and barely getting them folded before needing them again.

Ruth handled the chaos of a house chock-full of children well, but the work could wear out even an "atomic" personality. Ruth kept two long quotes taped to her cupboards for decades, until the paper became tanned with age. Every single day, she'd steal away to read the bolstering words of Walter Wintle's poem "Courage":

If you think you are beaten, you are; If you think you dare not,
>*you don't;*
If you'd like to win, but think you can't, It's almost a cinch
>*you won't.*

And when she wanted to remind herself of what her children needed most, she read the admonition of Ronald Russell:

A child that lives with encouragement
>*learns confidence.*

A child that lives with truth
>*learns justice. . . .*

The Lees worked hard from early dawn to after dark, and as the children grew old enough, they were assigned farm chores. Work and family time, school and sports activities kept them constantly on their toes. Everyone reconnected at the dining room table, even if it was later in the evening. The kids were expected to be in their seats before the supper prayer: "Come, Lord Jesus, be our guest, and let this food to us be blessed."

At one such dinner, Charles offered one of his frequent challenges.

"Okay, does anyone have a riddle tonight?"

"I do," Brian said, passing a bowl of mashed potatoes on to Deb.

"Go on, what is it?" Charles asked.

The table fell silent except for the scrape of forks on plates and the chewing of food. The circle of faces waited, wondering what Brian had dreamed up.

"What has windows and walks?" The gleam in Brian's eye piqued his family's interest.

They looked around, seeking the inspiration for the riddle.

"Um . . . the cuckoo clock?" someone said.

"Nope," said Brian.

Seven pairs of eyes sought an object around the room besides the glass of the windows, which clearly didn't have legs.

"A car?"

"No."

They studied the smug look on Brian's face, tried again and again, soon tossing out answers that couldn't possibly be right. No one in the Lee family liked to be duped by a riddle. The older two siblings especially couldn't allow their younger brother to beat them. Even little Jay tried babbling out words that he couldn't quite put together.

Dinner grew cold. Ruth knew it was time to end it.

"We give up," Ruth said, winking at her middle son. He beamed triumphantly and took a bite of his meal.

"What's the answer?" Tim asked. The entire family was waiting.

Brian looked up from his plate, eyebrows raised as he scanned the table.

Someone shouted in dismay. "He doesn't have an answer!"

Guilt flushed Brian's face.

"What? You don't have an answer to your own riddle?" Charles asked his son.

"I . . . no, I don't."

The room roared with groans and laughter in equal measure. The story of "What has windows and walks?" became legendary in the Lee family. Brian would never live it down.

Grandparents, uncles, aunts, and cousins were constants in the Lees' lives. Ruth's father, Peder, retired from his pastorate in 1962, though he continued to lead special prayer meetings and fill in for other pastors when asked. He also delivered clothing to Native American families in the Dakotas. Eventually arthritis and knee surgery slowed him down, and for the rest of his life he walked with two canes.

Brian often did chores for his grandpa Peder, like mowing the lawn and taking out the garbage, for which he was always paid. Peder would pull out fifty-cent pieces from the Old Spice deodorant decanter where he kept his change and hand them to Brian.

"You paid me too much," Brian once said.

"When I'm gone, I don't want you telling people your grandpa Peder was stingy," Grandpa responded.

Once each summer, Peder treated the entire Lee brood to dinner at Hokey's South Lawn drive-in, an outing the kids looked forward to every year. As they spread out over several picnic tables, they liked to retell some of the cherished family stories.

"Remember when Tim was four or five years old, and he followed his dog Duke down the frozen creek? We couldn't find him for the longest time. . . ."

"Remember when Brian got his finger bit by a mink, and then another one bit his rear end, not once, but twice!"

"What about the story of the Magic Carpet Ride? Dad shaking

that rug over the second-story railing in the garage, and the rail breaking. Mom walked by at that very moment, and it seemed like Dad rode the rug down, landing unharmed on the ground with the rug still in his hands."

"How about when Mom and Deb went shopping when Carrie and Jay were really small, and the saleswoman at J. C. Penney thought Mom was the grandmother? Deb said when they left, 'See, Mom, I keep telling you to color your hair!'"

All the children did well in school and kept busy participating in extracurricular activities and playing on sports teams. Ruth would pack up the younger children to hurry off to the various events: cheerleading, wrestling, track, baseball, scouting. Naps were often interrupted, dinner served late, schedules juggled. Charles would watch from the stands still dressed in his work clothes. But he and Ruth never missed a game.

The Lees could have posed for a Norman Rockwell painting. They were the epitome of a rural American family, with sons joining the military and each of the children earning college degrees. The family was garnering one accomplishment after another.

And there was one among them who reached for the stars and captured the sky.

Chapter Twenty

FROM CHILDHOOD, it was obvious that Mark was smart as a whip. He studied hard with no prompting and earned excellent grades. He excelled in sports, too. His younger brothers and sister idolized him. Busy with a procession of babies, Ruth was grateful for her second child's self-sufficiency.

On the same day that Alan Shepard launched into space in 1961, nine-year-old Mark and a friend were kept in from recess. To commemorate the launch, the boys took all the art clay the school had and molded it into projectiles. After wetting the clay in the water fountain, they threw the "missiles" onto the ceiling of their classroom. During the middle of class, as the teacher was explaining how to diagram a sentence, the clay missiles lost their grip and began to plop down onto students' heads.

The teacher pulled Mark aside and asked for an explanation. Mark told her that he thought the missiles would stay up there forever. She looked at him thoughtfully and told him, "You need to go to the library and learn about gravity."

So Mark went to the city library, found a book on Sir Isaac Newton, and prepared a report for class. A whole new world opened up. Mark began reading all the biographies and autobiographies the library had. While watching the Alan Shepard flight into space, he'd made a decision: he knew what he wanted to do when he grew up. And every step he took from then on would bring him closer to that goal. His elementary, junior high, and high school teachers all would unknowingly contribute to his dream.

Someday, Mark would travel in space.

He became a Boy Scout and achieved the highest ranking of Eagle Scout. He was pleased to learn that an extremely high percentage of astronauts had taken part in Scouting, and a large number of those were Eagle Scouts. After high school, he was accepted by the Air Force Academy. He earned a bachelor's degree in civil engineering and spent years flying fighter jets. He then entered MIT to earn a degree in mechanical engineering, specializing in advanced composite materials, something NASA valued.

One Christmas, Mark came home and began talking about NASA's astronaut program. Ruth was busy in the kitchen but finally began to wonder why he was going on about the subject. Then she realized: this was *Mark* talking.

She looked at him.

"You wouldn't want to go up into space, would you?"

Mark held her gaze. He spoke directly, as all the Lees did.

"Yes, I do."

After two decades of working toward a single goal, it was the first time Mark had mentioned a word of his plan to his family. They were surprised, but Charles and Ruth had always supported their children and encouraged their aspirations. They would support this idea too.

No one doubted Mark's abilities, so no one was surprised

when, out of more than five thousand applicants, he was one of just seventeen accepted as an astronaut candidate.

In January 1986, seven months after Mark completed his training, the shuttle *Challenger* exploded seventy-three seconds into its launch, killing everyone on board. The images of debris falling back to earth replayed on television screens across the United States and around the world. Excited schoolchildren had been watching the launch live in American classrooms as Christa McAuliffe became the first teacher to head to space. As a result, the tragedy—and the danger of space exploration—was magnified.

Mark, who had just become the first in his astronaut class to be assigned to a future space flight, called his parents. He needed them to understand just how dangerous this really was. His resolve had not wavered—neither did their support.

In late April 1989, the extended Lee family gathered on the narrow strip of Cocoa Beach, just south of Cape Canaveral. Mark was scheduled for his first space flight on the shuttle *Atlantis*. Two days before launch, NASA hosted the astronauts and their families for a beach house barbecue. Like all the guests, Mark's family members were examined by a doctor before being allowed into the house. The government took no chances that someone would pass along a sore throat or fever to a crew member.

Despite the unspoken sense that this might be their last time together, the mood at the barbecue was upbeat. As usual, Brian lightened the conversation with wisecracks, but they all felt the gravity of the occasion, the sense of purpose. After a couple of hours, the five *Atlantis* crew members had to leave. Ruth hugged her boy tightly, but she did not cry.

While the crew finished preparations, the families were treated to a tour of the Kennedy Space Center and a nighttime visit to the launchpad. Their buses were driven to the foot of the massive structure, now illuminated with brilliant lights. A guide explained the different components of the pad: The enormous fuel storage tanks. The sophisticated venting system designed to contain exhaust and contaminated water after the launch. The eight enormous bolts, four inches in diameter, that held the rocket boosters to the platform and that would split in two at ignition. The escape baskets, which could slide the astronauts into a bunker in case of emergency.

Ruth felt her heart racing as she studied all the vital pieces and complex parts that had to work perfectly together to take her son into space and bring him safely back home.

Above them loomed the massive external tank, nearly half the distance of a football field and weighing over a million and a half pounds, most of that liquid oxygen and hydrogen. Clinging to its sides were the two solid rocket boosters, which would power the launch during the first two minutes of liftoff, and the familiar white body and finlike wings of the orbiter *Atlantis* itself.

It was the most stunning sight that Ruth, who'd grown up climbing trees and marveling at her family's first washing machine, had ever seen. As she tilted her head back and looked at the fearsome expanse of machinery standing ready to transport her thirty-six-year-old son, it was astonishing to think that her family was a part of all *this*.

In the end, Mark's first launch was scrubbed at T-31 seconds due to a problem with a pump. The relaunch would take place in four days. While they waited, the Lee family visited Disney World, SeaWorld, Rocket Park, and the IMAX theater at the Space Center. They tried to ignore the tension knotting their stomachs.

Finally, on the morning of May 4, they boarded buses for the LC39 family viewing center. It was a warm day, with a bright sun heating the tarmac and glinting off the bus windows. Every one of the Lees wore a red shirt proclaiming, "Viroqua, Wisconsin, home of astronaut Mark C. Lee."

As the buses prepared to roll from the loading area on Merritt

Island, Uncle Ole stood up and addressed the people settling into the rows of seats. The extended Lee family filled over half of the bus that was packed with other astronauts' families and friends.

"Excuse me, and hello, I will be your tour guide this afternoon," Ole said in an exaggerated monotone.

"Here comes a sermon," someone tossed out, followed by a ripple of laughter.

"No, just a song." Ole cleared his throat, then winked at Ruth and laughed. "All joking aside. My name is Ole Nordsletten, the proud uncle of astronaut Mark Lee. A group of people up in Seattle like to call me Reverend Ole.

"I'm sure each of you has a million memories attached to those boys out there like we do. I remember Mark as just a little fella running around the farm out in Viroqua, Wisconsin. And now we're going to see them go down in history."

Ole took a deep breath as his eyes swept the faces on the bus, resting again on his little sister. He remembered the day his parents brought home little infant Ruth—the girl who always laughed at his jokes and brought an unquenchable sunshine to their family.

"This is a remarkable day, and I'm incredibly proud of my sister, Ruth, my brother-in-law, Charles, and of course my nephew Mark. I am sure each one of you feels the same for your astronaut. If there are no objections, I would like to offer up a prayer for a safe launch, a successful mission, and the safe return of our loved ones."

There were approving murmurs throughout the bus. Ole closed his eyes and in his deep voice sent his prayer beyond the shuttle's destination. Ruth thought of her parents and how amazed they'd be by all of this. Olava had been gone for almost thirty years, and her father had passed away in 1974 on the day of Mark's graduation from the Air Force Academy. It seemed impossible that he'd been gone fifteen years already.

Once they reached the viewing area, the family settled into the stands for a long wait. Loudspeakers broadcast feeds from mission control and launch control. A narrator explained what was happening as the launch timeline moved forward. Astronauts were on hand to answer questions. Three miles away, the shuttle shimmered through the heat.

From behind her sunglasses, Ruth stared at the launchpad. A light breeze ruffled her short hair. She knew that Mark was already in the shuttle crew compartment, lying flat on his back with his feet in the air, strapped in for hours of preflight checks and procedures. Her stomach clenched with a mixture of emotions. Excitement. Fear. Immense pride.

The crowd was silent as a pleasant male voice started the countdown. Everyone tensed, not knowing whether the count would be aborted, as it had been days earlier. But at T-14 seconds, as 300,000 gallons of water poured onto the launchpad to muffle the powerful sound waves, steam began to billow underneath the shuttle.

Ruth's heart was pounding so hard that she could actually hear it.

At seven seconds, bright flames ignited on the shuttle's main engines. Great clouds of steam nearly obscured the entire launchpad. Then the countdown completed: *two, one, zero . . . and liftoff.*

The sound hit the crowd a few seconds later. Even as they cheered, the noise thundered against their bodies, an insistent percussion. Ruth's eyes were locked on the shuttle, whose rockets were like infernos pushing it upward. She could feel her heart tugging toward them, toward Mark. Tears slid from beneath her dark glasses. Tears stained nearly everyone's cheeks—the majesty of the spectacle fairly demanded it. Nothing they had ever seen, or ever would see, had prepared them for the flames blazing under the rockets, colors of an intensity and brightness unlike any they'd witnessed before.

With memories of the *Challenger* explosion still fresh, the first two minutes were agonizing. But as the clock ticked on and the NASA feed continued its calm details, a sense of relief swept through the families. They hugged and slapped each other on the back, their eyes continually glancing skyward. All too soon, they were hustled onto buses and driven away.

Celebrations went well into the evening, with plenty of snacks and drinks to go around. The Lee family stayed riveted to the NASA channel on cable. Nerves dissipated as the shuttle safely reached Earth's orbit. Having already stayed extra days, most of the family scrambled to book flights and parted ways the next day. Ruth said good-bye to her children, her brothers, and her sisters-in-law. She and Charles flew back to Wisconsin.

After four days in orbit, the shuttle returned, landing in California. Ruth was relieved to hear Mark's voice when he called. He told her how bumpy the launch had been, like driving down a gravel road full of ruts. He'd been impressed by how small Earth appeared from space. It took just ninety minutes to go all the way around it in the shuttle. When he returned, the world felt smaller, the human experience both more trivial and more momentous.

During the next eight years Mark would go on three more space missions and would conduct four space walks, spending a total of thirty-three days in orbit and traveling around the earth 517 times. His parents and most of his siblings and extended family were present at every launch.

Especially harrowing for the family was his third mission in 1994, during which Mark performed an untethered space walk while flying an experimental jet-pack outside the shuttle. The walk produced stunning photos of Mark, in a brilliant white suit and gleaming gold-faced helmet, floating above the blue curve of Earth with the fathomless black of space behind him. Some hundred and fifty miles below, his anxious family listened to the NASA feed and waited for word that he was safely back on board the shuttle *Discovery*.

Traveling to space was an experience shared by only a handful of people in human history. Thanks to a certain stubborn determination and decades of focused work, the boy from Wisconsin had fulfilled his extravagant dreams.

＊ ＊ ＊

After the first shuttle launch in 1989, Ruth made her own changes. Her nest had nearly emptied out. For some time, she'd worked part-time doing bookkeeping for her church, but as Christmas approached, Ruth wanted to add funds to the holiday budget. She applied to be a seasonal employee at a busy store that had sprung up two miles away. In many ways, the new Walmart had now become the town center.

After the holidays ended, Ruth's manager asked her to stay. She enjoyed the bustle and energy of the place. It wasn't long before part-time turned to full-time. Ruth worked at Walmart for almost twenty years before retiring at the age of seventy-eight.

Ruth enjoyed chatting with customers, many of whom knew her family. It seemed as if the whole town of Viroqua eagerly watched televised reports of Mark's space travels. Ruth's other children had all worked hard to build successful lives for themselves, too. She couldn't have been prouder of each one.

As time marched on, Ruth acknowledged a truth about life: "You can only depend on change."

Life was more than she might have imagined as a girl sitting in the tops of trees. It had taken her far beyond her beginning at a home for unwed mothers in Sioux Falls, South Dakota. Ruth knew nothing about her conception, but sacrifice and prayers had prevailed against the tragic assault on a sixteen-year-old girl at Scatterwood Lake. Great beauty had risen from ashes.

Redemption had occurred, but something else was on its way, something that Ruth hadn't expected but which would bring her abundant joy. Something that a very old woman had waited for nearly all her life.

Restoration was coming.

Chapter Twenty-One

THOUSANDS OF MILES separated two women who shared the same DNA yet were as good as strangers. The miles would shorten not by their own doing, but by the curiosity of the younger generation.

Brian Lee was a tough and focused soldier, but he had always been close to his mother—and he wasn't afraid to show it. Even as a teenager, after a long day of school, football practice, and bagging groceries at the local market, Brian would stay up late with Ruth to watch Johnny Carson on *The Tonight Show*. With three other children still at home, this was mother and son's chance to connect, to laugh together over a shared pleasure.

Brian had intended to follow Mark into the Air Force Academy. He, too, had earned the rank of Eagle Scout and had excelled in track, football, and wrestling. His grades were also good. But sidelined by poor eyesight, Brian enlisted in the marine corps instead.

Two years later, Brian was accepted by the elite US Military Academy at West Point. He graduated as a second lieutenant; promptly married his high school sweetheart, Teresa; and then began an army career during which he would rise to the rank of lieutenant colonel. Brian earned an MBA from Syracuse University, and with dreams of flying still in his blood, he obtained his private pilot's license.

Brian spent five years working at the Pentagon. When he retired from the army at the age of forty-six, he was hired as an engineer by a defense contractor in Alabama. After years of bouncing around the country, Brian and Teresa and their two children could finally settle down. But Alabama was far from his parents' farm in Wisconsin.

The connection to his mother and father was as ingrained in Brian as rising early, stating the hour by military standards, and driving the precise speed limit at all times. Every day, unless he was overseas on business, Brian called home to check on his parents. When a problem arose within the family, and especially with his mom or dad, Brian couldn't get it off his mind. When Ruth had heart surgery in late 2005, he could think of little else.

It was bitterly cold for a day in the Deep South. Though she was accustomed to harsh Midwest winters, Ruth could not get warm. She huddled on Brian's couch, wrapped in a thick sweater. Charles had gone to bed, and Brian had lit a fire in the fireplace. Ever since her operation four months earlier, Ruth had struggled to shake the chill that settled in her bones.

As was their custom, she and Charles had stopped in Alabama to visit Brian and Teresa on their way back from a two-month "snowbird" trip to Florida. The annual tradition had started eight years earlier, on their fiftieth wedding anniversary. The couple would stay at the same hotel in Cocoa Beach that had hosted them during Mark's launches. Charles relaxed by the pool or dropped coins in the machines at the penny arcade while Ruth played shuffleboard and visited with fellow vacationers.

But after this vacation, in February 2006, Ruth's health issues were very much on Brian's mind. One facet had nagged at him for years. Whenever Brian went to the doctor or had a physical, he'd be asked his family's medical history. His reply was always the same—there was no information on his mom's side. As time went on, that answer bothered him more and more.

Brian had considered discussing this with his mother before but had needed time to deliberate first. He liked to analyze every angle of a situation—it was one of the reasons his employer valued him so much. Now he was ready to broach the subject. In typical Lee fashion, he spoke plainly.

"Mom, have you ever thought about researching your adoption records? Maybe we could find out more about your birth parents." He paused. "Maybe we could get some medical information, for *all* of us."

In the background, a news program played on the TV with the volume low.

"Well, yes." Ruth looked at Brian. The reference to her children swayed her. Ruth would do anything for her family. "But I wouldn't know where to begin."

"I can do some research and see what I can find out," Brian said. "If you say no, I'll drop the subject. But if you say yes, I'll lead the way."

"Okay," Ruth said. "Let's do it."

"Do you know anything besides what you've told me?" Brian knew from Ruth that his birth grandmother had been Dutch and that she'd obviously gotten "in the family way," but that was about it.

"I've never known very much," Ruth said. "The girl's name, my birth mother, was DeYoung or de Jong. . . . I'm not sure how they spelled it. And I have a letter."

"A letter?" Brian was surprised. This was the first he'd heard of it. "From whom?"

"From somebody at the place I was adopted from. They wrote to Mom and Dad when I was just a baby and mentioned my birth mother. Said something about Holland; she was from Holland, I think."

"Where is the letter?" Brian asked.

"Our safe-deposit box. At the bank."

"Wow." For a moment, he tried to imagine what that letter might say. "I'll need a copy of that. And then I can start searching on the computer."

"Okay," Ruth said. "I'll go to the bank and get it when we get home."

That night, after Ruth went to bed, Brian sat staring into the fire for a while, his thoughts flickering like the muted orange flames. *There's no turning back now*, he realized.

He was suddenly more curious than ever.

On Thursday, March 2, Brian arrived home from work and settled in front of his computer. His mother had called from Wisconsin after rereading the letter she'd retrieved from the bank. The letter was written to Brian's grandparents and was from Lutheran Social Services of South Dakota, or LSS. The supervisor of the Lutheran House of Mercy offered the requested information about Ruth's christening. The letter was signed: Miss Bertha Bragstad.

Brian found a website for Lutheran Social Services of South Dakota. He clicked on "Contact Us" and filled out a form with his name, phone number, and e-mail address. There was a space for comments. He kept it short.

I am helping my mother research her birth parents. She was cared for and subsequently adopted from the Lutheran Children's Home Finding Society of SD back in 1929. She would like to know what information is available through telephone or mail/letter request and what other information would require more official request through state/local agencies. Thanks. Brian Lee

The next day, he received a reply. To ensure he wasn't embarking on a wild-goose chase, Brian sent more detailed information—names, dates, and places—to the "post legal adoption specialist" at LSS. He asked if the woman could confirm that Ruth had been adopted through their agency. Were there any records?

The brief answer came the following Monday. The e-mail said that Brian would need to contact the clerk of courts to begin the process of unsealing the adoption records. But yes, it confirmed, Ruth had been adopted through their agency. That's all they could say.

Sitting alone in his office, Brian felt the elation of a detective getting a hit on a long-cold trail. His face broke into a wide grin. He immediately searched for a phone number for the South Dakota Department of Social Services.

One week later he received a petition for release of confidential adoption records, which he forwarded to his contact at LSS. And then he left town for a two-week business trip to his company's Boston offices. He thought about the search often. He wondered what his brothers and sisters would say—he hadn't told them about this mission yet. Would they be glad? Irritated? He was close to all of them, but this was uncharted territory and he couldn't guess their reactions.

On April 19, Ruth received a packet in the mail from LSS containing their waiver of hearing and the court petition. Brian told her to send it on to the South Dakota courts. They were inching ever closer.

The process was straightforward: fill out the correct paperwork, then wait for it to wind its way through the system. Brian was plenty busy with work and family—his two children were finishing up their spring semesters of college. But his mind was never far from the search. If all went well, he was about to collide with a huge piece of his history that he'd always wondered about.

He wanted to be realistic, however. The average life expectancy of someone born early in the twentieth century was some fifty-four years. His own mother was already in her late seventies. Whoever his birth grandparents had been, they were likely long dead. Perhaps they'd had other children, but if so, he'd have to tread carefully. He'd researched reunion stories. It seemed that for every glowing, heartfelt account there was a cautionary one to balance it, a tale of grievances and rejection.

He tried not to hope that somewhere, in a nursing home perhaps, one of his grandparents might still be alive.

Brian knew that he could expect to get at least *some* information. The Lutheran Social Services was a modest operation, but they'd undergone some modernization over the years. At some point, all of their records had been transferred to microfilm.

Even the files from early in the previous century.

On May 22, 2006—the day Ruth turned seventy-seven years old—the signed judge's order arrived in the mail. Brian forwarded it to LSS, along with a check for two hundred dollars. He waited again. Finally, at the end of June, just as Brian and Teresa were preparing to drive to Wisconsin for a wedding, Brian received a short e-mail. It said that the package with the adoption records had been mailed to his mother.

The e-mail concluded with a final, puzzling line: "Just to give you the heads up, the file is about 270 pages."

❋ ❋ ❋

On Wednesday, June 28, a mailman driving on a rural Wisconsin road pulled up to a black mailbox, one that had been propped back up a dozen times over the years after winter snowplows knocked it down. Along with bills and a flier from the local Walmart, he had to struggle to stuff a large manila envelope into the space. The return address was Lutheran Social Services in South Dakota.

Sometime later, Ruth Lee picked up the packet from the dining room table, where Charles had left it after sorting the mail. She ran one hand over the yellow envelope. It was nearly two inches thick, and heavy. The weight felt like an enormous book that had a story to tell—her story.

She laid the package back on the table and called Brian's cell phone. When he picked up, her words tumbled out.

"It came. The package with the adoption papers. It's so big! I don't know why it's so big."

She couldn't imagine why there would be that many pages to a perfectly legal adoption. Was something wrong? Had there been some sort of terrible medical issue?

Brian had been sitting at his desk, reviewing spreadsheets. He stood and paced now, pulse racing. He wished four states didn't separate him from his mother or that package.

"Do you wanna open it, Mom? Or wait until we get there on Saturday?" He and Teresa would be in Wisconsin in three days. He didn't know whether he preferred she wait or not. If he could've borrowed a plane and flown up to his parents' farm that very moment, he would have.

"Well . . . I don't know. Your father says to open it, but I think I'll wait."

"Whatever you decide is fine," Brian said.

Ruth left the package on the dining room table but soon regretted that choice. She passed by it all day long. She tried not looking at it, but that didn't help. It seemed to beckon her. Ruth resisted. The sheer size of the packet intimidated her.

Brian was on his way. He would help her sort it out, deal with whatever was in those pages. She told herself to wait.

After Charles went to bed on Friday night, Ruth's curiosity finally won out. She sat down, tore the flap open, and pulled out an enormous stack of photocopied pages. Flipping through them with unsteady hands, Ruth realized that none of the papers were in order. And there was such a confusing variety.

Official forms.

Legal documents.

A couple of photographs, but the copies were so dark and grainy that she couldn't make out the faces.

And letters. Letter after letter after letter after letter.

Ruth began to read them. Most of them, dozens of them, were from a young girl. A young mother.

My mother, the thought came suddenly. *Writing about a baby named Betty Jane. Writing about me.* Ruth had not heard or thought about that name since her childhood. The unexpected sense of connection pinned Ruth to her seat.

May 29, 1934

Dear Miss Bragstad

I hope you haven't thought I've forgotten you and Betty's birthday. Am so sorry I was unable to get these few lines to you in time. Never the less I do hope she had a happy birthday & enjoyed herself through the day. . . .

If you have heard or seen her please write and tell me. . . .

Ruth realized the date on this letter referred to her fifth birthday. Her birth mother had written a letter five years after her adoption? She picked up another letter.

September 1933

Our crops and all around amount to nothing. We did receive a small potato crop. Outside of that we shall have to buy everything.

Well there are some folks here that don't seem to realize yet we are in the midst of depression. Maybe they will before the close of winter . . .

Have you heard or seen anything of Betty Jane? I think of her often through the day. . . . Hope & pray they will always be able to think highly of her. . . .

Ruth's vision blurred. She blinked her eyes clear, kept paging through.

June 25, 1933.

December 4, 1935.

January 6, 1947.

1947? The year she graduated from high school, leaving the gym in that rare May snowstorm with Charles walking beside her. Her birth mother was still writing letters about her then?

Ruth's hands stilled. She stared at the window, blackened by the night outside and reflecting the harsh light over the table where Ruth sat. Certainty flooded her.

She loved me, with all her heart.

Ruth picked up her cell phone. It took her longer than usual to punch in Brian's number. By the time he answered, both her eyes had filled with tears.

"She never forgot about me, Brian," Ruth said. Her voice trembled. "These letters . . . there are so many letters!"

"Letters? There are letters?"

"Yes, so many. She kept writing for years . . . asking about me. . . ."

Brian felt a hard and painful knot in his throat. His own vision blurred. Whatever he had expected, it wasn't this.

"Does it say who she was, Mom? Did you get her name?"

"Yes." Ruth's gaze dropped to the page in front of her, a type-written timeline of Case No. 359, her case.

"Her name was Minnie."

Chapter Twenty-Two

LATE THE FOLLOWING NIGHT, Brian drove into Viroqua. After a long day on the road, he had dropped Teresa off at her parents', his mind fixed on the package waiting on his mother's table. Never before had he been so tempted to exceed the speed limit, just a little.

Ruth met him at the door of her farmhouse. After the usual greetings with her and Charles, Brian couldn't wait any longer. "Where's the file, Mom?"

"On the table," Ruth said as Charles bade them good night.

Ruth led the way into the dining room. Even after her description of the adoption file, Brian was startled by its thickness. He sat at the oval wooden table, and Ruth pulled up beside him in another chair. Brian began to read.

Some of the documents were hard to decipher, the words barely legible due to light ink and poor copying, especially the letters from young Minnie. But her handwriting was consistent, and it soon became familiar enough for Brian to decipher most of the contents. There were also a handful of letters to and from his grandfather, Rev. Nordsletten, to this House of Mercy where Minnie had stayed. He thought of his grandpa Peder with his quotable sayings and silver coins and tried to imagine him as a young married minister writing to this house, seeking a little girl to join their family.

Then something caught his eye. In the pages titled "child's history," there was a long paragraph under "disposition of case." He stared, leaned in toward the page as if that would give him a different truth.

He read the lines again.

Anger swept over him, hot and swift. Brian was a career soldier. His instinct was to protect, to defend. He had a daughter of his own, a beautiful young woman. He couldn't even imagine someone trying to hurt her.

There was no other way to put it than bluntly. He turned to Ruth.

"Mom," he said, "she was raped."

Ruth stared at Brian, eyebrows raised, lips parted.

"What?"

"That's what it says here. She was, uh . . . " he looked back at the paper. "She had been out with some friends, at a lake, and . . . some strangers accosted her. She was raped. They . . . " He checked the paper. "No, they never caught him."

Ruth flushed with anger. She sat for a few moments, wondering what to do with this startling information, but soon she was practically shaking. That man had done *this*. And however burdensome the fact was, that man was her *father*.

The news cast a distressing pall over their discoveries. Given that the documents stated the man was older than Minnie, he was surely dead by now. Even if they could find his identity, he could no longer be held accountable.

Ruth had lived almost eighty years protected from this truth. Her few imaginings of her parents had been of a young couple who had unintentionally conceived a child. Now she'd been handed the truth—her life had been created through a violent act. Her biological father had done a horrible thing. Ruth couldn't wrap her mind around it. She'd admired her adoptive father to such an enormous extent; it had never occurred to her that her birth father could have been so different. The contrast was staggering. It was impossible to process the tumult of emotions washing over her.

But one thing Ruth knew: it made her mother's love for her all the more remarkable.

※ ※ ※

After Brian arrived back at his in-laws' late that night, his mind raced. Reading the letters had created a deep affection for the young woman he'd never met, his grandmother, who'd loved her baby so much. Yet a powerful rage rose up against *him*, the man who'd fathered that baby. *How could he! My own flesh and blood. . . .*

But another thought kept pushing in. *If he hadn't done that, I wouldn't be here.* Mixed with the emotional conflict, pieces of new information flashed through his mind.

Information that could be used to find out who this Minnie had been.

According to the file, her birthday was November 10, 1911. Her given name was Minka. Her married name had been Disbrow, but there was no way of knowing whether she'd married more than once. She'd had at least one more baby, a girl named Dianna. The letters had stopped in 1947. There had been no new information in almost sixty years.

Too many thoughts swam through his mind. Brian barely slept.

Just after dawn, he pulled on shorts and a T-shirt and walked the half-mile back to his parents' house, breathing deeply of the cool air that was such a relief after Alabama's humidity. In his mother's familiar kitchen, he poured grounds into a paper filter and dumped an entire pot of water into the coffeemaker. It was going to be a long morning. Ruth puttered around the kitchen, preparing to go in to Walmart for a work shift.

Brian spread the contents of the adoption folder on the table. The task energized him. His pen scratched names and dates on the manila envelope. Locations, too, and time frames of where Minka had lived, and when. He arranged all the documents and letters in the correct order and then carefully read the letters again.

Finally, Brian laid his pen on the stack.

He had enough information to go on, enough to find somebody on the Internet. But he was in rural Wisconsin, and his parents had no computer. He would have to go back to his mother-in-law's.

An hour into his Internet search, Brian's excitement drained away. Whoever this Minka had been, there seemed to be no record of her at all. There was nothing in the Social Security death index or the obituaries. Nothing in birth notices for the daughter, Dianna Disbrow. He searched every place that had been listed in the file: South Dakota, North Dakota, Minnesota, Iowa, Rhode Island. He searched WWII records, looking for any mention of Minka's husband, Roy. Nothing.

He leaned back. Stared at the screen. He took off his glasses, rubbed the bridge of his nose. And then Brian thought of something he'd used before to get phone numbers, something much more convenient than a bulky phone book.

Whitepages.com. He put his glasses back on, then pulled up the website.

First and last name: Minka Disbrow. He had no city, state, or zip. He pressed "enter."

One result for Minka Disbrow. A California address. A phone number.

Brian's heart began to hammer. He stared at the name.

He called to Teresa.

"You have to see this," he said. They sat in amazement, staring at the data, realizing what it could mean. Ruth's mother could still be living.

Brian needed to be sure. On the screen, to the side of Minka's name and address, was an option—for a few dollars, he could obtain more details: age, relatives, past addresses, and more. This would allow Brian to back-check earlier addresses and some other information gleaned from the file. He glanced at his wife.

"Do it. You have nothing to lose," Teresa said.

Feeling slightly intrusive, Brian clicked on a link and typed in a credit card number to retrieve more detailed personal information. And there it was.

Minka Disbrow. Birthdate: November 10, 1911. Age: 94 years.

It was her.

* * *

Hours later, Brian's family sat together at the Lee house on the concrete patio next to their garage. Two of Brian's siblings, Deb and Tim, were visiting too, along with their families. The outside table bore the remnants of Sunday dinner, their ritual when they were all together. Tim had grilled bratwurst, and they'd had potato and fruit salads and baked beans. From their seats near the vegetable garden, they could see bright-green stalks of corn and pumpkin vines glowing in the remains of sunlight.

When Ruth rose to clear away the salad bowls and silverware, Brian and Teresa followed.

"We'll help you, Mom," Brian said. They made their way along the worn path to the rear porch. Although the rest of the family didn't know it, the three of them were anxiously waiting for a phone call. Earlier that day Ruth had left a message on an answering machine.

Minka's answering machine.

After Brian had found Minka's number that morning, he and

Teresa had driven to Walmart. He'd gone in, found his mother in the employee break room. He blurted out the news.

"I found your birth mother. She might still be alive."

Once home, Ruth had stared at the phone number Brian had written on the manila envelope. Her nerves flared, suddenly on edge. She knew that Minka, if she were still alive, would welcome this call. But what if she wasn't living? What if Ruth had missed her by mere months? She felt a stab of anxiety.

What if she'd found her birth mother but had already lost her?

She'd swallowed her fear and dialed the number. Ruth couldn't help feeling relieved when the answering machine picked up with a generic greeting. She left a faltering message that she immediately regretted. She wished she'd practiced it a little first.

Ruth, Brian, and Teresa jumped every time the phone rang that day. But the callers were only local friends. Brian thought of the many possibilities. Maybe Minka hadn't gotten the message. Or she was traveling, or visiting family members.

But what if she *had* received the message and hadn't wanted to call back?

Or what if the phone number was outdated, and they hadn't reached Minka Disbrow at all?

Throughout that day, Brian had gone in and out of the house, fiddling with projects. Like his mother, he was unable to sit idly when things needed doing. A section of the Lees' siding had ripped off during a recent storm. Brian climbed up a ladder to repair it. He fitted the white-painted boards back onto the wall above the porch and recaulked the seams, working up a sweat.

Every time he came back in, he spoke quietly to his mother.

"Has she called yet?"

Every time, Ruth shook her head.

They were distracted at dinnertime by the commotion of family arriving. The grill was fired up, the table was laid, drinks were opened. There hadn't been an opportunity for more discussion until now, as Brian and Teresa helped Ruth clean up.

"Mom, do you want to call again?" Brian asked when they were back inside, alone.

Ruth gazed around the kitchen, nodding, not looking at Brian.

"Yes, but let's just get the kitchen cleaned up, and then we can sit down and relax."

Brian did not argue or push.

"Okay. We'll help you. What do you want to do first?"

Together they scrubbed the bowls and silverware, covered leftovers with plastic wrap, wiped the counters. After they'd hung the dish towels back over the stove handle, Brian asked again.

"Do you want to call now?"

Ruth looked out the window. She touched the silver necklace hanging from her neck. She nodded again.

"Yes . . . but let's pick up the lawn chairs and clean up outside."

Teresa glanced at Brian. They followed Ruth outside. Scooping up napkins and paper plates, they tossed them into the fire pit. They straightened chairs as the rest of the family continued chatting next to the fire. Brian had the sense that his mother's nerves could gnaw away the entire evening.

"Mom, do you want me to call her?" he finally asked.

Relief washed over Ruth's face. "Oh, yes . . . would you?"

They entered the screened back porch, out of earshot of the rest of the family. Brian had already sorted through—and rejected—possible ways to begin the conversation.

Hi, I'm wondering if you possibly gave a baby up for adoption in 1929?

No.

Hi, I'm Brian, and my mother is your first child. . . .

No.

Hi, I'm your new grandson. . . .

Um . . . no.

Hi. My name is Brian Lee, and I'm calling from Wisconsin. I've been doing some research on my mother's adoption from 1929, and your name came up. I'm wondering if I may ask you a few questions.

Yes. That was better.

He looked at the envelope where he'd written Minka Disbrow's phone number. He punched in the digits.

Far away in California, the phone began to ring.

✳ ✳ ✳

Minka had stayed home from church that morning, something she rarely did. She'd been especially tired, and one of the preachers she liked to watch would be on the television soon. After lunch, she decided to take a nap.

She heard the phone ring, but that was the beauty of an answering machine—you didn't have to spring from bed like a jack-in-the-box to see who was calling. She let the machine pick up. She drifted off.

Some time later, refreshed, she got up and listened to the message, left by a female caller with a hesitant voice. It made little sense. There was a name and phone number, but the woman had not said much except that she was calling from Wisconsin.

Minka didn't know anyone in Wisconsin, although she supposed that it could be someone she'd met at one of the church conferences she regularly attended.

Minka hauled out her phone book, leafed through the front sections until she found the page listing state area codes. She ran her finger down, found Wisconsin. There were several area codes listed, including the one prefacing the number on the message. Minka considered for a minute, but she still couldn't remember anyone she'd met at a conference who was from Wisconsin.

Minka decided to ignore the message.

When the phone jangled again that afternoon, Minka lifted the receiver.

"Hello?"

There was a stranger on the other end of the line, an amiable fellow with a flat drawl that Minka couldn't quite place. To Minka's astonishment, he started asking probing, personal questions about her life, her history. She asked him to repeat what he'd just said. He did.

He was looking for his mother's birth mother.

The man mentioned South Dakota. He mentioned the House of Mercy.

Minka's heart lurched. But she had not reached ninety-four years of age by being gullible—she'd read magazine articles warning of thieves trying to steal the identities of senior citizens. She cut the man off with some questions of her own.

"What was your mother's given name when she was born?" she asked, doubt thick in her voice.

"Betty Jane."

For a moment, everything stopped. The silver clock ticking on the wall above the phone cradle seemed suddenly very far away.

Although that name had not been absent from her head or her heart for a single day since her daughter's birth, Minka had not heard it spoken in ages. That name had vanished six years earlier with the last person who'd known it—her sister, Jane.

"Where was she born?"

"Sioux Falls, South Dakota."

Minka's pulse thudded in her chest and in her ears. There was only one more question to ask, and her entire body strained toward the only answer she wanted to hear.

"When was she born?"

"May 22, 1929."

Minka had to force her voice into something louder than a whisper.

"I'm the person you're looking for. I'm . . . I'm your mother's birth mother."

And then the man said eight words. One word for each of the nearly eight decades she'd waited to hear them.

"Would you like to speak to Betty Jane?" he asked, and the years began to roll back, with lightning speed. Everything was rolling.

Minka's legs buckled beneath her.

Chapter Twenty-Three

MINKA SANK INTO a dining room chair, placed her left fist on the clear plastic cover she kept over her tablecloth to protect it from spills. She squeezed the phone so hard her wrist hurt, but she didn't notice the pain. She tried to remember to breathe.

A voice came on the line.

"Hello?" An older woman. A stranger. Her darling girl?

"Hello," the voice repeated. "This is your Betty Jane."

Minka would never remember exactly what she said next. For the next minute or so, there was too much commotion in her head and in her heart. She introduced herself as though they had never met. As though she had not spent every day of the last seventy-seven years missing this person.

Minka drank in her daughter's voice. Her mind thudded: *Betty Jane. Betty Jane.*

". . . we have six children," the voice was saying. Minka tried to stay with every word. "Two girls and four boys . . ."

"Six children?" Minka said. Her number of grandchildren had

just doubled. Betty Jane began to list the children's names, their occupations. They were all grown, of course. Minka listened with a kind of numb astonishment to the cascade of details about these people who were her blood.

A business owner. Air Force pilot. Four-time shuttle astronaut. Army. West Point. A teacher. A NASA contractor. Another teacher.

It was too much to take in. NASA . . . West Point . . . educators . . .

Astronaut?

Minka would have to process it all later.

In Wisconsin, the Lee family was in an uproar. After he'd handed the phone to Ruth, Brian had hurried outside to his siblings and father. His usual deliberate way of speaking gave way to obvious excitement.

"Hey, guys," he said, raising his voice. "Guess who Mom's talking to?" He knew they'd never guess. "She's on the phone with her birth mother. In California."

That got their attention. Brian had recently told his siblings that he was looking for their biological grandparents, but he hadn't kept them updated on his progress. Until the last twenty-four hours, he hadn't believed he'd find much.

"She's talking to her right now, on the phone."

Deb stared at him. "No kidding," she said.

"She's still alive?" Charles asked.

"Yes, still alive," Brian replied. "I just called and asked her a bunch of questions—well, actually, I started to, but then *she* grilled *me*—and it's her, all right." He placed both hands on his hips, exhaled. "I can hardly believe it."

Deb stood up and began moving toward the house.

"I'm gonna go back in too," Brian said. "To hear what they're saying."

He and Deb hurried across the grass, up the slight incline to the house. When they entered the screened porch, Teresa looked up and smiled. Ruth sat at the table with a pen and paper that Teresa had fetched. Ruth was scribbling words and numbers down, nodding and saying "Oh!" a lot.

From her California apartment, Minka offered some details about her own life. Her husband, her children, her career. There was simply too much to fit into a few minutes.

Minka could hear voices in the background from time to time. She remembered the first voice over the line. The one she'd thought might be trying to con her.

"Oh, is that my grandson?"

"Yes, Brian. He's the one who found you."

Minka didn't want to hang up. She wanted to grab this moment, hold it fast, and not let go. If she hung up, might she discover this wasn't real? If it was a dream, it was one she didn't want to wake from.

They exchanged addresses. Betty Jane—if she'd said her new name, Minka hadn't heard it—promised to send pictures of her family and childhood pictures of herself. Minka's heart soared.

"Be sure to put my apartment number on the envelope," Minka said repeatedly. There were only four units in her complex, but although her neighbors were dear friends, practically family, Minka couldn't bear the thought of having any delays when the mail came.

She didn't want to wait a single extra second to see her Betty Jane's face, only imagined all these years.

As the conversation wound down, Ruth's family heard her give her address and offer to send photographs. She repeated her phone number. Then Ruth said good-bye. As she hung up the phone, she looked at her family with an astonished smile. Tim and Charles had made their way up and crowded onto the porch.

"What did she say?" Brian asked.

"Well . . . let's see. She grew up in South Dakota. Was married to a World War II pilot, but he died. Had a boy and a girl, but her son died a few years ago. She used to work for a school district as a cook. And then she worked for Kmart. She goes to church. And she takes care of her apartment complex. She sounds very healthy."

"Is she gonna send you pictures?" Teresa asked.

"Oh, yes," Ruth said. "And she wants to see pictures of all you kids and old pictures of me. I'll have to get some out. . . . I'll have to find them and make some copies at the store." She glanced at the paper in front of her. "I wrote her address down. She told me to make sure to include her apartment number. She mentioned that a couple of times. And I told her . . . I said I'd go see her."

"I'll go with you, Mom," Brian said immediately. Ruth looked up at him.

"I want to meet her too," he said. "We'll go together. As soon as we can."

It was clear to them that, although the search was over, this journey was just beginning.

✳　✳　✳

Minka sat at her table, holding the phone for a long time. She barely noticed the tears streaking her cheeks. Her mind brimmed over with all she'd discovered about Betty Jane—her *heart* brimmed over with the knowledge that she'd just *spoken* to her. After all these years, after everything.

This new reality was wonderful. It was like the day when she'd first held her newborn baby, the day the world had shifted, opened, turned from dark to color. Everything had changed. *She'd* changed with it.

At the end of the call had come an impossible wonder. Six weeks earlier, when Minka had prayed her foolish prayer, she'd promised not to interrupt her daughter's life. She'd asked

God for a mere glimpse of Betty Jane, had dared to hope for a photograph.

But now her daughter wanted to meet her.

"We will set something up soon," Ruth had promised.

Minka didn't know how long she sat there, breathing prayers of thanksgiving, reliving the conversation. But finally she turned the phone back on and punched in a familiar number. Every person she had ever told about her firstborn child was now dead. There was just one other living person who knew the secret; but it hadn't been through Minka's telling, and they'd only spoken of it once.

In Oregon, Minka's second-born daughter, Dianna, answered the phone.

"Guess who called me?" Minka blurted out.

"Um . . . Cathy? Gary? Grant?" Dianna's own children seemed the likely answers to such a question.

"Betty Jane."

The name meant nothing to Dianna. She'd never heard it before.

"Who?"

"Betty Jane. My . . . my baby."

Decades earlier, when Dianna was just a teenager, Roy had taken his daughter out to lunch and spilled a slew of family secrets. Perhaps he'd been drinking, perhaps he'd just been trying to cause trouble. With a slight sneer, he'd told Dianna that her mother had had another baby once and had given the child up for adoption.

It was shocking information to a "good girl" whose life revolved around church. Dianna eventually worked up enough courage to ask Minka about it. After a long pause, Minka had merely said that, yes, it was true; but her first daughter had gone to a good home, and that was that. She never offered any additional information.

Now, on the phone, the whole story spilled out. Dianna had never heard her mother this excited.

"They want to come see me, honey, and they want to meet you, too!" Minka's voice danced. "They seem so nice. I can't believe this."

❋ ❋ ❋

Days later, Minka received a thick envelope in her mailbox. As soon as she saw the Wisconsin address, she hurried inside to rip it open.

There was a letter from Ruth, but Minka's eyes jumped to a stack of photographs. Her bent fingers trembled. Tears filled her eyes. At long last, she was looking at her little girl, the one she'd only imagined over the many days and decades.

There was Betty Jane as a laughing, chubby baby. Minka studied every detail of her face and hands, remembering the softness of her skin.

There she was as a girl with bare feet and flowers in her curly hair, squinting into a bright sun, her adoptive parents standing close behind her.

There she was as a beautiful young woman with bare shoulders and dark lipstick, gazing over her shoulder with a serene expression.

There she was with her husband and six growing children, all wearing seventies-style clothing, Ruth's hair going gray.

Minka examined each photo, holding them close so she could take in every detail. One of Ruth's sons looked almost exactly like Dianna's son Grant. Ruth bore a striking resemblance to Minka's own mother, Jennie. Every picture gave testament to a good life, a full one. It was everything she'd ever hoped and prayed that God would give her darling Betty Jane.

This was why she had let her go. So that Betty Jane could have all of this.

But it was hard to make the mental adjustment. After so much time, even though she'd tried to "age" Betty Jane in her mind, Minka realized she'd always expected to get a little girl back.

The wound was still deep. It always would be. As she did every time she thought of giving up her baby, Minka wept.

✷ ✷ ✷

Ten days after their first phone call, Brian composed a long letter to Minka.

Dear Minka,

Wow!!! What a whirlwind 2 week period. My head is still swimming and only can imagine yours is as well. I know Mom has been on an emotional roller coaster, as I'm sure you have been as well. But I must say this research has been a labor of love and based on what I have read in the adoption file, it has all been worth the time spent researching . . .

I must say right up front that you must be an amazing person!! I am glad to be able to call you my Grandmother!!! I am sure it has come as a shock to know that your family multiplied by about two times overnight . . .

Brian gave some background information on his siblings and himself, his wife, and their children. And then . . .

I could probably write and write all day, but then nothing would get in the mail. So I will conclude with this, enclose pictures and begin to plan for a reunion between you, Mom, and Dianna (I hope). I believe we should waste little time in planning this reunion . . .

With love,
Your (new) grandson, Brian

Minka held the letter, read it again. *Oh yes, please come today!* she wanted to say.

Brian's schedule was the busiest, but after another phone conversation, they all settled on a date. Friday, August 18.

Minka now had several weeks to prepare those who loved her for this bombshell. None of her dearest friends or oldest acquaintances knew that Betty Jane existed. Minka's own grandchildren hadn't the slightest idea. She knew she would have a lot of explaining to do. Right now, her lifelong preference for privacy seemed to be coming apart at the seams.

But Betty Jane had come back. Nothing else really mattered.

✳ ✳ ✳

August finally arrived. The day before the reunion, Minka's grandson Grant, a high school teacher and father of twin toddler girls, flew down from Oregon. He came to support his grandmother and to videotape the reunion. His mother, Dianna, would join them after a college class she was taking wrapped up. Grant had been dumbfounded by the news of Ruth's existence and shocked to hear about the rape, as were all of her grandchildren. But they were also thrilled to see their grandmother bursting with joy.

Minka spent Thursday in a whirlwind of baking. She'd learned that Ruth had an insatiable sweet tooth and loved chocolate, lemon, and licorice. Minka made fruit bars in a sturdy metal pan, lemon bars, and snickerdoodles. She bought the biggest tub of red licorice she could find.

That night, Minka didn't sleep much. Her mind raced. She wished that her mother and Jane, even Honus, were still alive to share the excitement. Her fondest dream, the one she'd held since 1929, was about to come true. It may have seemed silly, given her age, but somehow it felt as though Minka was at a new beginning in her life, rather than near the end of it.

By dawn Minka had given up on sleep. She rose, tidied up, set the table. She laid out donuts, cookie balls, and nuts. She cut up watermelon, cantaloupe, and honeydew. Grant, a tall and gentle man, pattered around offering soothing conversation. Together they went outside and cut pink bougainvilleas, which Minka spread on the dining room table between two candles.

Her guests were coming at 9:30 that morning. Minka wanted everything to be perfect.

Twenty-six miles north, at a hotel near the Orange County airport, Ruth hadn't slept much either. She had no memory of her birth mother, hadn't spent the last seventy-seven years missing her or decades writing letters in search of her. But she now knew that Minka had been waiting for her. Ruth realized with wonder that through every memory she could recall in her seventy-seven years, Minka had been thinking of and longing for her.

Lost in her thoughts, Ruth spoke little. Brian went out for coffee and pastries. Teresa moved quietly in the background, getting ready. Ruth sat at the desk in their shared room. She picked up a pen, opened a greeting card. She wished to get this just right, but no words could completely capture what she felt.

> *Dear Mother Minka,*
>
> *The time is finally arrived for us to meet face to face and I can't hardly wait. I know it is an answer to prayers and that's why I am giving you an angel of prayer. The time will go by all too fast, but there will be other times I'm sure. Teresa put together albums for you and Dianna from us. She is such a special daughter-in-law . . . "daughter" as I call her.*
>
> *With love,*
> *Ruth*

Brian came back with donuts and a big bouquet of flowers wrapped in pink cellophane: white daisies and pink roses and delicate lilies.

"I thought you'd like to give these to her," he said.

"Oh, those are beautiful," Ruth said, walking over, touching the wrapper, smelling the roses. "She'll like those." At least, Ruth assumed she would. She really didn't know much about her mother. But who didn't like roses?

It was almost 9. They rode the elevator down. Brian went to get the car. Ruth stood in the lobby of the hotel, looking into the dining room. She could see people inside, eating breakfast and drinking juice. The woman she'd soon meet was like any of these people—a stranger. Ruth wondered if she and Minka looked alike. *If we stood beside each other, would people guess we were mother and daughter?*

Ruth took a deep breath and looked down at her outfit. At least she looked nice for this special day. She'd dressed carefully in white slacks, a solid-colored shirt with fancy embroidery at the neck, a good watch, and jewelry.

At her apartment, Minka puttered around, tidying her guest room and fussing again over the table. She finally dressed, choosing white slacks, a solid-colored shirt with fancy embroidery at the neck, a good watch, and jewelry.

And then she paced and fiddled. She swept the sidewalk and straightened the chairs on her patio. She decided that the light fixture above the garage was not clean enough, so she unlocked the laundry room, retrieved a red shop rag, and then rubbed at the light until all the dust and bits of cobwebs were gone. For good measure, she wiped down the placard displaying the street numbers.

Finally, there was nothing left to do but watch the clock.

And wait.

One final time.

Ruth was quiet on the drive down the freeway. From the driver's seat, Brian commented on how much had changed here, how many buildings had sprung up. Although he'd since traveled the world, Brian hadn't driven these roads in thirty years, not since he'd been stationed at the marine corps base in nearby Twentynine Palms.

He pulled off the freeway, following directions he'd printed from a website. Teresa helped navigate. These coastal roads were twisty, leading down to the ocean, and twice Brian almost made wrong turns. Finally they saw Minka's street. Each of them felt a jolt of adrenaline.

Brian turned the steering wheel, passed an empty dirt lot, saw a driveway. A tall man stood on the concrete, holding a video camera and waving excitedly.

Brian pulled in. And then they saw her—an old woman striding along the walkway toward them, her smile as bright as a prairie sunrise.

Chapter Twenty-Four

THE CAR WAS PULLING IN.

Minka's heart seemed ready to hammer right out of her chest, but her legs carried her forward. Off to the side, she saw Grant already in the driveway with his video camera.

Faces flashed through the car windows. She squinted at the front passenger seat, but Betty Jane was not there. Through the tinted back window, she saw a blaze of white hair. Minka stepped forward, opened the rear door, and was met with a great spray of flowers.

From behind them, she saw her daughter's face, the one she'd seen only in photographs, and heard the voice she'd heard only over the phone.

Everything disappeared behind one longing. To get her daughter into her arms. And then, she was.

Minka's sight blurred. Her voice stuck in her throat. Her arms wrapped tightly around her girl, hands clenched against her back. She'd waited more than 28,000 days for this, her daughter safe in her embrace. The joy of it was boundless.

Betty Jane. Her Betty Jane, returned to her at last. The infant, the little girl, the teenager, the young mother, the grandmother. Here was Betty Jane as a chubby baby, playing dress up, losing her first tooth, putting on lipstick, wearing a wedding dress, expecting her first baby, her fourth, her sixth. Here was Betty Jane as a new grandmother, an empty nester, an elderly woman. Here was everything all at once, a lifetime in a moment.

Minka had missed every second of it but she had waited, she had waited forever and she had kept her promise, she had never forgotten—and now, impossibly, her Betty Jane had been given back to her.

Finally Minka let go a little, pulling back to see that dear face again—a face as lined as her own, and familiar only from recent photographs. But Minka believed she recognized those pale blue eyes. She looked into them, and then her daughter pressed in again and kissed her cheek. Minka managed to speak, her words pushing through a throat thickened by the weight of a million *I love yous* that had never been spoken.

"You're as wonderful . . . as I thought you would be," Minka said.

Her daughter was pressing flowers into her arms, and Teresa came forward for a hug, and then here was Brian, the grandson who had brought her girl home. The moment whirled around Minka; she tried to capture it but was swept away.

She hugged Brian, gripping so tightly that Brian's first, laughing words were, "Not so hard, Grandma!"

Overcome, Minka began to shake and nearly stumbled. Ruth and Brian put their arms around her, steadying her. They turned toward Teresa's camera for a picture.

"The power of God . . . " Minka said, thinking of the decades of prayer that had led to this very moment.

"Wow," Teresa said as she lowered the camera and took in the two women. They didn't look like strangers meeting for the first time. There was something weaving them together, undeniably, right before their eyes.

"How about that," Brian said.

Grant had been videotaping from the moment Minka came down the walkway. He struggled to keep the camera level as he received hugs and gave welcomes. Emotion was thick in his throat too.

Minka leaned her forehead against Ruth's face. They held each other.

"This is something, isn't it," Ruth said. She beamed. "Seventy-seven years."

Minka's thoughts bounced back and forth between those perfect days with her newborn daughter at the House of Mercy to Betty Jane at this moment, back to the day of good-bye and now together again.

"You finally got back into your mother's arms," Minka said, squeezing her daughter. "It took you long enough," she gently teased.

Minka gripped the bouquet in one arm, Ruth in the other.

"What a glorious day," Minka said.

"Yes, it is," Ruth agreed. "Yes, it is."

"Well, come in," Minka said, sighing with contentment. "You might as well get acquainted with your home."

Minka stood at her door and motioned them inside. Brian carried in Ruth's suitcase—she would spend the next three nights here. Minka's apartment was small but comfortable. Most of the furniture was of an older style, but the colors were still bright, the fabric clean. The knickknacks were things that Minka had found "cute" and that she'd had for a long time: a ceramic bird, an angel holding a cluster of pink flowers.

She'd chosen glass tables that allowed the light to shine through and dried flower arrangements that could be kept fresh with dusting. There were plenty of lamps, lots of comfortable chairs in which to sit and read. The décor reminded Brian of his mother's house.

Minka's well-worn Bible sat next to her favorite spot, along with a notebook, a pen, and a book of word puzzles, which she sometimes worked on late into the night. "I like to keep my mind busy," she explained.

As Minka fetched a glass vase for the flowers, Ruth and Brian walked around the living room, looking at photographs displayed on the shelves. Many of them were of Ruth and her children.

"How come our pictures are up already?" Brian asked. "How did we rate that?"

Minka gestured to Ruth. "My daughter." She poked Brian, began to laugh. "It's because of my daughter that you rate!"

Brian and Ruth began to bring out the things they'd brought for Minka. There were albums brimming with Lee family photos. A thick folder holding a complete copy of the adoption records—all 272 pages in protective sleeves, including all of the letters Minka had sent over so many years. The letters had been penned during such turmoil and so long ago that Minka couldn't remember the words they contained.

Ruth presented Minka with the card she'd written at the hotel and the ceramic angel figurine. Then Brian and Teresa gave a second angel figurine and their own card.

Minka,

    This Angel of the Heart is a reminder of how you always carried Ruth in your heart. We feel so lucky and so fortunate to have found you. God was watching over us and guiding us to this very happy day. Brian loves having a Grandma Minka.

                        All our love,
              Brian, Teresa, Annya & Taylor

Minka gazed up at her new grandson and granddaughter-in-law and thanked them.

"And there's more," Teresa said, giving Minka handwritten letters from each of Ruth's six children—letters of love and thanks. Minka matched letters with the faces in the albums, trying to memorize the names. These were her family. Her grandchildren. And their letters to her, offering a warm welcome into their lives, were beyond a treasured gift. She had no words for such joy.

After lunch, visitors arrived at the small apartment. Minka's army of friends had been stunned to discover the elderly woman's secret. They'd marveled at how she beamed talking about her long-lost daughter and the miracle of her return. Minka had invited them to stop by to meet Ruth, with the admonition that they couldn't stay long. They came in droves, bearing gifts of cookies, bread, and soup. Soon Minka's friends were hugging Ruth, Brian, and Teresa like they were their family too.

Minka introduced Ruth with her arm around her daughter's waist.

"This is Ruth!" she announced over and over, then couldn't resist adding, "This is my Betty Jane." Ruth, always comfortable with strangers, smiled and laughed, learning names as she discovered each person's connection to Minka. She repeated tidbits from her biography: where she'd grown up, how many children she had. "Yes, six children!" she'd say with a laugh at the wide eyes.

Minka was unaware that she kept watching Ruth's face, searching it for all she'd missed, memorizing the curve of her cheeks, the sparkle of her eyes.

Brian and Teresa mingled, chatting with Minka's friends, while Grant roamed with his camera. "Yes, it is remarkable, isn't it?" they all said.

Late that afternoon, Grant and Brian drove to the airport to pick up Dianna. She was finishing her bachelor's degree at a college in Oregon and could stay only one night, but she wanted to meet her sister. Before she even got inside the apartment, Minka and Ruth were pulling her in for hugs. "I always wanted a sister," each woman said. Minka was radiant.

Ruth and Dianna were both grandmothers now. But that night, for the first time ever, Minka and her daughters would all sleep under the same roof.

✸   ✸   ✸

On Saturday morning, Minka made breakfast for everyone while grandsons Grant and Brian made repairs to Minka's apartment, sealing a leaky shower and installing a new garbage disposal. Then, after a round of hugs, Grant and Dianna reluctantly left to fly back to Oregon. The rest of the group went for a long drive down the coast.

As the freeway jogged close to the shoreline, Ruth watched the white-capped waves below and listened to her mother talk about her long life in this tropic-like part of the country. Ruth had never been to the Pacific coast before.

They drove past San Onofre, where a massive nuclear generating station clung to the shoreline, a bleached-out local eyesore. They passed Camp Pendleton, where thirty years earlier a young Brian had done rifle training with the marines. Minka talked about one of her volunteer projects, putting together care packages to send to deployed troops. At times, Minka's garage was filled with donated items waiting to be sorted.

Only two months before, Minka had been navigating these freeways herself. But then her "wheels" broke down, and she'd sold her car to a repair shop. At the age of ninety-four, her driving days were finally over.

Already, Minka and Ruth fit together like two halves of a friendship necklace. They patted and fussed over each other. Whereas most people, even with loved ones, come from opposite sides of a conversation to meet in the middle, these two seemed to think and move as one person.

Brian and Teresa noted how alike mother and daughter were—it was uncanny. Minka and Ruth were both hard workers who loved to serve others and always stayed on top of things. They had good instincts and could peg a person immediately. Although both were frugal, they loved to decorate themselves with jewelry. And during overlapping years, Minka had worked at Kmart and Ruth at Walmart. They even dressed alike, with no prior arrangement.

Minka and Brian had instantly settled into a loving banter that would define their relationship. Brian would tease. Minka would cut her eyes at him, then look pointedly at a companion as if to say, *What am I supposed to do with him?* Then she'd throw the teasing right back at him.

It had been twenty-five years since Brian's grandma Lee had died. Teresa's note was correct; he loved having a grandma again.

✳ ✳ ✳

That evening Minka's granddaughter Dawn came to meet the Lees. Having lived with Minka for many years, Dawn thought she knew most everything about her—she'd been stunned to learn of Minka's first child and the story surrounding her conception. But any concerns Dawn might have had for her grandmother vanished within seconds of seeing her. Minka simply glowed. And Dawn adored Ruth immediately.

Minka's longtime friend Charlotte had invited them all to her home, which sat on a cliff overlooking the ocean.

While Dawn and Teresa drove away on a coffee run, Ruth and Brian walked with Minka to her friend's house, savoring the warm evening and the delicious togetherness. Next door to Charlotte's place was Jane's old apartment building. Both sisters had been close to Charlotte, whose name they always pronounced in the German manner, "Shar-LOT."

Minka paused in front of Jane's old driveway.

"This is where Jane lived," she said softly. She glanced at Ruth and Brian. "You would have liked her." Minka's heart still tugged toward this stucco building with the red tile roof. Oh, how she wished that her sister were still here, that she could have met Betty Jane at last.

Teresa and Dawn arrived at Charlotte's with Starbucks beverages, and they all settled on the deck outside, in white chairs covered with bright-blue cushions. Far below, stretching over waves where surfers bobbed in the day's last light, was a historic local pier that at the time of Ruth's birth had been used as a smuggling point for bootleg liquor.

When the air outside cooled, the older women went back indoors. Charlotte and Minka gave Ruth a tour of the expansive home. Then they sat together in the living room to look at photo albums. Charlotte was eager to share stories.

"Minka is a genius with decorations, really," she said. "Every year I asked her to plan my Christmas parties."

"Yes, dinner parties," Minka chimed in. "Sit-down dinners for, oh, forty people."

"Right here?" Ruth asked, gazing around the fancy living room.

"Oh yes, right here," Minka said. "In the early years I helped with the food, too. Did the appetizers and such. But then the parties got too big, so Charlotte hired caterers and I just did the decorations."

"Look at this," Charlotte said, pointing to a photograph of a miniature sailing ship. "She did that. Those were the party favors one year."

"Oh, my, that's beautiful!" Ruth said, bending closer. She touched her fingers to the plastic covering the photo. "Look at those little sails. All that detail."

Minka watched Ruth's hands moving over the album. Her own mother, Jennie, had been gone for nearly fifty years now, but Minka remembered everything about her.

And Ruth's hands were a carbon copy of Jennie's.

"Here's another one," Minka said. "This year," she tapped a picture, "was snowmen. Every year we had a different theme."

"And you made all of it?" Ruth asked, charmed.

"Oh, yes. We'd go to the craft store, months in advance," Minka explained.

"Oh, I love doing crafts," Ruth said. "I would've loved to have helped. One year I helped Teresa decorate her house for the Tour of Homes, when Brian was stationed in Illinois. We had a theme too . . . old-fashioned teddy bears."

"Minka can do anything," Charlotte said. "She sews, and does beautiful flower arrangements—"

"Oh, I love flower arranging too!" Ruth said. "And making pretty things. Every year I decorate our pumpkin stand at the house."

"Sounds like an inherited trait," Charlotte said with a smile.

❊   ❊   ❊

That night Minka stayed up late baking an angel food cake from scratch and cutting up fresh strawberries. Sunday was Teresa's birthday, and Minka realized this would be their first family celebration together.

The following morning, she had Brian pull out the enormous box Minka's grandchildren had dubbed the "bling box," the one holding all of her and Jane's jewelry. After selecting a batch of necklaces, she called Ruth and Teresa into her bedroom.

"Do you like jewelry?" Minka asked. She was pretty sure she knew the answer. They'd been oohing and aahing over one another's accessories for two days.

Ruth stopped, looked at Minka, raised her eyebrows.

"Do I like *jewelry*?" Ruth said emphatically. She looked at the display, moved closer.

The large box was filled with smaller boxes, dozens of them. Each container held clusters of earrings, rings, and necklaces, separated neatly by color. There was jewelry with elephants on it. Copper jewelry. Shell necklaces from Hawaii. Family heirlooms. Dangly earrings. Sparkly watches. Even a person who didn't like jewelry could get caught up looking at the variety.

Ruth happened to have a deep and fervent love of jewelry. Almost as though she'd been born with it.

"I want you each to pick something out," Minka said. "You can have a necklace to take home with you. Whichever you'd like." She pointed to Teresa. "Since you're the birthday girl, you get to pick first."

After careful deliberation, Teresa chose a gold necklace with a single pearl pendant. Then it was Ruth's turn. She ran her fingers over each strand, examined the stones and metals carefully, and decided on a heart with colored stones on it.

In all the excitement, Minka completely forgot that she had another gift for Ruth. Long after her guests departed, Minka would remember the item that was still tucked away in her closet. She would have to wait for another visit to finally give Betty Jane the gift that Jennie had brought back from Holland in 1930—a pair of little wooden shoes for the granddaughter she'd seen only once.

❋ ❋ ❋

The three days of Ruth's stay were stuffed full with time together, from coffee in the morning to late-night talks around the living room. There were no awkward silences or uneasy moments. Mother and daughter were perfectly in sync.

Despite Minka's attempt to capture every moment, Monday came too quickly. She'd tried to slow time before, back in a house for unwed mothers, but then as now, nothing stopped the ticking clock.

Ruth, Brian, and Teresa had noon flights to catch, to Wisconsin and Alabama.

"We will be together again very soon," Ruth said. Her bags were at her feet, and she held Minka's hands. Minka nodded, feeling at peace. God had granted her blessings beyond what she'd asked, and Minka had no doubt that this was not the end.

"We'll get you out to Wisconsin next. You can meet the rest of the family," Teresa said.

"It will happen." Brian's voice was confident.

"I believe it," Minka said. Never had she felt so complete. She'd carried the loss of her child through the many years until it was simply part of her, an ache she lived with through the decades. She'd loved so many people, lost them, worked as hard as the days allowed her. And now she was given new life, amplified.

As Brian carried the luggage to the car, Minka and Ruth walked together to the driveway. The hugging began with Teresa. Next Minka held Brian, the boy after her own heart, the one who had given her the greatest gift of her life, here toward the end of it.

Then Minka turned to her daughter. She was trying to remember to call her "Ruth," but in Minka's heart, she would always be "Betty Jane." The daughter who'd been lost to her and was now found.

"Well, here we are," Minka said, smiling.

"Yes," Ruth said. Their identical blue eyes held each other. "It has been wonderful. So wonderful."

As they hugged, Minka held on. Her throat was tight, but she willed herself not to cry.

"I love you," Minka said, savoring the words, the fact of speaking them, the joy of their being heard. "I am so glad . . ." Her voice caught, but she pushed on. "I'm so glad Brian found me."

"Me too, Grandma," Brian said. He didn't like good-byes, refused to even *say* the word *good-bye*. "We'll see you again soon."

They delayed at the car as long as they could. Brian turned on the engine, rolled down the car windows as Teresa got in front. Ruth settled in the back with her hand out the window. Minka took a few steps away from the car, and they waved, calling out good-byes as Brian backed out of the driveway.

Minka squinted in the sun, watching them drive away. After noticing her daughter turn around for one last look, Minka stood there unmoving for a long time. Then she walked back to her quiet apartment.

The moment Minka stepped in her doorway, the words came.

Now you can forgive him.

She stopped dead in her tracks. She was used to hearing God's voice, to following His direction. And she knew exactly whom He was talking about.

Mack.

She had spent very little of her life thinking about Betty Jane's father. She hadn't harbored hatred or bitterness for the man. She'd decided long ago to focus on what *she* needed to do, what her own responsibilities were. She'd not really connected Mack to the nearly unbearable pain of giving up Betty Jane, the years of grief and loneliness that followed. But now she realized that Mack *had* been responsible, not just for the loss of her innocence but, far worse in her eyes, for the loss of her baby girl.

So for the first time in forever, she thought about the man who had changed everything in a few minutes. Maybe afterward he'd straightened himself out, had a family, regretted that hot August afternoon. Maybe Ruth had other siblings somewhere. There was no way of knowing.

For a moment, Minka imagined Mack as an old man on a May morning in 1989, watching the shuttle *Atlantis* blazing across his television screen as it headed to space. Had he ever imagined that his own grandson was on board?

Likely not. It was a thing beyond imagining.

Okay, Lord, Minka prayed, *I forgive him.* And she felt the weight and sorrow of the last seventy-seven years lifting from her body, from her very soul. This was the wonder that only God could bring. He gave the forgiveness itself, the peace that covered the offense, and the healing that swept it away.

✳ ✳ ✳

In the car, Ruth and Brian and Teresa felt as if they were pulling against a taut line that sought to draw them back.

"That was better than I could have ever hoped," Brian said, thinking of the reunions he'd read about on websites and in news articles. This weekend hadn't unfolded like any of those stories. They weren't feeling their way around the edges of new relationships. It was as though they'd grown up together but had been busy lately. As though it had simply been too long between visits.

If brought into a room together, they would have all agreed, including Grant, Dianna, and Dawn, that from their first moments together, each had felt something magical and mysterious occurring.

Early in one century, a mother had given up her daughter. Early in the next century, she'd gotten her back. But this was not a group of strangers. They never had been.

They were family.

This was home.

Chapter Twenty-Five

RUTH WAS BEHIND the wheel, alone, when the road and sunshine disappeared.

She'd been driving along the open countryside of Highway 14, coming home from the airport in Madison with thoughts of her just-completed visit to see Mark and his family. She was wearing a pair of earrings that Minka had given her—stones in a gold setting—and a cross necklace she'd bought to match.

As she came down a hill near Readstown, she blacked out. Her car dropped into a ditch, hit a culvert, and launched into a dry creek bed.

She came to, disoriented and holding the steering wheel. As a passing motorist called for an ambulance, Ruth found her cell phone and called Charles to tell him she was okay and not to worry, but to come and help her.

The news shook up the entire family, Minka especially. The minute Minka heard the news, she marshaled her prayer partners and took to her own knees. She did not sleep easy until it was clear that Ruth would be okay. They learned later that Ruth's episode was due to a new mix of blood pressure medication. Minka felt sure she couldn't have survived losing Betty Jane just seven months after getting her back.

But Minka didn't believe God had returned Betty Jane only to take her again so quickly. Especially not with a birthday party to attend.

Minka had missed all seventy-seven of her daughter's birthdays. She was not *about* to miss the next one.

In May 2007, the Lee siblings chipped in to buy Minka a plane ticket to Wisconsin. She flew into the small airport in Madison. Brian arranged for Dawn to come, too, to help Minka navigate changing planes at the Chicago airport.

Minka couldn't wait to see her daughter again, to see where she'd lived since her junior year of high school, to become even more deeply a part of her life.

Their August reunion had opened up Minka's world in so many ways. Shortly after Ruth's visit, Minka was invited to speak at a banquet for a local crisis pregnancy center, and the appearance led to her volunteering at the center every week—a work she was determined to continue until she could no longer move. Every Monday now, she went to the center to pray for the frightened young women who came through the clinic, girls whose pain she knew too well. Minka also made it her mission to support and encourage the director of the center, whose competence and kindness reminded her so much of Miss Bragstad.

Viroqua was bucolic, all rolling farmland, blue skies, and puffy, white clouds. It was much cooler than Southern California, but Minka was too busy to notice the chill.

First she met Charles, Ruth's mate of almost sixty years, who mildly quipped that it was interesting to have a mother-in-law again after nearly five decades without one. Minka liked him immediately.

Ruth helped Minka get settled into an upstairs guest room, the biggest and most comfortable one, where the morning's first sunlight fell brightly on hand-braided rag rugs. Being in Betty Jane's home was strange and wonderful. All these years when Minka had tried to imagine her girl moving throughout her day, she'd had to picture her in an unknown kitchen, living room, or garden.

Now she walked through the spaces that had sheltered Betty Jane for so long, the rooms that had watched over her daughter's family. She brushed her hand along the railing of the stairs, thinking of the years her daughter had walked these steps, the small children who'd charged up and down them. She studied paintings on the wall, wondering when they had been chosen. She gazed out the window at the views her daughter had taken in for decades.

These were Betty Jane's things.

She felt a pang at the thought of all the grandchildren she had not rocked to sleep here, the drowsy warmth that had not filled her lap, the tousled hair she had not smoothed. There had been so many children's secrets that had not been whispered in her ears. So many Christmases and birthdays and snowfalls she had not witnessed.

She pushed the sad thoughts aside. All a person ever had was the now, and her now was filled with joy.

And then her grandchildren came to meet her. Here was Deb, the oldest and shortest of Ruth's children, who kept busy with church committees, her small business, and gardening. Deb marveled at her grandmother's height and her firm grip.

Here was Mark, the famous grandson who'd traveled more than thirteen million miles in space, and his two cherubic, curly-headed boys. Minka told him proudly that her husband had been a pilot too.

Here was Tim, a middle-school teacher, and his two boys. He'd come to meet Minka straight from a track meet, where he'd done double duty as coach and official. Tim found it poignant, in light of his new grandmother's strong faith, that her daughter had been adopted by a minister.

She met compassionate, free-spirited Carrie, a special-education teacher who loved to read.

Jay, who lived in Texas, was the only grandchild not there. But Minka had met him a few months earlier when he'd flown to California and stayed in her home for a weekend. They'd ordered Chinese takeout, gone to a farmers' market a few blocks from Minka's apartment, attended church together.

For Minka, who had always been bothered by her own lack of education, it was particularly satisfying that all six of Ruth's children had earned college degrees, four of them advanced. Minka recognized bits of herself in each grandchild.

Like Minka, Ruth's children were determined. They liked privacy but were generous with their time and thrived on doing things for others. Several of them loved tending to plants. Above all, perhaps, they were hard workers. As she took in their faces, heard them joke with each other and share family stories with her, as she saw how the house was still their home even as they reached middle age, Minka's heart felt as if it might swell too large.

It almost hurt to love this much. This family, *her* family, was more than she had dared to hope for.

In all the decades she had spent wondering about Betty Jane's family, imagining what they were like or what they'd think of *her*, Minka could not have dreamed up such a loving welcome. The Lee family enfolded her as though she'd always been a part of them.

✳ ✳ ✳

As Minka had done in California, Ruth arranged an open house. Deb, Teresa, and Tim's wife, Beth, helped Ruth clean house, cut up fruit, bake cookies. They set the table with plates and napkins in Minka's favorite bright yellow, laid out photo albums of their families and of the first California reunion. Friends came by the carload to meet this birth mother, amazed that she didn't look anything close to ninety-five. Guests flipped through the notebook holding the papers from the adoption file, perusing the old documents.

Ruth took Minka to meet her coworkers at Walmart. She had not yet returned to work after her March accident, but her friends there knew about the previous year's reunion with Minka. When the two women entered the store, they were surrounded by people eager to meet this mother of such monumental faith.

On Saturday, the family drove to French Island in LaCrosse to attend the Deke Slayton Airfest. Mark would be presenting that year's Distinguished Wisconsin Aviator Award, and his family was treated to seats in the VIP tent. They watched as a biplane and a helicopter performed tricks, diving and leaving a trail of smoke behind them. They saw the Blue Angels, the navy's elite stunt team, fly four blue-and-yellow Hornets in impossibly tight formation against a cloudy sky.

Minka watched her grandson, the hometown hero so comfortable in the spotlight, as he shook hands and patted backs and chatted with spectators and dignitaries and old friends.

That night the Lees had a family picnic at the farm, just like the evening when Ruth had first called Minka, less than a year earlier. They ate barbecue, beans and salads, and a lemon pie baked for Minka by Teresa's mother. There were more stories and laughter and joking. Minka took in how her new son-in-law, Charles, seemed to be the steadying force of the family, focused and unwavering in his work around the farm. He and Ruth appeared quite different in personality, but they were the timeless example of how opposites worked well together. Brian gave Minka further insight into his parents' relationship, telling stories that made everyone laugh.

"One time Dad was making something in the kitchen and ran

out of vanilla extract," Brian said. "He asked Mom, 'Ruthie, do we have any more vanilla?'

"After thinking a minute, she said, 'Oh yes, we bought some in Mexico back in 1986 when we visited Brian and Teresa after Taylor was born. I know we have it. I'll look in the basement for it.'

"Dad replied, 'Oh, we don't have that. It's been much too long, and it was probably thrown out.'"

The room was alive with chuckles from the Lee children and grandchildren, who knew exactly where this story was going.

"Now the gauntlet was thrown down," Brian said with a laugh. Charles stood off to the side, arms crossed at his chest, shaking his head. Minka caught a slight grin on his lips.

"So Mom marched downstairs and, within a few minutes, surfaced with the bottle of vanilla they bought in Mexico in 1986."

"That's our parents," someone said from across the room.

Minka reveled in the stories, the effortless way the family interacted, and the love woven through it all.

✳ ✳ ✳

Sunday dawned balmy and clear. Minka and Ruth woke early and ate breakfast together, then crossed the street and walked to church along the road's shoulder. Immanuel Lutheran was the same congregation where Peder Nordsletten had come to minister in 1945—Ruth had attended the church ever since. For the last thirty-eight years, the church had used this building, located just 175 yards from Ruth's front door.

Two days later, on May 22, 2007, a year to the day after Minka had prayed her unreasonable prayer, she sat in a restaurant in Wisconsin with Betty Jane in the chair to her right. Her new family surrounded the large tables, which had been pushed together to fit everyone.

There was a cake for Ruth. Minka finally watched her daughter blow out her birthday candles and make a wish for the future. Silverware clinked and voices rose in laughter and light shone off water glasses as they were raised to lips. The scene was simple and ordinary and perfect. Waiting had been worth it. Her daughter had been worth it.

There was one more important visit to make before Minka returned home. On an overcast morning, Charles drove Minka and his wife to Viroqua Cemetery, where Ruth's parents were buried. It was a spacious park in the countryside, ringed by evergreens. As Charles and Ruth bent to pull a few weeds, Minka gazed at the double headstone.

Olava Nordsletten, 1884–1960. Peder Nordsletten, 1886–1974.

Over the years, Minka had tried to picture this couple a thousand times. In the photographs Ruth had since shown her, they looked older than Minka had imagined, with serious but kind faces. So many times she'd wished to trade places with them. She'd spent long nights aching to hold Betty Jane on her lap, to brush her hair, to kiss her good night. But Minka was abundantly grateful—this couple had been as good to her precious Betty Jane as she could have wished.

Watching her white-haired daughter brush dirt off their headstones, Minka felt an eternal link to these people. Minka had given Betty Jane life. The Nordslettens had given her a wonderful home and a faith-filled heritage.

Someday we will meet in heaven, and I will thank you. I will thank you for loving her. I will thank you for teaching her about God, for showing her how to live a good life. I'll thank you for being kind, for raising her to be a thoughtful and giving person.

Minka would soon say good-bye once again, to fly home to California. The farewell would be hard but joy filled. After nearly eight decades apart, she and her Betty J.—the "sweetest little girl in the world"—had been reunited. Nothing could ever really separate them again.

❋ ❋ ❋

The century before, in a wooden church on a windswept prairie, a young Dutch girl heard the Reverend Kraushaar read ancient words from a German Bible. She had understood the words from the book of Job, about God giving and taking. But she couldn't have guessed how thoroughly those words would come true in her own life, or how great the cost of their fulfillment would be. She couldn't have known that a few years later, on a blistering day by a lake, she would be split into two pieces, a tear that would not be mended until she'd reached the other end of her life.

How could she understand it then—that one of her greatest blessings would come only through her greatest wound? Or that her faith, whose seeds were even then being planted in a stubborn, curly-headed farm girl, would sustain her through more earthly days than most humans were granted?

Der HERR hat's gegeben, der HERR hat's genommen;
der Name des HERRN sei gelobt.

In her own life, the Lord had taken first.
And then, a lifetime later, the Lord had given back.
Blessed is the name of the Lord.

Reunited: Author's Note

WHEN GRANDMA PRAYED her birthday prayer for Betty Jane in May 2006, my first son was only five weeks old. I was shocked a couple of months later when my brother Grant called to tell me that Grandma had found her long-lost daughter—someone we hadn't even known existed. He and my mother, Dianna, were preparing to fly to California for the reunion.

Often, while nursing my son, I'd try to imagine having to give him up, an agony I now knew Grandma had endured. The idea was so unbearable, so inconceivable, that it caused me to weep every time I thought about it.

As thrilled as I was that Grandma had finally gotten her daughter back, I was living in the sleep-deprived fog that accompanies the first months of motherhood. During the next few years, I enjoyed getting occasional updates about their relationship, but my life was too consumed by babies and toddlers for me to pay attention to much outside my own home in Oregon.

But Brian Lee and I started exchanging regular e-mails, and he and Teresa—the brand-new cousins we'd never met—began send-ing yearly Christmas presents to my boys and to Grant's twin girls.

As Grandma was celebrating her one hundredth birthday in 2011, an Associated Press article about her reunion story went viral. Brian and I wrote to each other, discussing how crazy all the attention was. He mentioned that this story would make a great book.

Early in 2012, with the blessing of Brian, Grandma, and Ruth, I began researching and writing *The Waiting*.

As the months rolled by, Brian and I began talking regularly by phone and video chat. We texted constantly. Although we'd never met in person, in time he became like my third brother. He gave me a hard time. I called him a variety of pet names. Typical family stuff.

This past November, we finally met. Brian, Teresa, Ruth, and I flew to Southern California to meet with Grandma and a crew from Tyndale, our publisher, to sit for interviews and photographs. On that day, Stephen Vosloo took the book's exquisite cover por-trait of Grandma holding the picture of Betty Jane that she'd car-ried so long.

By this point, I'd been writing about Betty Jane for nearly two years. I'd read hundreds of pages of letters Grandma had written about her baby. I'd worked on scenes depicting those agonizing moments when she gave up Betty Jane, as well as stories about Grandma crying into her pillow during all the years that she kept her memories locked deep in her heart. Every day as I wrote, I looked at a copy of the photo of Grandma and her baby, which I'd pinned above my computer.

And now I was going to meet Betty Jane, at last.

Walking around the corner into the lobby of Grandma's church, where Ruth and Brian waited, was a surreal experience. There stood "Betty Jane," white-haired and smiling and *little*! (Evidently only some of us got those oversized DeYoung genes.)

I'm fairly stoic, and it was a bit awkward to have cameras there, but tears filled my eyes as I hugged Ruth tightly. Hugging Brian was like greeting one of my closest friends whom I hadn't seen in a while.

Over the next few days I got to watch Grandma and Ruth and Brian together, and it was one of the biggest treats of my life. You would have thought Grandma and Brian had known each other forever—their nonstop clever banter delighted Grandma to no end.

And I'd never seen two people interact the way Grandma and Ruth did—like the closest of sisters but with zero friction. Almost every time we got together, without planning to, they dressed alike, right down to their beloved "bling." They patted each other and took care of each other and kept track of each other's handbags and fussed over each other in exactly the right measure.

My mother says that there was always a bit of sadness around Grandma, which is gone now. We agree that we've never seen her happier.

Since that visit I've communicated with all of Ruth's children by e-mail and have spoken to Mark and Jay on the phone. Brian and I continue to antagonize each other nearly daily. And Ruth and I stay in contact. She prays for me when I'm sick. When the temperatures in Wisconsin get too bitterly cold, I text to make sure she's staying warm.

Long before we knew anything about "Betty Jane" or my grandma's painful past, my brothers and I agreed that our strong, tireless, selfless grandmother was the most extraordinary person we'd ever known. It is no surprise to us that her first daughter, and that daughter's children, are extraordinary as well.

✳ ✳ ✳

In the years since their first reunion, my grandma and the Lees have slipped seamlessly into the close relationships typical of any loving family whose members live far apart. Brian calls Grandma every Wednesday to chat.

"This is Lieutenant Colonel Lee," he'll say, "reporting in to higher headquarters."

"It's about time!" Grandma says triumphantly.

He has also become a sort of extra caretaker for her. During one of her visits to his home in Huntsville, Alabama, Brian noticed that Grandma's military dependent ID card carried an expiration date. He took her to his local garrison and had her card updated to an "indefinite renewal" status.

Grandma visits her family all around the country—she flies to Portland to see us, to Huntsville to visit Brian. Though she can't make up for all the years she didn't know six of her grandchildren and their families, she's made it a point to be at some of the key events in their lives. She flew to Houston when Jay had a baby baptized at his Lutheran church, and to Georgia when Brian's son graduated from college and was commissioned into the army.

In the years following the reunion, my family noticed an intriguing phenomenon. As Grandma approached her hundredth birthday, she seemed to be aging *backward*. Her volunteer activities continued apace. She traveled to Nashville to attend church conferences.

For her centennial birthday celebration, Jay and Brian flew to California to surprise her. The Piedmont School District in Oakland, which is still paying for all her health care, sent a representative more than four hundred miles south to congratulate her. (I couldn't help but wonder if they wanted to make sure she was still really here!) The following spring, Ruth and Grandma flew to Brian's house to celebrate their birthdays together—Grandma's recent one hundredth, and Ruth's upcoming eighty-third.

In fall 2013, just before Grandma turned 102, she and my cousin Dawn flew to Georgia to celebrate Brian's son's wedding with the extended Lee family. Shortly before taking that trip,

Grandma had joined a local gym with plans to work out several times a week. She told me, "I want to keep up my strength." During her first visit, she rode the exercise bike for fifteen minutes. "It was hard," she said, "but I just kept my mind on something else." She continues to manage her little apartment complex too.

Last year when Grandma was here in Oregon for a visit, I went by my mom's apartment to pick her up. I noticed Grandma wasn't wearing her eyeglasses, and I asked her where they were.

"Oh, I don't need those anymore," she said. "My vision has gotten better—I can see fine now. When I wear the glasses, it's just to cover the bags under my eyes."

It seems fitting that Grandma's sight is better today than it's been in years. After seeing so much of the hardness of life, she now savors each glimpse of its beauty.

Afterword

WHEN I WAS BORN IN NOVEMBER 1970, Grandma was nearly sixty years old. In my earliest memories of her, she already seemed old. I never tried to imagine her as anything else. But once I became immersed in this book project, I realized that I had to bring her to life at every age. And so, for the first time in my life, I sat with her for hours, asking questions and then listening as she reached back through time to grasp scenes from a world long disappeared.

Cooking apples on the back burner of Uncle's cookstove until the fruit began to dance, soft and hot and ready to eat. Listening to snow squeak under her boots as she walked miles to school in the bitter cold, squinting in sun that glared so brightly off the snowdrifts it made her eyes water. Climbing into the dairy's towering wooden silo to tramp down oats during summer afternoons, chaff swirling in the stifling air.

The cascade of details uncovered an entire life, more than just the years I'd witnessed. Now, I saw the stubborn, curly-haired little girl who battled the same shyness I felt in childhood, and then the innocent teenager, grieving the loss of a baby she could not keep. I saw a hardworking young woman coming into her own while the world around her spun into the chaos of war. I saw the newlywed who tried to hold on to her dreams and her handsome husband, as both came apart in her hands, and then the single mother, working hard while harboring age-old regret over all that she couldn't give her children.

The more I learned, the more I couldn't wait to share Grandma's story through this book. The publishing team and I worked at a blistering pace for six months, racing against a clock that I was convinced still had plenty of time left on it, even as Grandma celebrated her 102nd birthday. The book's hardcover release was set for May 6, 2014.

That April, I received a package from Tyndale House Publishers containing my first copy of *The Waiting*. My hands shook as I opened the envelope. Tears filled my eyes. The book was more beautiful than I'd imagined, a worthy tribute to the most extraordinary person I'd ever known, my dear grandma. Every hour I'd labored over the story, for more than two long years, had been spent to honor her.

Two weeks later, I boarded a plane to California with that copy of *The Waiting* tucked in an overnight bag at my feet. Grandma, Ruth, Brian, and I were being interviewed by *Today* show contributing correspondent Jenna Bush Hager, a segment scheduled to be aired May 9, the Friday before Mother's Day. Grandma hadn't seen the actual book yet; we wanted to keep everything a surprise. When I'd given her the manuscript to review, I'd purposely left out the chapters covering Ruth's childhood. I wanted to save them, because I knew she'd savor every detail they contained, each little glimpse into the life she hadn't been able to share with her daughter.

I met the Lees at John Wayne Airport in Orange County, and we all drove to Grandma's apartment. Grandma greeted Ruth and me at the door with tight hugs, but before Brian and his wife, Teresa, made it into the apartment, Grandma had sunk back into her favorite chair. She looked thinner than usual and was wearing a thick sweater even though the day was warm. Seeing her this way was startling.

After a few minutes, I knelt beside Grandma's chair and pulled out the book. She gripped it in her strong hands, passing her crooked fingers over the photo of her and Betty Jane on the cover. I showed her the dedication page and the beautiful photo insert. I flipped to the acknowledgments, read them out loud. She was most satisfied by my final thank-you: *To God, whose book this really is.* "Yes, that's right!" she said, nodding firmly.

Over the next few days, during huddled conversations with other family members, I pieced together the grim details that Grandma had only reluctantly doled out. Doctors had recently discovered a mass in her throat and had scheduled an MRI for later that week. She was having difficulty eating.

"That's the problem," I insisted. "She isn't getting enough nutrients." So we fetched chicken from her favorite Chinese restaurant, cut it into small pieces, and hovered near her while she ate. Just five months earlier, as I'd watched Grandma pedal away on a bike at the gym, she'd seemed invincible. *She's going to be in the news,* I'd thought, *for living to at least 115.* Now doubt crept in.

Grandma rallied for the television interview, which was taped in a sunny hotel room a few blocks from her home. The "uneducated" (as she still referred to herself) former milkmaid wasn't nervous being interviewed by the daughter and granddaughter of former US presidents—she took it in stride. When the crew headed outside to get footage of Grandma and Ruth strolling arm in arm near the beach, the cameraman had to ask the two women to retrace their steps because Grandma had been charging along too quickly. All of us watching from the sidelines couldn't help but smile.

Still, when we got back to Grandma's apartment, we could see how much energy the day had cost her. As we prepared to fly home the next day, we were all worried. Grandma was still living alone. I couldn't help wondering, *Once we are gone, who will make sure she gets enough to eat?* I wanted desperately to believe her vitality could be restored with just a little more food.

Two weeks later, when the TV segment aired, we urged Grandma to leave her apartment "just until the media attention dies down." We didn't want her to be inundated with phone calls. She packed a small bag and headed to Dawn's, where she'd long had her own room. None of us knew that she'd never see her apartment again.

Her tumor grew. As usual, Grandma refused to complain, even when swallowing became more painful and meals were reduced to protein shakes and fruit juice. She said she was willing to undergo treatment, even something as intrusive and painful as chemotherapy or a feeding tube. At heart she was still the little Dutch girl with the inexhaustible spirit. There were more doctor visits, but when you're 102, medical options are nonexistent. Even a biopsy was out of the question.

Within days, Grandma could no longer walk unassisted. Friends stopped by for short visits, and Grandma taped a video message for members of her beloved church. Dawn's family provided gentle, around-the-clock care, postponing work assignments and rearranging school schedules. The rest of us checked in often, getting updates from Dawn when Grandma was too tired to come to the phone. From Wisconsin, Ruth worried and prayed. She wanted to fly out to see her mother again, but the April trip had been physically hard on her; she was suffering from painful edema that her doctor was still trying to reduce with medication. Ruth spoke to Grandma as often as she could.

"Are you sleeping well?" she'd ask. "Have you seen the doctor lately? Did he have any news? I wish I could come see you. Make sure you get enough rest. I love you."

"Oh, I'm doing okay; I'm just a little tired," Grandma would reply. "I've been able to drink some new juice that Dawn bought—it's cranberry lemonade. My pastor came by for a nice visit. I love you, too, honey."

Dawn called us cousins in early June. "Come," she advised. "Do it sooner rather than later." My brothers and Brian and I booked flights immediately.

Inconceivably, Grandma's journey was near its end.

When we arrived at Dawn's house, we found Grandma tucked into a recliner near a tall window, where bright sunlight filtered through the blinds. Even in a big, fluffy robe she looked smaller than ever. She was too tired to bother with lipstick or her cherished bling, but her eyes were clear, eager to see us. In one hand she clasped a small "prayer stone" with a cross etched into it, a recent gift from Teresa.

We took turns sitting on the floor at her feet, holding her hands, wrapping the sadness in small talk. At one point, after my brother Gary fled outside because he could not contain his tears, Grandma noticed his absence and asked where he was. We made excuses, said he'd had to take a phone call, but Grandma's mind was as sharp as ever. "My sweet Gary," she said softly with a sigh.

The following day we gathered to say good-bye to her (words I can scarcely type, all these months later). Each of us knew that her extravagantly long life had been a rare gift. We were grateful that she hadn't had to suffer through a long illness, that her memory would remain undimmed to the end. But we couldn't help longing for more time.

Grandma was too weak to get out of bed, so we bunched up around her. I lay across one end of the bed, patting her feet through the covers. We tried to chat, tried to smile brightly despite the heartache.

Grandma had something on her mind.

"I'm sorry I couldn't bake cookies for you," she said hoarsely, with obvious effort. Speaking took what little strength she had left. "I wanted to make you some snickerdoodles."

We smiled more brightly. I patted more vigorously.

"I found a lady who makes cookies," Grandma continued. "You can give her the money for ingredients, and she'll bake things. So I want to give her some money, and she can make cookies for you."

We came undone. All five of us grandchildren—grown men and women with half of our own lives behind us—began weeping. Grandma looked around the room, at the tears flowing down our cheeks. "Why are you all crying?" she asked softly.

But she knew; of course she knew. The room was filled with the knowing. This was our final farewell, and all our love for her, enough love to move a thousand mountains, wasn't enough to keep her here.

We each had a private moment with her. I held her face, kissed it over and over. I told her I loved her, that I'd see her again someday.

Less than a week later, shortly after midnight on June 16, 2014, with Dawn's family surrounding her, Grandma passed quietly into heaven. The prayer stone that Teresa had given her was still in her hand, a symbol of the eight years she'd been granted with her Betty Jane's family. In the days that followed, all of her belongings were given to charity, per Grandma's instructions, except for a few keepsakes each of us chose.

The memorial service was held at Grandma's home church in California, where she'd become such a beloved mentor that a life-size painting of her hangs in the lobby. Brian Lee and I wrote the eulogy, both sides of her family now linked forever. When the pastor invited people to the microphone to share memories of Grandma, they came one after another, telling stories that all had the same theme: This woman loved God, and she loved people, and she lived to serve both.

It was immensely hard for her family to grasp that she was gone—it still is. For some of us, she was our chief matriarch all our lives, her presence as solid and certain as the daily sunrise, and we could not conceive of a world without her. One day, overcome with tears in public, I fled to the nearest bathroom to sob in a stall. I was only able to regain composure by reminding myself, *You are Minka's granddaughter. Her blood is in your veins. You have the strength to handle this, to handle anything.*

The Lees had enjoyed eight precious years with her—years during which her love for them, nurtured in secret for so long, was met by their newfound but deep affection for her. It had been fifty-two years since Ruth had said good-bye to her adoptive mother, and now she was caught off guard by the intensity of this fresh grief. The previous fall, when we'd done the photo shoot in California, Ruth and Minka had shopped together for holiday decorations. They'd had so much fun picking out ceramic turkeys and placemats printed with pumpkins, and they'd fixed Grandma's table for Thanksgiving early. Now Ruth could hardly bear the thought that all of Grandma's pretty treasures, cultivated over decades and displayed with such care in her tidy apartment, would never again be arranged by her beautiful hands.

Ruth has found solace, partly, through this book. As readers in Wisconsin spread the word, requests began to come in for Ruth to appear at reading clubs and women's groups to share her reflections. Ruth continues to go to them all, to bookstores and living rooms and church halls, carrying with her the entire adoption file—letters and documents and photographs that she's carefully laminated. She talks about Minka, their reunion and years together, and the remembering comforts her heart.

And it comforts all of us to see the reactions to Grandma's

story. Strangers send e-mails, write reviews, and post comments on the Internet. They mention they cried over the book. They say they've fallen in love with Minka and are moved by her life— moved to love, to act, to forgive. Each tribute, each heart that has been touched, bears witness to the influence that one ordinary person can have when he or she chooses to live with integrity, generosity, and love.

As for me, I now often accessorize with some of Grandma's precious "bling." I've never worn much jewelry, but I love wearing her pieces, feeling linked to her in that small way. And with the rest of the family's blessing, I brought home the one thing of hers I always wanted—one of the paintings she'd done in Oakland so many years ago. It hung on her living-room wall for forty years. Now I look at it every day.

The painting is of a thatched-roof cottage near a river. The water rushes past, rough, but the house is sturdy on the bank above—it's not going anywhere. Grandma, who always loved her bright colors, had painted splashes of vivid orange on the shutters and near the roof. A formidable wall encloses the yard, but there is an archway built into it, with the door flung wide open and a stone pathway leading right through.

Everyone is invited in.

She's thrown open the gates on her messy, beautiful story, with its heartaches and triumphs, and she inspires us all to find our own courage and hope, and above all, faith.

May we each live a tale that needs to be told.

May we never stop with the telling.

About The Waiting:
Bringing the Story to Life

You may be wondering: how does a person write a book that contains *so* many details from events that happened as many as one hundred years ago?

Beginning in early 2012, I exchanged dozens of pages of Q&As with Grandma and conducted hours of audio interviews with her. She proved to have an amazing memory (a trait she passed on to both of her daughters). Every time she supplied a story or detail from her childhood that I could check—such as the distance between two farms or the name of a neighbor—I found that she had been incredibly accurate.

Of course, I did double-check everything. A historical project like this requires a huge amount of research, and during the last two years I spent countless evenings and weekends tucked away in the library (away from my rampaging little boys), looking up obscure facts and writing scenes until the library staff turned out the lights. Any place in the narrative where I mention what the weather was like on a particular day, or describe the garments someone wore or the medicine they took, or what a building looked like, or what kind of birds were in the air or plants were on the ground, you can be sure that it was all researched.

In April 2013, my brand-new literary agent told me that in order to put the book together as quickly as possible—so that Grandma would have time to enjoy it—I'd need to get help from an experienced collaborator. Cindy Coloma (who, poignantly, had *just* had a baby) was hired, and we began to split the researching, writing, and editing duties.

Cindy and I have added historical details to the narrative. We've also extensively interviewed both of Grandma's daughters—Ruth and my mother, Dianna—for details about their childhoods.

Brian supplied me with a copy of Betty Jane's entire adoption file. It was a treasure trove, containing more than one hundred letters—hundreds of pages—of personal correspondence between Grandma and the House of Mercy, and between the HOM and Betty Jane's adoptive parents, the Nordslettens.

All the scenes in this book came either from Grandma's (or Ruth's) recollections or from the adoption file letters.

Cindy and I did have to re-create conversations, especially in the early chapters of the book. In these cases, we made sure that the characters conveyed only things that were factual, and we kept the dialogue true to the personalities and views of the people conversing. Wherever we attributed feelings, thoughts, or words to a person long deceased, such as Miss Bragstad or Reverend Kraushaar, we did so after carefully reviewing their letters and talking to Grandma.

Ruth, Brian, and Teresa read all the chapters about the Lees and edited them for accuracy. Grandma reviewed the entire manuscript and made a few minor changes, but otherwise vetted everything in it.

This project was truly a labor of love. At the same time, I approached it with some trepidation. After all, Grandma was a strong woman who was rightly protective of her life story. Also, because we lived hundreds of miles apart, she wasn't immediately available to review each chapter as I finished it. So when I finally flew to California with the first fourteen chapters for her to read, I gave her a highlighter and asked her to mark anything that wasn't accurate. I braced myself, thinking I might have to make changes in every paragraph.

When she returned the manuscript, I discovered that she had changed *three words*. Then she told me she loved it and couldn't wait to read the rest of it. That, to me, was the highest praise I could ever receive.

Acknowledgments

To MINKA DISBROW, my beloved grandmother. Thank you for living a story that needed to be told, and for loving our family so well, for so long. Words cannot express how much I love and admire you, but here are 86,000 of them that sure tried.

Ruth Lee, you would be eternally dear to me just for the joy you brought Grandma, but I've adored you from the moment we met. Thank you for being so generous with your story—and your life.

In so many ways this book would not exist without Brian Lee. Thank you for finding Grandma, for loving her, for wanting this book to happen. Thank you for your financial support; your tireless work to get me a hundred little details, at all hours; your commitment to accuracy. I only wish we'd known each other all along.

To my writing partner, Cindy Coloma. I could not have hoped for a more perfect person with whom to share this journey. Thank you for caring about this story, for talking me off a few ledges, for shouldering work when I couldn't. Your abilities amaze me.

Dianna Disbrow Huhn. Thank you, Mom, for providing so many specifics for the Minneapolis and Oakland portions of this story, even the painful sections. And thanks for your unflagging encouragement and prayers during this whole journey.

To my first and best friends—my brothers, Gary Huhn and Grant Huhn. Thank you for sharing my life, for loving Grandma's story, and for being my biggest fans, always.

Charles Lee, Debbie Lee, Mark Lee, Tim Lee, Carrie Lee, Jay Lee. Thank you for sharing your memories with me, and for being such an integral part of this story. And special thanks to Mark for verifying the technical aspects of the shuttle launch so I didn't look like a clown.

Dawn Disbrow Medina. Thank you for patiently answering questions and filling me in on your years with Grandma. And thank you for faithfully watching over her all those years.

Thanks to Teresa Lee for supporting this project—and Brian—in every way, for reading drafts and correcting errors, and for being such a sweetheart.

Jerry Huhn. I have no doubt that my stubborn ability to keep going with this project was due to years spent running wind sprints in the rain, under your expert coaching. Thank you for teaching me how to persevere, and for taking such loving care of my boys on several occasions so I could steal away and work.

Special thanks to both my parents for nurturing my love of reading early on, and therefore giving me the most enduring passion of my life.

To Janet Grant, my stalwart agent, who loved this story as much as I did, and who turned this dream into reality. Thanks for guiding me every step of the way.

To the entire Tyndale House team, who fell in love with Grandma's story and poured their hearts into bringing it to the world, especially Sarah Atkinson, Kim Miller, and Bonne Steffen, our editors extraordinaire. You made our words clearer and better.

And to our designer, Nicole Grimes, whose creativity made this book more beautiful than I could have dreamed.

To my author buddies, especially Karen Spears Zacharias, my first writing mentor, for providing encouragement and much-needed doses of reality; and to Billy Coffey, who read early versions of chapters and told me just to "jump" when I got scared. You both inspire me daily.

To all the brilliant writers whose words have made my life richer in a thousand ways, and especially Rick Bragg, who told me that this story would make a great book and that I should write it.

To Lavelle Huhn, Jason Dougherty, Catherine Huhn, and Samuel and Samantha Koch, who have made our family so much better.

Rodney Schoen. Thank you for giving us a glimpse into Grandma's childhood with your personal photos, and for telling me more about Uncle's family.

To all my friends, who tolerated my virtual disappearance during the last two years and cheered me on, especially Laurel Lundberg, Sunia Gibbs, Wendy Dillree, Karen Streelman, Kim Spalding, April White, Tami Richardson, Connie Helland, and Heidi Larson, who fed my family, cleaned my home, and killed house spiders so I could work in peace. And to Susan Askew, who would have loved all this more than anyone.

To my in-laws, Dave and Betty LaGrow, for entertaining and feeding my guys countless times while I was holed up working.

Thanks to the many people who assisted my research and answered my questions, including Marcia Sylvester, Zion Lutheran Church; Kathie Allstot, Riverside Cemetery; Pastor Joanne Nagele, Warner Lutheran; Ken Webb; Pam Videen, Minnesota Historical Society; L. J. Dean, National Railway Historical Society; William Brown, National Oceanic and Atmospheric Administration; Dale Kaiser, Oak Ridge National Laboratory; Diana Farmer, National Climatic Data Center; Gretchen Sharp, Aberdeen Public Schools

Foundation; Jeannet Bouma, Community of Heerenveen; Mary T, Find a Grave.

Barbara Rolph, for checking (and correcting) our German phrases, and Janneke Jobsis-Brown, Annelien de Haan, and Bouk de Vries Jobsis, for setting our Dutch phrases right.

My deepest thanks, forever, to my husband, Dan, for loving me, for shouldering so much extra work, and for never once acting like this dream was crazy; and to my boys, Cameron and Connor, for giving up "Mommy time" during this project, and for being my joy. Home, for me, is wherever the three of you are.

And, above all, eternal thanks to God, whose book this really is.

About the Authors

CATHY LAGROW first fell in love with books as a young girl, when she often chose to lose herself in a story rather than play outside. That love has never waned. She estimates that she's read more than two thousand books, and she habitually collects new titles much faster than she can read them.

Her previous writing endeavors include her blog, *Windows and Paper Walls*; a story for *Chicken Soup for the Soul* titled "A Good Mother"; and a weekly column for *All the Church Ladies* on a website created by journalist Karen Spears Zacharias.

In 2006, just after the birth of her first baby, Cathy and her family learned the secret her grandmother Minka Disbrow had been carrying for almost eighty years—that at age seventeen, she'd given up a baby for adoption. Cathy's mother, Dianna, is Minka's second child, born nearly eighteen years later. Cathy began working on *The Waiting* in early 2012.

Cathy has been married to her high school sweetheart, Dan, for almost twenty-five years. She is a licensed, nonpracticing

US Customs broker and a piano teacher. She lives in Oregon, where she's often found in the kitchen baking or curled up in a chair reading. An avid runner, she sometimes runs literal circles around her two small boys at the neighborhood park. Nearly everything fascinates her.

This is Cathy's debut book.

CINDY COLOMA is a national bestselling author who has written twelve novels, including: *Beautiful* (2010 Christy Award finalist for Young Adults and 2011 Revolve Young Adult Tour featured book); *The Salt Garden* (one of *Library Journal*'s best genre books in 2004); *Song of the Brokenhearted* (2013 ECPA bestseller with coauthor Sheila Walsh); *Orchid House* (2008 ECPA bestseller); and *Winter Passing* (2001 Christy Award finalist and Romantic Times Top Pick).

Cindy has collaborated on fiction projects with bestselling author, singer, and speaker Sheila Walsh, and as a ghostwriter with a former federal prosecutor and TV legal-news analyst.

Her nonfiction projects include collaborations on memoirs such as *The Waiting* (May 2014, Tyndale Momentum) and *It's a Wild Life: How My Life Became a Zoo* (June 2014, Medallion Press), a book about an exotic animal zoo in Michigan, and the *Nat Geo Wild* television program. Cindy developed and wrote the nonfiction book *Renting Lacy: A Story of America's Prostituted Children* (coauthored with former Congresswoman Linda Smith) and has also written over one hundred published articles.

Cindy is a speaker, book doctor, and writing coach. She's spoken at such events and conferences as the World Book Fair in Frankfurt, Germany; Simpson University Faculty Retreat; LittWorld in Tagaytay, Philippines; and many others. In her local area, she has co-led a writers' group for sixteen years.

With five children ranging in age from their early twenties to a baby boy, Cindy's life is always full of laughter, joy, and toys to trip over. She can't own enough books or watch enough movies, has more travel dreams than possible for a human (including underwater and outer-space itineraries), but loves home best of all. She and her extended family have lived in the Redding, California, area for over thirty-five years.

Online Discussion *guide*

TAKE *your* TYNDALE READING EXPERIENCE *to the* NEXT LEVEL

A FREE discussion guide for this book is available at bookclubhub.net, perfect for sparking conversations in your book group or for digging deeper into the text on your own.

www.bookclubhub.net

You'll also find free discussion guides for other Tyndale books, e-newsletters, e-mail devotionals, virtual book tours, and more!